Streetwise™

MANAGING
PEOPLE

Books in the Streetwise™ series include:

Streetwise™ Customer-Focused Selling
Streetwise™ Do-It-Yourself Advertising
Streetwise™ Hiring Top Performers
Streetwise™ Independent Consulting
Streetwise™ Managing People
Streetwise™ Small Business Start-Up

Streetwise™

MANAGING

PEOPLE

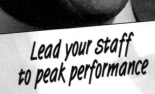

*Lead your staff
to peak performance*

Bob Adams
with Dr. Lillian Arleque, Naomi Deutscher, Gerald Felski,
Dr. Colleen Jones, Claire McCarthy, Judy Perry, and Dennis Zaia

Adams Media Corporation
Holbrook, Massachusetts

Published by Adams Media Corporation
260 Center Street, Holbrook, MA 02343

ISBN: 1-55850-726-4

Printed in the United States of America.

J I H G F E D C B

Library of Congress Cataloging-in-Publication Data
Adams Streetwise managing people : lead your staff to peak performance
p.   cm.
Includes index.
ISBN 1-55850-726-4 (pbk.)
1. Personnel management. I. Adams Media Corporation.
HF5549.A33   1997
658.3–dc21   97–34287
CIP

Inside photos: Photodisc™ Images ©1996, Photo Disc, Inc. and BodyShots™ ©1994..
Cover photo: ©Ken Fisher/Tony Stone Images. Cover background photo Superstock.

This book is available at quantity discounts for bulk purchases.
For information, call 1-800-872-5627 (in Massachusetts, call 781-767-8100).

Visit our home page at http://www.adamsmedia.com

TABLE OF CONTENTS

Managing People

TABLE OF CONTENTS

TABLE OF CONTENTS

TABLE OF CONTENTS

TABLE OF CONTENTS

TABLE OF CONTENTS

Managing People

TABLE OF CONTENTS

TABLE OF CONTENTS

1

THE TWENTY-FIRST CENTURY MANAGER

Today's worker is a new breed: more self-reliant, independent, and creative than any previous generation. The new worker is also expecting more from their employer—more focus on quality of life issues, more autonomy in their work, and more recognition that they are an important "stakeholder" in the organization. To succeed, companies will have to make a huge effort to capture and hold the attention and interest of the new workforce.

THE 21ST CENTURY MANAGER

The successful company of the twenty-first century will be managed by a new breed of manager, a person skilled in achieving objectives by maximizing the productivity of a company's most valuable assets, its human resources.

The twenty-first century manager may well be the hero of the new millennium and an identifying characteristic of the successful company.

The successful company will be a learning organization, one that encourages, supports, and enriches the intellectual and emotional capacity of all its employees.

The successful company will recognize the partnership between technology and employees as a major asset.

Companies that achieve success will use the most unique asset of a company, its human capital, in ways that offer the company strategic advantages in the marketplace.

The best companies will embrace change as a lifelong, ongoing process for the individual and the organization.

Forward-thinking companies will train leaders as carefully as automotive schools train mechanics to maintain, diagnose, and repair high-performance automobiles.

The successful company will be lead by individuals who have retained the ability to look at all situations as opportunities to create excitement and enthusiasm in meeting new challenges.

The successful company of the twenty-first century will be driven to increase stakeholder value and profitability while creating a working environment that encourages and nurtures the growth of personal creativity and development as well as nurturing a sense of well-being for all members of the organization.

Ultimately, the successful company will create a quality of life that balances the needs of the individual and family with the goals

> In the 21st century, successful companies will recognize human capital as their most unique asset.

THE 21ST CENTURY MANAGER

and objectives of the organization. Those organizations that value people as the cornerstone to achieving the objectives of the company will be the most successful.

This book is dedicated to helping you create a successful company through managing its most valuable assets, its people!

HISTORY

The growth and development of the modern economic world has been identified most consistently with high-volume, mass-produced, standardized products and services. This traditional concept of production was carried over to management and characterized by autocratic management practices that have been the norm for most of recent history. After World War II the traditional concept was refashioned and redesigned. The new management approaches might have clever names, but in the final analysis they were merely variations on the basic concept, which is an approach that subordinates employees to the management hierarchy.

This traditional concept included a clear yet unwritten and unspoken sensibility. A person who worked for a company for many years had an understanding that they would be guaranteed a job until retirement as long as their performance was deemed acceptable. There was an implied contract that motivated a variety of productive behaviors by employees. At retirement, the employee would receive a gold watch and the good wishes of management and coworkers.

Wrapped into this sensibility was the understanding that when the company did well the employees would benefit and would be treated to special awards, bonuses, incentives. Not unlike children waiting for Father to return home from work at the time the ice cream truck is on the street, the general theme of business management was paternalistic in nature.

Companies consistently sent this message: "Follow our specific directions, and if we do well, we will take care of you." This has been the basic management message that has driven our modern economy until the recent decade of reengineering, downsizing and rightsizing.

During the time this consistent management message dominated our economy a number of management techniques, schools, fads,

> Management has been autocratic until recent times.

THE 21ST CENTURY MANAGER

or directions have appeared. Many of these management schools have disappeared from view as quickly as they emerged. Others have captured the imagination and the sensibility of companies and have had varying degrees of impact. Some of these include:

- Managerial grid: Manager's styles are identified as either people-focused or task-focused.
- Management by objective (MBO): Performance is measured by one's ability to complete various well-defined work tasks.
- Quality circles: Management puts together teams and focuses them on improving product and service quality.
- Total quality management (TQM): Management establishes an ongoing process of monitoring and continually improving quality.
- Self-directed teams: Management establishes diverse teams to achieve specific objectives independently, within the broad guidelines.
- Management by walking around (MBWA): Managers stress communications by walking and talking with employees throughout production to ensure everyone is on the same page and working toward the same goals and objectives.

Management styles developed to lead the baby boomer generation.

The various management styles of the past forty years are the result of an attempt to respond to the needs of the generation that grew up after World War II. This is the generation that grew up as children of parents who were raised in the Depression. These parents had experienced the horrors of a world war (some of them *two* world wars) and emerged feeling that they had paid their dues. These parents worked hard to protect their children and ensure that they never had to experience comparable difficult times. Similarly, business management was clearly directed toward a paternal, controlling style. "Management will take care of everything" became the prevailing feeling.

Today these baby boomers who now staff our organizations are faced with a management challenge such as never existed before. The world has changed, and more importantly, many of the people who

THE 21ST CENTURY MANAGER

> Today, managers need to empower employees to direct themselves.

make up the workforce no longer share the same sensibilities as the baby boomers and their parents. The challenge today is to adapt management strategies in this new environment to achieve the highest degree of productivity, quality, and profitability.

The management style embodied in the traditional concept, which has been successful in managing our present leaders and the baby boomers, is no longer appropriate to the emerging workforce that drives the economy of today. In the past, managers directed and controlled employees. Today, managers empower employees to direct themselves.

QUALITY OF LIFE

Issues surrounding the quality of life a company offers its employees are frequently a major factor in job selection. Employees searching for jobs are very aware of the options made available to employees by the various companies with which they interview. Savvy companies utilize this knowledge to create benefits packages that incorporate special quality-of-life programs and benefits. Successful companies are paying attention to many of the details that make the life of employees more enjoyable and in turn make the employees more satisfied and more productive.

> Quality-of-life factors now play a major role in job selection.

Companies that recognize the dilemma of a family in which both spouses work or the demands upon a single working parent are way ahead of the game in developing strong alliances with employees.

Companies that have employee assistance programs or strong human resources departments to support and help employees are usually able to recruit and retain employees more effectively than companies that do not offer such a supportive environment.

In their efforts to please employees, some companies have even gone to the enormous expense and trouble of designing and contracting for high-quality restaurant-type food in the cafeterias that serve their employees. These modern cafeteria dining rooms have everything from soup to nuts, including vegetarian, ethnic, and heart-healthy food choices. Additionally, these facilities are subsidized by the company to allow employees to enjoy restaurant-quality food at a

THE 21ST CENTURY MANAGER

fraction of the retail cost. Many single employees utilize this benefit to reduce their grocery bills by eating their main meal at work.

Companies encourage and frequently make special vacation packages available to employees to promote the importance of high-energy, active vacations. These packages are also designed for entire families. When companies encourage and support entire families vacationing together, it makes it a bit easier to justify expecting the employee to work so hard and so long when not on vacation.

Companies are spending considerable amounts of money on leadership training and team-building training to help employees become better at the jobs they do. In most cases these skills have a direct impact on the employee's quality of life. They allow the employee to better understand the interpersonal dynamics in the workplace and thereby empower the employees to actively improve the work environment. Many of these skills are directly transferable to life at home. In many cases, companies are helping employees to develop interpersonal skills and abilities that they can apply to their family life. In this respect the training and development provided by employees benefits not only the company and the employee but also the family of the employee. Everyone wins.

> Leadership and training programs positively impact employees' quality of life.

CHANGING WORKFORCE

The emerging workforce is a "horse of a different color." Most new workers do not fit neatly into the description of the post-World War II worker or the me-generation children of these workers. The employees of the successful company of the twenty-first century share some very distinctive characteristics.

The workforce of today is highly distrustful of institutions. Having lived through some of the most traumatic periods of modern history, they do not believe that the traditional institutions will be watching out for them or taking care of their needs. Examples of this trauma abound.

> The workforce of today is highly distrustful of institutions.

- Germany: The economic crisis in Germany following unification.

- France: The economic pressure on the farmers in France.

THE 21ST CENTURY MANAGER

Today's workforce is highly independent, self-reliant, and creative.

- Russia: The political problems of the breakup of the Soviet Union.
- Latin America: The lack of stability in many of the governments.
- Africa: Continued conflicts and abject poverty .
- Canada: The pressure and fear of Quebec succession.
- Mexico: The impact of a neighbor on the brink of economic challenge.
- U.S.A.: The downsizing and reengineering of the American workforce.

Change is the norm, and we must be equipped to embrace change in every possible form. We must embrace the opportunities change presents and use these opportunities to create new, innovative solutions to old problems.

Today's workforce is highly independent, the result of both parents working or a single-parent upbringing. Today's workforce is self-reliant and well skilled at the daily tasks of solving the many problems of daily life. This emerging group is able to work independently, solving problems with available resources by stretching the boundaries of creativity and existing guidelines and rules.

Our twenty-first century workforce is highly computer literate and innately understands the enormous potential of the technology available and yet to be developed. They have grown up with computers. They understand bytes and chips better than their parents understood interest rates and credit lines.

They are the MTV generation. They are the independents. They are the children who need and must have the $100 athletic shoes, the name brand jeans, and they want them NOW. They really don't have time to wait for someone else to make a decision. They will change jobs as quickly as they switch the channels of the TV or files in the computer.

Each of these traits and characteristics of the new workforce is powerful in and of itself. When wrapped in the mantle of an enormous need for immediate feedback and gratification, the prospect of managing this workforce offers some exciting and difficult challenges.

THE 21ST CENTURY MANAGER

CHALLENGES

The twenty-first century company will achieve success when it is able to communicate throughout the organization in a fashion that captures and holds the attention and interest of the new workforce. The company must be interactive, engaging employees whenever and however possible. It must be an exciting place to work for people who are interested in the product, service or commodity. The successful company must be perceived as "hot" and "cool" and able to grab the attention of future workers. Change will be a constant within the successful company of the twenty-first century. Change generates excitement, excitement generates interest, interest generates creativity, creativity generates innovative ideas, and innovative ideas generate new concepts, which in turn create new products, services, and commodities to reach the emerging markets of the world.

People managers will need new guidelines for this new environment.

VALUES

Don't worry! The challenge is great, but this does not change the core values that have been the foundation of our economy. As a matter of fact, a recent survey indicated that the new generation of workers aged twenty to thirty-three have a higher degree of recognition that "hard work is the key to getting ahead" than the forty-nine to sixty-two-year-old group surveyed.

Although this new group of workers recognizes the need for and the value of hard work, there is a big difference between the existing workforce and this emerging group. The twenty-first century workforce will work hard but they will not—repeat, *will not*—work to "pay their dues" or "wait quietly" until management decides to take action.

Remember, these are the independent souls who are experienced at making decisions on their own, who are able to solve problems as they occur using the resources available. They know what is possible and realize that the old adage "the early bird will get the worm" still applies. They want to know exactly what is going on and how they will be involved. They want to experience personal gratifi-

> Companies must capture and hold the attention of the new workforce.

THE 21ST CENTURY MANAGER

> A company that can create a relationship with workers that incorporates the sensibility of partnership and shared values will emerge as the next success story.

cation for their efforts. They want to be on the receiving end of continual learning and development.

Due to the many factors that differentiate the new workforce from their predecessors, the tactics by which we arrive at the successful company of the future will need to change. Fortunately, the core values that glue the tactics together will remain the same.

The traditional values of security, loyalty, and playing by the rules are being replaced by new values of challenge, fun, independence, and opportunity. But that does not diminish the fundamental core values that hold both the traditional and the new values together.

Trust, harmony, and honesty are the fundamental core values that drive our world.

A company built on trust, harmony, and honesty will achieve higher levels of success than a company that chooses to ignore these fundamental core values.

The company that does not promote these basic values sends a message of exclusion and distrust to its employees. A company that can create a relationship with workers that incorporates the sensibility of partnership and shared values will emerge as the next success story.

According to former secretary of labor Robert Reich, "today a new compact is slowly emerging. In it, employees have responsibilities for making their companies as profitable as, and companies have responsibility for making their employees as valuable as, possible."

LEARNING

To build this relationship, successful companies must become learning organizations. No longer can a company speak of the training department. In reality every aspect of the successful company serves as a learning/training opportunity. Learning should be happening between peers and coworkers as part of the normal and everyday work process. The responsibility for learning and growing is a shared responsibility of all members of the company: the employees, the managers, the teams, and the organization as a whole.

THE 21ST CENTURY MANAGER

Because they are so experienced at using the available resources to solve problems and make decisions, they value education and learning as means to an end. They want to learn, but they do not want to learn and grow according to some predetermined plan designed by someone else. Personal growth and development are critically important to this group, and they expect it to take place in rapid-fire progression with steady feedback and solid support.

PARTNERS AND COACHES

Successful businesses of the future will think more in terms of employees as partners in managing the business. The term "partner" creates images of an equal, valuable contributor to the organization. Although each employee may not have legal status as a partner with shareholder ownership, successful businesses consider each employee a stakeholder in the business. This is a fine line that cannot be too carefully managed. It's part of their internal public relations spin that all companies must manage every day.

If you call employees stakeholders and never give them the opportunity to stake their claim to the internal processes, then you have created a negative situation. Employees will now see the term is a farce, and they will ignore all attempts to bring them into the process.

If you actively involve employees in the decision-making process, if you actively solicit input from a variety of employee sources, you will see employees behaving as stakeholders, concerned about the future of the company.

Your employees have the potential to be the very best partners you could imagine. They are emotionally vested in your company. With a consistent level of coaching from you and the management team, you have the potential to make great progress. The manner in which you coach will have a direct result on how well your employees buy into the stakeholder sensibility.

The process of managing people entails following some basic, commonsense tactics. Whenever you plan to work with employees to help them reach higher levels of performance through coaching, you will need to display these basic characteristics:

> Successful businesses of the future will think more in terms of employees as partners in managing the business.

> Your employees have the potential to be the very best partners you could imagine.

THE 21ST CENTURY MANAGER

- **You must be consistent in everything you do.** Your employees must be able to rely on you to behave in similar ways when similar situations occur. You cannot be mercurial and up one day and down the next. For some managers this may be the hardest characteristic to master. Don't even begin to consider yourself a good coach until you have mastered this trait.
- **You must be scrupulously honest.** If you are proceeding with employee coaching because you think it is the trendy thing to do or because everyone else is doing it, then stop before you begin. You must sincerely believe that this is the best and most appropriate way to help your employees. Don't lie; everyone will know that your heart is not into what you say is important.
- **Demonstrate your passion for your company, your product, and/or your service.** Your enthusiasm must be visible to everyone who comes in contact with you. You must be totally committed to making your company the very best. You must be committed to making your employees the very best. Your passion and commitment will shine through and will have a positive impact on all your employees
- **Support the training efforts of your company.** You must invest both time and money to support your company's training efforts. The employees want you to follow up with information, support, and clarification that will strengthen the required skills you have identified through your coaching. Give your employees lots of opportunities to practice the skills and behaviors you are coaching them to develop.
- **Be flexible and able to make adjustments as necessary.** Recognize that the strategies you have created may need to be modified at a moment's notice due to a client or customer request. Don't be too rigid in the way in which you deliver your coaching or your supportive training. Build all your programs on a flexible base with clear objectives.

Basic characteristics for successful coaches.

THE 21ST CENTURY MANAGER

NEW ROLE OF THE MANAGER

The effective manager today must really see his or her role as that of a coach.

COACH = TEACHER = EDUCATOR = TRAINER

The ideal manager/coach must have a broad range of skills:

- The successful coach must be well regarded and respected for what he or she does and has accomplished.
- The successful coach works closely with employees in various situations.
- The successful coach has skills and abilities desired by others.
- The successful coach understands and articulates the culture, mission, and values of the company.
- The successful coach is sincere in relationships with employees.
- The successful coach allow the relationship to develop as the employee develops.
- The successful coach is trusting and respecting.
- The successful coach sets clear objectives and gives honest feedback.
- The successful coach empathizes with employees; he or she has been there and can relate to what they are experiencing.
- The successful coach offers professional and personal support and guidance.
- The successful coach serves as a role model, leading by example.
- The successful coach allows for individual agendas and respects the needs of the individual.
- The successful coach talks with and not to or at the employees.
- The successful coach identifies and communicates the objectives to be reached and how the efforts will be measured.
- The successful coach allows others to grow and develop without fear or concern about his or her own status.

The ideal coach will have many skills.

THE 21ST CENTURY MANAGER

- The successful coach makes available both formal and informal feedback on employee progress.
- The successful coach constantly identifies opportunities to improve and plans ways to achieve improvement.

Are You a Good Coach?

Can You Identify the Most Successful Coaches Within Your Organization?

Think about how you can make your company a more successful company in the twenty-first century by coaching and partnering with your employees.

FUTURE LEADERS

The future leaders of our companies are already working in these companies. As Ken Blanchard and Spencer Johnson stated in *The One-Minute Manager*:

The key to developing people is to catch them doing something right and then reinforce that action.

The challenge for your business is first to determine what is considered *right*. People need and want to know what is expected of them. They want to do things *right* and are waiting for you to give them a good definition of and guidelines about what you expect.

Thus the first step in this process of developing people is to determine what you and your company consider right or expected. Having identified these key practices, behaviors, and skills, management must then catch people doing these things <u>right</u> and reinforce these desired activities through positive feedback.

Some of these behaviors will be directly linked to skills and abilities necessary in your future leaders. And you will have the opportunity to identify and train these future leaders daily.

STYLES OF LEADERSHIP

There are many forms of leadership, and each style can be viewed as positive or negative, based on the perception of the observer. Consider the following four leadership styles and the way in which each can be perceived as both positive and negative.

> The key to developing people is to catch them doing something right and then reinforce that action.

THE 21ST CENTURY MANAGER

Leadership Style 1

Makes decisions on own and takes responsibility for these decisions. Transfers information about the what, why, and how to do something and expects that it will be accomplished. Recognizes those who follow directions and succeed.

Based on the perception of the observer, this style can be considered either directing or dominating.

Leadership Style 2

Makes decisions based on input of others. Involves other people in responsibilities. Seeks information for solving problems. Recognizes people who contribute to solving problems.

Based on the perception of the observer, this style can be considered either problem-solving or overly involving/democratic.

Leadership Style 3

Helps others think through the problems. Supports other people as they solve problems. Asks questions to assist other people in problem-solving. Recognizes people who seek and/or accept support.

Based on the perception of the observer, this style can be considered either developing or excessively accommodating.

Leadership Style 4

Allows people to make decisions on their own. Limits communication to basic briefings and updates. Recognizes people for accepting responsibility for solving problems.

Based on the perception of the observer, this style can be considered either delegating or abdicating.

You and your organization must decide what type of leadership style is most appropriate for your company. Then you must identify and develop the employees who display the greatest potential to become your future leaders.

Look for employees who display some of the following characteristics:

- They conceive and select innovative ideas and keep these ideas in balance with reality.

> Implemented properly, any of these four leadership styles can succeed.

THE 21ST CENTURY MANAGER

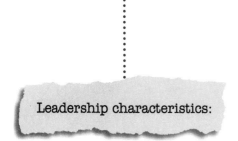

Leadership characteristics:

- They connect processes, events, and systems within the big picture.
- They evoke trust from others and place trust in others to enable them to succeed.
- They focus on a goal and direct their energy to meet the goal.
- They understand and master their own emotions in a way that instills confidence, motivates, inspires, and enhances group effectiveness.
- They know how to market and sell the company's products, services, and programs.
- They know how to coordinate the efforts and subparts of their organization.
- They know how to manage and deploy capital, both internally and externally.
- They know how to employ, deploy, and shape the talents of people within their department.
- They know how to set long-term and short-term objectives for their department.

Use this check list of leadership traits to identify some of the future leaders within your company. Then determine what you must do as a coach and as a leader to develop these people to their maximum potential.

DELEGATION

Today's organization is faced with downsizing, reengineering, and rightsizing. There are fewer and fewer employees to accomplish the tasks that must be accomplished. The challenge is clear.

We must become more efficient and we must be prepared to let other people do some of the things we did in the past. In other words, we must learn how to delegate and feel comfortable with delegating.

The most common concern attributed to delegation is the fear that the work will not get done the way we wanted.

THE 21ST CENTURY MANAGER

STOP!

Can you identify the objective of the particular task?

Can you clearly identify the end product?

Is there more than one way that this task can be accomplished?

Are you prepared to let go and let someone else make this task happen?

If you can answer YES to all the above questions, then you should be ready to delegate that particular task to another employee.

When the task or objective is clearly defined with specific outcomes, it is very difficult for a skilled employee to make a mistake.

The problems arise when an unskilled employee is asked to complete a clearly defined task, or when a skilled employee is asked to complete a poorly defined task.

The second of the two scenarios is the more common. A highly regarded and highly skilled employee is selected to take over a project or task that has not been clearly defined. The supervisor is delegating this task to the skilled employee, but because the project does not have a clear objective, the potential for problems and eventual failure is enormous. Once the project or task fails, the supervisor then can say, "I just can't delegate anything to anyone, not even the best person in my group."

This is a tragic situation that can be avoided if supervisors and employees are willing to have an honest and open conversation about the project and what is really expected.

Frequently the supervisor makes such a fuss over the fact that he or she is selecting Employee A to take over a task or project, that Employee A does not want to appear incompetent by asking very important questions, such as "What exactly do you want me to accomplish?" "What problems have you had in the past?" or "What resources will I have to accomplish this task?"

Delegation can be a powerful vehicle to advance the mission of your company and to develop the future management and leadership of your organization. As in all endeavors, it must be well planned, well communicated, and well implemented.

To succeed in management today, you must be able to "let go" and delegate.

THE 21ST CENTURY MANAGER

PRODUCTIVITY

The successful businesses of the future are going to be well-oiled machines that obtain the greatest productivity from the least amount of employees without burning them out.

The secret will be in maintaining the balance between achieving task accomplishments and nurturing the relationships that support the organization. The successful company of the future will be equally concerned about both the employee's productivity and the well-being of each employee's family life.

This balance will be a key factor in the formulas used to measure productivity in the twenty-first century.

In the past, employees did exactly what they were told. If they were not given instructions, nothing would happen. If they were given incorrect or incomplete instructions, they would comply even though they knew that the product would not meet standard specifications.

Today we expect employees to make minute-by-minute decisions related to their work tasks. Employees are for the most part asked to direct their own work flow and to keep productivity up even when required resources are limited or not available.

In the future, the emphasis will be on increased independent actions and decision-making by each employee. Increased pressure to perform and deliver flawless products and services will place employees under ever greater pressure. The ability to reduce this pressure and translate it into developmental opportunities for employees will set apart the successful managers and companies of the future.

> The secret will be in maintaining the balance between achieving task accomplishments and nurturing the relationships that support the organization.

> In the future, the emphasis will be on increased independent actions and decision-making by each employee.

STAFFING

Staffing is a perennial problem for all organizations. It will never go away, and it will constantly change, making it very difficult to design a solution or a plan that will always work.

For staffing to be a business-as-usual issue, your company must have a strategy that defines actions to be taken in a variety of circumstances and a process that creates new actions when the rules change, which they will.

THE 21ST CENTURY MANAGER

Key to any staffing strategy is a knowledge and awareness of who and what your company is, its mission, its culture, and its values. Without a clear sense of these three components all your efforts will be only marginally successful.

To begin, collect the written mission statement for your company, a description of your company culture written by a respected and senior member of the organization, and a list of core values that support the mission and culture. These documents should be a part of the materials you have available for interested potential employees.

Once these documents are available, you will need clearly defined job descriptions for all positions, but most importantly, for any jobs you are seeking to fill. Without a job description that honestly explains the job duties and responsibilities, a potential candidate cannot make an informed decision about the position. Without an informed decision, the candidate may take the job only to discover that it is not what was expected and will quit. Now the entire process must begin again. Do it right the first time and save lots of time, money, and lost productivity.

The staffing process is very critical to a successful organization. Be sure to put adequate time and planning into the staffing process to ensure that the best people are brought into your company.

The way in which you design and present your advertising to recruit staff is the first impression many people have of your company. Let your job advertisements be the first good impression you make. Depending on the positions you are filling and your type of organization, the design and copy of your ads can make a big difference.

Select your words carefully. Use an image that will be clearly identified with your company. Generally your logo should be used in the ads to maintain a consistent image of your firm in all print media.

In the past, recruiting ads tended to be very basic information about the job, with lots of job-related detail. Now we find the ads have a greater amount of information about the company and why the company is a good place to work. There is a stronger emphasis on the company's quality of life and values. And there is a greater amount of selling of the company as part of the recruiting process.

> A staffing strategy is essential for effective hiring.

> Recruitment ads are increasingly emphasizing the company, not just the job.

THE 21ST CENTURY MANAGER

21st-century companies must carefully balance factors such as production, profits, and employee needs.

CONTINUOUS IMPROVEMENT

Whatever the twenty-first century brings to the business community, one thing will be for certain: Every successful business will incorporate some type of continuous-improvement process into their operating strategy.

Today's modern society is obsessed with self-improvement and constant improvement. Our economy is driven by individuals who want to improve their looks, their wardrobe, their investments, and their status. They want their children to go to prestigious schools and want to have the best brand-name products and services. These same people want their companies to improve constantly. They want to know that the organization for which they work is the best, is the top dog in the marketplace.

In parallel, business has recognized the importance and value of the continuous-improvement process. The Japanese have successfully implemented this process, becoming the role model for American industry.

The process of continuous improvement has become part of the future of business. It is the lifeblood, preventing business from cycling back to older, less intelligent, and less efficient forms of management.

BALANCE

For a twenty-first century business to survive, there must be a keen sense of balance in the company's leadership. Balance implies a constant weighing of all factors that make a business successful. No one issue—production, profits, or employee needs—can overtake the importance of the others.

What a business does today that appears to be insensitive with regard to employees may be necessary for its future survival. The real test will come when we observe the company over a period of time and notice how these insensitive activities are balanced by later initiatives to make things right.

Employees in the midst of this constantly changing environment know when the scales are tipping and when they need to tip back the other way. Companies and managers able to maintain this steady balance will be the long-term success stories of the twenty-first century.

CHAPTER

2

COACHING
FOR
MANAGERS

Coaching is critical to managing the new workforce. Coaching requires managers to direct employees by influencing them—not by controlling them. Effective coaching can boost morale and productivity tremendously by making employees feel empowered and by creating the feeling of "ownership" of their work.

COACHING FOR MANAGERS

WHAT DOES COACHING INVOLVE?

Coaching is the continuing evolution of one-on-one management communication skills designed to effectively achieve both company success and employee professional development objectives in a rapidly changing work environment. It is a process of using questions, active listening, and support to assist the employee being coached in developing fundamental self-assessment skills that result in increased productivity, skills levels, and overall job satisfaction.

THE TRADITIONAL APPROACH

Coaching and managing are part of the same family of management communication tools but essentially represent very different approaches for obtaining a desired result. A traditional approach, or management by directive, is based on the supposition that upper management possesses the knowledge, information, and decision-making rights, and employees exist to carry out management's orders and directives. Essentially, employees are not expected to think but only to do as they are told. While this management model has been significantly altered over the years, the core of this management style still is found in many companies today.

THE ESSENCE OF COACHING

In addition to proactive communication, coaching is based on influence and leadership and represents a management communication style that accepts employees as valuable and contributing individuals. An employee who has had successful coaching is capable of solving most problems on his or her own if involved in the process and encouraged to contribute and take intelligent risks. He or she must be heard and supplied with the appropriate information, tools, and support. The effectiveness of coaching is derived from the value placed on the input of employees, an implicit trust and confidence in their abilities.

ORGANIZATIONAL BENEFITS

A company that uses coaching techniques with its employees will see several direct and measurable benefits. It has a more confident and motivated work force with high-quality output. Coaching

> The effectiveness of coaching is based upon an implicit trust and confidence in the abilities of the employees.

COACHING FOR MANAGERS

develops employees who are capable of doing a broader and more flexible range of work, thus enriching the employees' professional development while freeing managers to concentrate on strategic direction and planning for the company.

BASIC TENETS OF COACHING

1. Management does not have all the answers.
2. The power to create and implement solutions and generate new ideas and approaches is vested in those who are closest to the customer, problem, or process—most often the employees.
3. Power is generated through the acceptance of responsibility and accountability and encouragement of self-discovery.
4. The right answers are those that create superb performance results, high quality and productivity, and outstanding long-term customer satisfaction, regardless of the source.
5. Actions and decisions are reached through consideration of all information, which is openly shared by everyone involved.
6. Knowledge, creativity, and innovation reside in all members of the team and can be encouraged and developed.

> The creativity and insight of employees should never be overlooked.

SUCCESSFUL COACHING SESSIONS

1. SKILLS NEEDED TO PRODUCE SUCCESSFUL COACHING SESSIONS

- *Active listening skills.* The use of active listening skills enables a manager to "shift into neutral," clear his or her mind of other distractions, and give 100 percent attention to the employee. Active listening improves his or her ability to hear not only what the employee is saying but also what the employee is feeling, which is equally important. In other words, it enables the manager to "hear" what is *not* being said.
- *Understanding goal-setting methods.* A manager must understand how to set reachable goals for employees with different skill sets and abilities. He or she must evaluate various

methods of achieving goals and objectives and determine which ones apply most effectively to his or her department.

- *Good probing and questioning skills.* It is critical that a manager develops a good set of questions and techniques to probe the employee's thought process and determine how he or she approaches a problem or issue. To be a good coach, managers need solid information about the individuals being coached.

- *Skilled understanding and use of feedback techniques.* Feedback allows the manager to make better decisions on how to coach the employee, including what to say and how to say it. Language is critical here—even the choice between using "but" rather than "however" can set a framework for the employee to absorb and understand your message.

- *Ability to suspend judging individuals and responses while listening.* Managers should understand that all judgments and assumptions about an individual's capabilities should be suspended while coaching their employees. They may even want to suspend judgment at all times to ensure that they gather accurate information.

- *Empathy.* Some employees need more coaching than others, especially if emotional issues are involved. It is necessary that managers show empathy, especially during difficult times at the company.

> Skilled coaching is based on good listening and understanding.

2. HOW TO PREPARE THE MANAGER AND EMPLOYEE FOR THE COACHING SESSION

For the Manager

- *Clear your mind of everything else going on, and focus on* this *session with* this *employee.* Coaching is built on the effective use of carefully selected questions versus statements. When your mind is cluttered with many other distractions, you cannot effectively coach.

- *Define specifically what the coaching session will cover and the time involved.* By establishing parameters for the

COACHING FOR MANAGERS

session, you set the employee's mind at ease and enable him or her to focus on limited areas of responsibility.

- *Choose the most productive location for conducting the session.* Location is important because it sets the tone for the session. Coaching an employee in the manager's office can detract from coaching, especially if the manager is sitting opposite the employee at a desk. Also remember that coaching done immediately following the action being coached is often most effective.
- *Inform the employee of the time, place, and goals of the session.* Good coaching starts with clear expectations and communication between manager and employee.
- *Be relaxed and cordial, and try to alleviate any perceived anxiety of the employee.* The manager has the responsibility to create a positive and supportive coaching environment to eliminate undue stress and nervousness.

Mutual trust is essential to good management.

For the Employee

- *Relax and perform to the best of your ability.* By its very nature, coaching is built on a platform of mutual trust. When done correctly, many issues and differences between the employee and employer disappear. Trust your manager, and expect to be trusted in return.
- *Trust your own ideas and judgment.* Coaching is based on a team effort of the manager drawing out the innate skills, knowledge, and creativity of the employee, which are often never tapped into without coaching.
- *Use your creativity to find ways to improve performance.* Put your ideas out on the table. You are the closest to the job or problem and probably have excellent suggestions to offer.
- *Be honest and open, and avoid defensiveness.* Both employee and employer must work diligently to establish and maintain open channels of communication for coaching to be effective.

COACHING FOR MANAGERS

3. THE COACHING PROCESS

Since each coaching session is a discrete event, the process generally follows these guidelines:

- *Set a specific time period and length for the session.* When you set these parameters in advance, you will find it easier to cover all the topics on your agenda, and your coaching session will likely meet with success.

- *Define and agree on the coaching topic and the specific goals for that session.* The ideal coaching situation involves actually observing the employee doing a task, then following up immediately with coaching on what you observed.

- *Begin with an opening question that defines the employee's understanding of the task at hand and the boundaries within which he or she has authority to act.* Coaching is effective in part because it recognizes that employees are people rather than just "business assets" and, as such, have thoughts and feelings. Your probing will address both of these dimensions; in other words, "How do you 'feel' about this project?" and "What do you 'think' about this problem?" can elicit two very different responses.

- *Listen actively.* Clear your mind of other agendas, suspend judgment, focus on both the feeling and thoughts in the response, acknowledge your attention with verbal and non-verbal signals, paraphrase as appropriate, and probe for clarification and confirmation of your understanding.

- *Offer support or acknowledge understanding of the response.* Even if you receive what you consider to be a totally "left field" response, you still can acknowledge that you understand what the employee is saying. That acknowledgment does not imply you agree, yet it indicates your active involvement.

> Employee suggestions should always be acknowledged, if not agreed with.

- *Probe again in the direction that you want the self-discovery process to head.* Your questions should lead the employee toward learning how to solve the problem without you actually providing a solution.

COACHING FOR MANAGERS

> Acknowledge learning gains, creative ideas, and progress toward improvements.

- *Repeat the process until the employee reaches the desired conclusion (or leads you to an alternative approach that you may not have considered but can accept with an open mind).* There will be some instances in which, after several well-structured questions, the employee "just doesn't get it." In this case, it's okay to state a more specific direction and proceed from there. You're striving for structured leading, not a guessing game.
- *Give recognition.* Acknowledge learning gains, creative ideas, and progress toward improvements.
- *Agree on a next-step plan, noting what has been agreed to.* This next-step plan will form the basis for the next follow-up coaching session.

COACHING SCENARIOS

SESSION 1: CUSTOMER COMPLAINT

Setup

In this scenario, the manager has received a telephone complaint from a regular customer who recently experienced quality problems with the company's product. The customer indicated that the employee treated him with disrespect and conveyed an attitude that dealing with the complaint was a "bother."

Manager: Chris, we need to talk about the recent customer service situation you handled with Mr. Johnson.

Chris: You mean the complaint? He was really unpleasant and not very easy to deal with.

Manager: Chris, I understand that some people can be very difficult to deal with and can challenge our patience. Let's review what happened. Tell me about it from your perspective.

Chris: The guy just would not stop complaining about the fact that he could not get the X-14 to work properly. I tried

COACHING FOR MANAGERS

to walk him through the installation process, but he just wouldn't listen. He kept insisting it was our problem, not his.

Manager: I understand. Now that a little time has passed since your conversation with Mr. Johnson, let's look back at the situation and analyze it from a nonemotional perspective, okay?

Chris: Well, okay, sure. But what good will that do? Haven't we already lost Mr. Johnson as a customer?

Manager: Not necessarily. Meanwhile, what we'll do is work together to develop a strategy and a script so that when this situation presents itself again, everybody wins: you, the customer, and the company. Sound like a good approach?

Chris: I'm willing to try anything at this point.

> Instead of first criticizing the employee, the manager adopts a problem-solving style and approach.

Commentary

The dialogue worked because the manager, while dealing with a difficult customer situation, was willing to keep an open mind to the fact that there are usually two sides to every story. He employed active listening skills, created a nonthreatening environment for the coaching session, suspended judgment of his employee's customer interactions before having all the facts, and used this opportunity to create a learning situation for his employee. In addition, he supported his employee by developing a plan to create a way of avoiding future similar situations.

> Keeping an open mind can diffuse a volatile situation.

SESSION 2: DIFFICULTY DELIVERING ACCURATE MONTHLY REPORTS

Setup

In this scenario, the manager is meeting with an employee who is having trouble creating monthly reports that accurately reflect data gathered using a generic questionnaire. The manager has just asked the employee to join him in his office to try to work out a

COACHING FOR MANAGERS

solution to help the employee refine his methodology in gathering the data.

Manager:	Good morning, Joe. I've been reviewing your latest reports, and there seems to be a problem with the data you've been gathering and the final conclusions in the report. Can you give me your insights on what you think may be happening here?
Joe:	Well, the questionnaire that I get from research is generic. When I confront a special situation, like the Avac Company report, I can't seem to make the adjustments necessary to reflect Avac's data in the overall report.
Manager:	That can happen. But it's important for you to understand, Joe, that your reports affect not only external customer buying decisions but the performance of your entire department. What do you see as the impact on the rest of the department and external customers when your reports become skewed?
Joe:	Well, I have to admit, I had no idea that the skewed data had such a negative effect on the department and the customers. Certainly data must help customers make solid buying decisions and uphold the reputation of our department as a producer of accurate reports. If I don't do the job properly, we stand to lose business and customer confidence.
Manager:	That's right. Let's take a look at how important your job is and how it supports the overall success of our entire department. What are the specific problem areas that seem to be giving you the most trouble?
Joe:	The questions don't seem to fit their specific type of work, and they're measured on different criteria.
Manager:	Based on your experience to date, what changes in the questions do you believe would help solve the problem?

COACHING FOR MANAGERS

> Joe: I think that if we change the reporting format to include a step-by-step interview process, which can be used with special situations, I will be able to draw the proper conclusions and combine them with the generic formats for more accurate final reports.
>
> Manager: I'm glad you understand the importance of this matter. Let's take a moment to outline a plan to help you understand how to best utilize this new method. I'll expect progress reports from you on a weekly basis, and by all means, ask as many questions as you need to fully grasp what we're doing.

Commentary

This situation worked because the manager took time to carefully understand the problem that his employee was facing. He set up an environment in which he clearly stated the problem to the employee, then utilized active listening to try to understand the problem from the employee's point of view. Based on what he learned, the manager was then able to use his questioning skills to lead the employee to understand the impact of his actions and also to begin developing possible solutions to resolve the problem. He followed up with a mutual commitment to monitor progress.

SESSION 3: HANDLING ADDITIONAL JOB RESPONSIBILITIES

Setup

In this scenario, the manager and employee are meeting to review a new set of job responsibilities that the employee is taking on for the first time—above and beyond what she is already handling. The manager recognizes that because of staff reductions, the employee is being asked to shoulder more of the workload, and the employee is not happy about it.

COACHING FOR MANAGERS

The manager gives the employee all of the background facts.

The manager asks for input.

Manager: Hi, Cindy. As you know, because of the elimination of one department position, you're being asked to handle some additional work. My goal this morning is to review specifically what needs to be done, and I'd really like to hear your thoughts as to how we can achieve the new workload objectives.

Cindy: Mr. Snyder, this just isn't fair. How am I supposed to do the work of two people when I'm working flat out just trying to do my own job?

Manager: I understand your feelings, Cindy, and I empathize with your situation. In regard to being fair, we want everyone to understand that, based on current business and financial conditions, if we had not taken the steps to reduce the number of positions, we could not have protected the jobs that you and the other team members still have. It was a tough but also fair decision to cut one job for the good of the department. Our challenge now is to design ways to continue to do the work we need to do with the current employee levels. Let's review the new responsibilities you'll have and figure out how we'll get them done.

Cindy: There just aren't enough people to handle the work as you've laid it out. There has to be a different way.

Manager: Given what we need to accomplish, do you have any suggestions for getting it done?

Cindy: Well, looking at my two sets of responsibilities, there seem to be several redundant tasks that could be eliminated. That would save several hours a week.

Manager: Good, let's use that as a starting point. What else do you suggest?

Cindy: Maybe we've been following procedures in the job that aren't really necessary to meet our customers' needs. You know, we're doing it just because "we've always

COACHING FOR MANAGERS

done it that way." I bet that if you asked others in the department, they'd say the same thing.

Manager: Let's do that. I appreciate your positive approach to a difficult challenge. I wonder if you've taken time to think about the personal gains you'll get out of this, too.

Cindy: What do you mean by "personal gains?"

Manager: You've been doing your current job for several years now and have it done it very well. But maybe it's lost some of its challenge and stimulation. What new skills will you have to use now to master this new challenge?

Cindy: Well, even though I'm not happy about this change, I never really had a chance to use my creativity in my current job. I'm looking forward to using this skill to solve these and other problems as they appear.

Manager: Sounds great, Cindy. You're already showing new skills and abilities that may even position you for a different job in the future. We should talk once the restructuring is complete.

Commentary

This situation is faced almost daily by managers who are short on resources and long on workload. The manager recognized that the employee is not happy about the change, which can't be avoided, so he immediately outlined for the employee what caused the situation so she had all the facts—what specifically needed to be done—then asked for her thoughts, input, and ideas. This helped generate ownership on her part of the solution. He demonstrated empathy and fairness and led the employee into an open discussion of possible options of how to not just blindly do "double duty" but to look at the restructuring and eliminating of unnecessary work to achieve the objective. He also helped her see additional self-fulfillment opportunities in the new work, thus appealing to intrinsic motivating forces.

> A dialogue, rather than a monologue, enables listening.

COACHING FOR MANAGERS

QUESTIONS AND ANSWERS

1. **Why should I be concerned about coaching?**

   Coaching is a communication tool that can make your life as a manager much easier, more rewarding, and more satisfying. Coaching can help build employer-employee relationships with minimal internal conflict, reduced stress, and more win-win solutions for employers, employees, customers, and vendors. These benefits should be worth any investment of your time.

2. **Can you contrast some of the differences you see between coaching and management?**

   The essence of the difference lies in the approach management takes in communicating with employees. Management's approach to attaining its objectives is controlling and directing. Coaching is based on attaining objectives through the use of influence and leadership skills. In contrast to the controlling and directing approach, in many ways, coaching is the opposite approach to attaining the same results.

3. **What's wrong with how I'm communicating with my employees now?**

   Perhaps nothing. It's vital to remember that the use of coaching in the workplace is equivalent to use of a new tool. Using new tools with outdated directions or (mindsets) is a recipe for ineffectiveness, lack of productivity, mediocre results, and possible failure.

4. **Who is involved in coaching employees?**

   The managers and employees are the usual participants. Effective overall use of coaching skills, however, can be extended to working with vendors to create partnerships in the design, construction, supply, or delivery of the most effective solutions. It also can be used with customers to resolve customer-satisfaction issues and build long-term, profitable relationships. At its basic level, coaching is a respectful, participative, and mutual communication process

> Coaching attains objectives through influence, rather than through control.

COACHING FOR MANAGERS

designed to honor the diverse and valuable input of many perspectives in solving problems.

5. **When do I use coaching skills?**
Coaching is used in all steps of the management communication process.

Up-front. It provides for thorough and comprehensive input from employees and managers, often resulting in more effective solutions, quicker results, more "buy in," higher quality, and higher team spirit and morale. This is especially important today in light of employment security and trust.

Ongoing. It keeps everyone on the team involved and contributing to the project or task success. Mistakes or less effective methods are caught and corrected earlier in the process, resulting in higher-quality results and higher employee or team member self-confidence and self-esteem.

On completion. It creates an open environment in which completed projects can be effectively reviewed and critiqued and fosters learning that can be employed in successfully completing the next project.

> Coaching builds trust and morale because employees feel their views and suggestions are getting heard.

6. **What are some individual benefits of using coaching?**
Coaching builds trust as a result of people feeling that their ideas and suggestions are heard; therefore they feel ownership in their company's and their own success. Morale increases as well.

Employees learn and become adept at the process of self-assessment. They become skilled at self-analysis and critical thinking and build increased self-esteem and confidence in their ability to really make a meaningful contribution.

Coaching also improves performance. It helps employees develop the skills to examine each step of a process they are involved in and encourages new and better ways to do a job. Each improvement also helps employees discover hidden skills and abilities they then apply to their jobs.

COACHING FOR MANAGERS

> To benefit from coaching some control must be sacrificed.

7. What are some of the benefits of coaching for the company?

The benefits include the following: increased productivity. higher quality, higher morale, less turnover, lower costs, higher profits, customer satisfaction, faster problem-solving, and less downtime for additional training and development.

8. What do I have to change as a manager to use the coaching process?

As a manager, your first step is to recognize that coaching is different from what may be your traditional management communication style. You must recognize that to receive the benefits of coaching, you must be willing to give up some of your control because coaching is based on leading and influencing rather than directing. You achieve results through questions rather than directives and through listening and supporting rather than controlling. The new method may feel uncomfortable at first, but you'll get the hang of it soon enough.

9. How do I get started with my employees?

If you have not been using coaching to communicate with your employees, they'll probably wonder what's going on when you start. Therefore you should have a meeting with them to explain your reasoning and your goals and share with them what changes and benefits they can expect. It's not unusual to be greeted with some degree of skepticism and suspicion, which is okay. After they understand the process, most employees welcome the opportunity to be heard and to have input into their daily work processes and team activities. They'll begin to feel more important.

10. What are some of the drawbacks of coaching?

The "drawbacks" are really a matter of personal perception.

- Coaching does take more time and patience than giving directions, but the results for the whole organization will be significant.
- Coaching can appear threatening for managers who are not secure in their own self-image or job skills and may be uncomfortable in letting go of control.

COACHING FOR MANAGERS

- Managers might be very attached to what they did to get promoted and be leery of letting go of those "trophies of accomplishment."
- The "what are they going to need me for now?" syndrome may set in if the manager helps his or her employees grow and develop.

11. **How will I know if I'm coaching the wrong way?**
Be alert to feelings of emotional involvement of wanting to prove that you're right and the employee is wrong. Also, be aware of being judgmental: not listening, thinking of your own responses while the employee is still talking, formulating mental arguments, making more statements than questions, and letting your mind wander to other tasks you have scheduled for your day or week.

> You will need to work at not being judgmental.

12. **How do I help employees develop the ability to evaluate their own ideas and suggestions?**
One very good way is to use open-ended questions to help them think through the implications of their suggestions. This method of questioning helps develop a "mental balance scale" that employees use to evaluate the pluses and minuses of their ideas.

    Another way is to suggest that they evaluate their ideas from the perspective of another person involved, such as a customer, supplier, or fellow worker, and determine how they might respond to the suggested approach.

13. **How can I suggest ideas without "backing myself into a corner" by taking a position?**
One way to prevent this problem is to suggest ideas from an "approach" perspective rather than a firm decision; for example, you might ask, "What would happen if we approached the problem from this perspective?" Then, if the perspective approach doesn't work, you only have to suggest a new approach. No face is lost, and no solution becomes the "wrong one."

> Use open-ended questions to help develop employee suggestions.

STREETWISE
advice

◆ **Actively listen to your employee.**
Mentally prepare yourself to participate in a communication process that is based on actively listening to "the other person." The process is largely a dialogue rather than a monologue. Using active listening skills is key to coaching success. It means that you suspend the all-too-human tendency to apply judgment and carefully listen to what the other person is both saying and feeling about the coaching topic.

> Open communication between manager and employee is key to effective coaching.

◆ **Establish open lines of communication.**
Remind yourself that when you use a coaching technique, the objective is to establish and maintain open channels of communication. The goal is to create a comfortable environment in which performance levels can be examined and evaluated rather than explained and defended. Open communication is based on hearing and reviewing performance at three separate levels: performance that would be deemed as proficient, competent, or deficient.

◆ **Give feedback.**
Feedback should be included on performance observations at all three levels (i.e., the levels of proficiency, competency, and deficiency) whenever possible. Feedback on competency and proficiency is important to keep a balanced focus on the overall spectrum of performance and not fall into the trap of focusing only on deficiencies. Your employees will appreciate having some positives to build on.

◆ **Be patient.**
Patience is required for successful coaching. Most managers tend to "tell" rather than "ask" because they think they know how to do something better than their employees. They're afraid "asking" might make them look weak to the employees, or they simply find "telling" quicker and easier. If you want to succeed in coaching, you must relearn some asking approaches. It's a short-term investment for a long-term gain.

◆ **Conduct follow-up sessions.**
Be prepared to follow up on your mutual commitments to progress. If you've set measurable goals for a future date, plan to meet regularly to update the progress toward those goals. Remember that coaching is an ongoing commitment, and both you and your employee are responsible for maintaining momentum toward successful coaching results.

CHAPTER

3

MOTIVATION

Good communication and empowerment are great starting points for positive motivation. When employees run into problems, be prepared to help guide them to solutions while avoiding taking control or leaving them stranded without help. Use the self-assessments and questionaires to help improve your own motivational style as well as your ability to motivate specific employees.

MOTIVATION

MOTIVATIONAL TECHNIQUES

Threats, intimidation, nonspecific criticism, and humiliation are several examples of how some managers attempt to motivate their employees. Often without realizing it, managers use fear to get employees to produce or to toe the line. The implicit assumption behind this approach is to get people to respond to demands, deadlines, and responsibility by using fear as a motivator, without realizing that, in fact, it's very much the opposite—a demotivator.

FEAR

Fear can be a powerful motivator, but people usually respond to the pain that fear creates with distrust, blame, resentment, anxiety, stress, and a lack of enthusiasm and commitment, all of which negatively impact productivity. In the short term, fear may get the job done, but as a long-term strategy, it fails miserably because people will look to leave a situation where fear is an ever-present part of their jobs. On the other hand, when people receive praise, encouragement, and recognition, they respond with increased effort and enthusiasm.

> Fear and intimidation only serve to de-motivate employees.

EXTRINSIC AND INTRINSIC MOTIVATORS

Employees are motivated to complete tasks when they perceive the outcome will be a satisfaction of one or more of their basic human needs such as security, acceptance, respect, fun, power, fulfillment, choice, or self-esteem. Some managers make the assumption that employees are solely motivated by rewards such as money, benefits, titles, and recognition. These rewards are commonly referred to as extrinsic motivators; while they are important, they don't satisfy all of the basic human needs. In fact, they often provide only short-term results and behavior changes. To ensure long-term motivation, managers must create a work environment that provides employees with the opportunity to satisfy all of their needs. Such an atmosphere will foster the development of intrinsic motivation, where employees will be motivated by their own inner drives rather than extrinsic motivators such as money and titles.

MOTIVATION

Positive reinforcement through open communication is a good motivator.

MOTIVATION SCENARIOS

COMMUNICATION
Setup

Communication is the heart and soul of motivating employees. Employees are demotivated when they are unsure of manager expectations and priorities. They're motivated when managers provide clear expectations, instructions, information, and time frames, creating within the employees a sense of security, respect, power, and control in their jobs. Furthermore, managers need to communicate encouragement during the process as well as acknowledgment and appreciation on achievement of outcomes.

Demotivator

Manager: Sarah, I'm very disappointed in your ability to complete your responsibilities on schedule. We have to meet this deadline. If you don't get that report on my desk by Friday, there will be serious consequences.

Sarah: But I'm trying very hard—*[manager cuts her off].*

Manager: No buts about it. I want that report by Friday morning at nine!

Sarah: I'll do my best. *[appears upset and puts her head on the desk in frustration]*

The demotivator offers no help or suggestions.

Motivator

Manager: Sarah, you seem to be having problems meeting deadlines.

Sarah: Yes, I am. I can't ever seem to stay on top of them.

Manager: We both know that your ability to maintain your schedule is critical to the functioning of our department. Therefore, I'd like to sit down with you to make sure we agree on priorities, brainstorm possible solutions, and determine what information and resources I can provide to help you solve this problem. I'll also continue to

The motivator offers to help find solutions.

MOTIVATION

update you with any information that may impact task priorities.

Sarah: Thanks. *[feeling understood]* I want to do a good job, but I have so many responsibilities, I don't know what to do first. Can we have that meeting today? *[with enthusiasm]* I really want to hit that Friday deadline.

Manager: Well, my schedule is pretty tight today. Why don't we meet over lunch — around 12:30. Does that work for you?

Sarah: Sounds great.

PRESENTING A CHALLENGE

Setup

Productivity increases when employees are presented with growth opportunities and challenges. Most employees, when given the chance to leave their comfort zones, benefit from the stimulation and enjoyment of a new challenge. They experience a sense of acceptance, fulfillment, power, and recognition.

> Challenging employees with new situations encourages growth and creativity.

Demotivator

Manager: Jeff, the quality of your work has been slipping for the past couple of months. It seems like you don't care about your work, and to tell you the truth, if you can't do the job, I'll have to find someone else who can!

Jeff: *(apologetically)* I just can't seem to get into it anymore. I don't know what's wrong.

Motivator

Manager: Jeff, you've been working for us for a long time, and I can see it's time we give you some new challenges.

Jeff: Great. I'd like a change of pace.

Manager: I'd like you to take part in a mentoring program that we've just established here at the company. You'll be responsible for working with new employees in the department, helping them adjust to their new jobs and

MOTIVATION

> Creative problem-solving motivates employees to take responsibility for both the problem and the solution.

> A motivator guides the employee to a solution—but lets the employee actually find the solution himself.

new responsibilities. In particular, I want you to monitor their training and development and suggest methods or programs that will help them and the company improve productivity within the department.

Jeff: I can't wait to get started.

CREATIVE PROBLEM SOLVING

Setup

When an employee experiences a lack of freedom, choice, and control in his or her job, the response is usually to play the role of victim and blame others rather than take personal responsibility. Creative problem-solving, based on the philosophy of employee involvement in task analysis, decision making, and self-generated solutions, motivates the employee to take ownership of problems and responsibility for the success of the resolution.

Demotivator

Manager: Wayne, even though you've been hired to work from nine to five, we need an employee who's committed to getting his work done—even if that means coming in early and staying late. There are any number of people who would love to do what you do for a living. *[Manager leaves room]*

Wayne: *[under his breath with resentment]* Yeah right, and if I had a better manager, I wouldn't have this problem. I'm going to start looking around for something better.

Motivator

Manager: Wayne, you seem to be having problems completing your projects within a normal working day.

Wayne: Yeah, I just don't know how to finish what I start on any given day.

Manager: Well, I have an idea. During the next week, I'd like you to make a list of all your responsibilities and the ways you get your work done on a daily basis. Then analyze what you do to get the work done to determine if there's a better or more efficient way to complete it.

MOTIVATION

Wayne: It'll be a long list, but I think I can do it.

Manager: Also, keep a log of how long it takes to complete a task without interruptions. If you determine that you're constantly being interrupted, think of at least two solutions you believe will decrease the number of interruptions.

Wayne: I've never kept a log before but I am certainly willing to give it a shot.

Manager: Good! One week from today, we can meet to discuss options and decide how to increase your productivity and eliminate the continuous need to extend your workday.

Wayne: In the back of my mind, I knew that there had to be some way to improve my productivity, but I didn't think I had any input into the way work gets done around here. I'll get a list of solutions to you early next week.

COACHING

Setup

Frequently, employees don't have the strategies in place to complete a task. Consequently they're less motivated and often experience stress and a feeling of being overwhelmed. Managers who coach employees enable them to experience a sense of power and purpose. More importantly, during the process managers often help employees discover personal success strategies they can utilize on future projects.

> Clearly defined explanations encourage effective results.

Demotivator

Manager: Kathleen, I've given you more than a week to work on this project, and it looks like you spent a total of two hours on it. I want you to redo it. *[condescending]* I know you can do better than this!

Kathleen: *[Manager leaves and phone rings; Kathleen starts speaking]* Hello! *[pause]* Oh, hi, Terry. *[pause]* Nothing's wrong, just the same old thing. No matter what I do, it's never right! I give up. I can't read minds.

MOTIVATION

Motivator

Manager: Kathleen, it appears you and I weren't on the same wave-length about the outcome of this project.

Kathleen: How so?

Manager: I think it would be helpful for us to sit down and discuss the nuts and bolts of the project. I want to clarify my expectations for you and provide you with specific information and instructions that will help you produce a more polished product.

Kathleen: That sounds like it would be really helpful.

Manager: Good. Then, every Wednesday morning at nine, we can meet to review your progress, reexamine goals and deadlines, troubleshoot, and assess your need for additional resources. Is that plan acceptable?

Kathleen: Yes. I feel much better about the project now. I know I've messed up, but I feel confident my performance will improve with your input and support.

> The motivator takes the time to very clearly outline expectations and guidelines.

CONTINUOUS TRAINING

Setup

Employees become discouraged and demotivated when they lack the skills necessary to complete their responsibilities. By providing continuous training and growth opportunities, managers motivate employees by enhancing their self-esteem, which enables the employees to experience feelings of power and control in their jobs.

> The availability of training and growth motivates employees to improve their performance.

Demotivator

Manager: Sharon, you've been my administrative assistant for two years, and I've never seen such poor-quality work. You assured me that you could handle producing the company newsletter, but if you can't do the job, I'll have to find someone else to do it!

Sharon: *[with anger]* I can't do it the way you want it done because you expect me to use the new page layout

MOTIVATION

program, and I haven't had the time to read the manual or go through the tutorial.

Manager: I can't accept any excuses. I want to see that newsletter finished and ready to distribute.

Motivator

Manager: Sharon, you've been my administrative assistant for two years, and you've always given me quality work. But it seems you're having trouble creating the newsletter. Is there an issue or a problem that is holding you back?

Sharon: Yes, I'm having trouble learning the new page layout program.

Manager: What if I make arrangements for additional training or pair you with another employee who could mentor you until you feel totally comfortable with the new software?

Sharon: That would be a huge help. I really want to give this newsletter a professional look. With someone to help me learn the software, I'm sure I'll be able to do the job.

> The motivator recognizes that most employees want to do the work and will succeed with clear guidelines, proper training, and adequate resources.

MOTIVATION

MANAGER SELF-ASSESSMENT

MANAGEMENT STYLE SELF-EVALUATION

Overview

The purpose of the self-assessment is to give you, the manager, an opportunity to assess your managerial style in regard to motivational strategies. By examining your responses in each of the five categories, you can develop an action plan to improve the motivational environment you create in the workplace.

Read each question and place a check in the column that best describes you. Check "Frequently" if the statement is true 70 percent or more of the time. Check "Sometimes" if the statement is true 40 percent to 69 percent of the time. And check "Rarely or Never" if the statement is true 39 percent or less of the time.

	Frequently	Sometimes	Rarely or Never
A. Communication			
1. Do you make an effort to keep your employees informed and updated with information that will enable them to complete their job tasks?	_____	_____	_____
2. Do you inform employees of your priorities?	_____	_____	_____
3. Are you clear about your expectations in regard to outcomes?	_____	_____	_____
4. Are employees aware of their specific tasks and responsibilities?	_____	_____	_____
5. Do you discuss time frames and establish agreements regarding completion dates with employees?	_____	_____	_____
6. Do you acknowledge and recognize employees for their contributions to your department, organization, and/or company?	_____	_____	_____
B. Coaching			
1. Do you meet with employees to discuss progress and/or problems?	_____	_____	_____
2. Do you provide support and resources to your employees?	_____	_____	_____
3. Do you provide direction and guidance to your employees?	_____	_____	_____
4. Do you regularly provide constructive feedback in regard to job performance and goal accomplishments?	_____	_____	_____

MOTIVATION

5. Do you encourage employees to participate in setting their own performance goals? _____ _____ _____

C. Continuous Training

1. Do you provide opportunities for employees to update or learn new skills? _____ _____ _____
2. When you give employees new tasks and responsibilities, do you provide them with the training and support necessary for their success? _____ _____ _____
3. Do you encourage employees to create a career development plan and provide them with the training to advance within the organization? _____ _____ _____

D. Creative Problem-Solving

1. Do you include employees in decision making when an issue impacts them? _____ _____ _____
2. Do you involve employees in problem-solving in the department and encourage them to provide solutions? _____ _____ _____
3. Are employees involved in assessing and refining the effectiveness of processes and procedures? _____ _____ _____

E. Challenge

1. Are employees enthusiastic about and satisfied with their jobs? _____ _____ _____
2. Are the talents and skills of employees being fully utilized? _____ _____ _____
3. Are most employees satisfied with their levels of responsibility? _____ _____ _____

Totals: Frequently   _____

              Sometimes   _____

              Rarely or Never   _____

MOTIVATION

Use the test results to improve your ability to motivate people.

Scoring

If you scored between 15 and 20 on "Frequently," congratulate yourself; you're doing a great job in creating an environment that fosters motivation in employees. You can improve your "motivational quotient," or MQ, by setting goals to improve in all the areas that you did not mark "Frequently."

If you scored between 9 and 14 on "Frequently," you're doing a good job but you need to focus on the questions you marked "Sometimes" or "Rarely or Never," because they're pointing out areas where you need to set goals and make changes in your behavior.

If you scored between 0 and 8 on "Frequently," you definitely need to focus on this self-assessment and view it as a diagnostic tool to assist you in improving the environment that you create for your employees. Begin by noting the questions you marked "Rarely or Never." These are the areas you need to improve first. Then focus on the questions you marked "Sometimes," and determine how you intend to implement these strategies on a more frequent basis.

EMPLOYEE QUESTIONNAIRE

This assessment provides managers with suggested questions designed to be utilized in a one-on-one meeting with an employee who lacks motivation. The specific purpose of these questions is to help managers discover and eliminate any demotivators by clarifying job expectations and time frames, setting priorities, disseminating information, creating goals and providing feedback, generating solutions, and discussing growth opportunities and career development. In addition, managers will gather valuable information regarding the employee's preferences and strengths that can be useful in designing a position that may be more suited to the employee's unique wants and values.

1. What are your current roles and responsibilities?

2. How are you using your time? (percentages on each task)

3. What activities in your job description do you devote the most time to? Why?

4. What job tasks do you enjoy the most?

5. Do you enjoy working with groups or prefer working alone?

6. Do you understand how your job contributes to the success of this organization?

7. Do you have suggestions on ways to improve your productivity or the productivity of your organization?

8. Do you have a career development plan? What new skills would you like to learn?

9. Are there any resources or information you need to help you achieve your present goals?

10. What do you see yourself doing for this company in the future? One year from now? Two years? Three years?

> This questionnaire gives you insight to an employee's perspective on motivational issues.

MOTIVATION

EMPLOYEE ASSESSMENT TOOL

Overview

This assessment is designed to assist you, the manager, in determining whether you're effectively incorporating the key components of a motivating work environment into your department based on employee feedback. Give this chart to your employees to complete. Once the employees complete the short analysis, you'll be aware of specific areas in which you need to implement new strategies. Patterns may emerge indicating weaknesses in your style as well as indications of specific individual's needs.

	Frequently	Sometimes	Rarely or Never
A. Communication			
1. Do you feel that you are kept informed and are not "in the dark" about your job?	_____	_____	_____
Aware of priorities?	_____	_____	_____
Clear about expectations?	_____	_____	_____
Sure of responsibilities?	_____	_____	_____
Clear about time frames?	_____	_____	_____
2. Do you feel that you receive adequate acknowledgment of and recognition for your contributions?	_____	_____	_____
B. Coaching			
1. When you are having difficulty with a task, do you receive:			
Support?	_____	_____	_____
Direction?	_____	_____	_____
Feedback?	_____	_____	_____
2. When you are given a new responsibility, do you receive:			
Support?	_____	_____	_____
Direction?	_____	_____	_____
Feedback?	_____	_____	_____
3. Are you involved in setting your own performance goals?	_____	_____	_____

MOTIVATION

C. Continuous Training

1. Do you feel that you have all the necessary skills and
   competencies to perform your job?
   _____   _____   _____
2. When you are given a new task or responsibility,
   do you receive adequate training?
   _____   _____   _____
3. Are you given opportunities to learn, grow, and develop to
   expand your career options?
   _____   _____   _____

D. Creative Problem-Solving

1. Are you given opportunities to:
   Participate in decision making?   _____   _____   _____
   Provide solutions?   _____   _____   _____
2. Are you involved in determining methods and
   procedures?
   _____   _____   _____
3. Do you experience a sense of power and control in
   your job?
   _____   _____   _____

E. Challenge

1. Do you experience feelings of achievement and
   satisfaction in your job?
   _____   _____   _____
2. Do you feel that your skills and talents are being utilized
   in your job?
   _____   _____   _____
3. Are you comfortable with your level of responsibility?
   _____   _____   _____

TOTALS:

Frequently   _____
Sometimes   _____
Rarely or Never   _____

MOTIVATION

An emotionally nurturing
work environment
motivates.

QUESTIONS AND ANSWERS

1. **How do you motivate employees to reach for higher goals?**

   People have a place that I refer to as their comfort zone. It's a place that's familiar and risk-free. Reaching for higher goals means leaving the comfort zone, and leaving the comfort zone means taking risks; if the risks are too big, fear will demotivate, and no action will take place. Through coaching, a manager can encourage an employee to set goals that would take him or her out of this comfort zone. When the risks are reasonable and the goals achievable, the employee will experience feelings of accomplishment, power, and self-esteem and subsequently will be motivated to set more goals outside the comfort zone.

2. **Joe is my top salesperson, but he never completes his paperwork on time. His procrastination is interfering with the productivity of the entire office. How can I motivate him to get his paperwork turned in on time?**

   Explain how the problem is interfering with company productivity, and assign Joe the task of finding at least two solutions to the problem. If he's unable to find agreeable solutions, analyze the task and procedures to discover new strategies for dealing with the problem. For example, because he dislikes the task, he probably procrastinates and finds himself overwhelmed. One solution could be to make it a daily task of thirty minutes rather than a weekly task of two to three hours; another solution could be to pair Joe with another salesperson or employee who is paperwork-efficient so they can share organizational strategies; and a third solution might be to consider Joe's people personality. Is he is the most productive in people-stimulating situations? Arrange a work environment that accommodates that need.

3. **How do I motivate an employee who is going through a family crisis so he or she maintains productivity?**

   Employees only have so many points of attention they can give their work. When there's a family crisis, even though they're physically present in the workplace, most of their attention is given to the family crisis; therefore, productivity diminishes. Short-term decreases in productivity can be ignored; however, with a prolonged crisis, the manager should meet with the employee to express concern and support as well as offer options in regard to time off. The manager can't control the crisis but can provide a caring and supportive work environment. When people feel understood, they free up points of attention that subsequently will be refocused on the completion of work tasks.

4. **Our company has just gone through a major layoff, and the remaining employees are being asked to take on new responsibilities as well as continue previous tasks. How can I motivate them?**

Before you can motivate people to take on new responsibilities willingly, you must provide time for expressions of anger, resentment, and fear of the future. People need time to vent their feelings in either a group or a one-on-one situation. Once that process has taken place, managers must commit to open and honest communication, particularly about the company's financial future and direction. Managers also need to coach individuals about new roles and responsibilities, use creative problem-solving to redesign tasks and procedures for more efficiency, and offer continuous training so employees feel capable of performing new tasks.

5. **Because of the restructuring of our industry, the long-term employees are feeling resentment that all their years of dedicated service no longer ensure job security. How do I motivate them to continue their commitment?**

Job security, as many employees once knew it, no longer exists. The only real security exists within the employees and is expressed in the trust and beliefs they have about themselves. Managers can help build that trust and those new beliefs by encouraging employees to view themselves not just within the boundaries of a specific job but also to see them-

> When job security is compromised, management must work to re-establish trust.

MOTIVATION

selves from a broader view—in charge of their own personal career development. By meeting with employees and pointing out strengths and weaknesses, managers can guide them to consciously plan their own careers by learning new skills, taking courses, and enrolling in long-range development programs. Employees will be motivated to continue their commitment when they realize that taking responsibility for their career development will replace their lost feelings of job security and also provide them with choice, freedom, power, and a sense of purpose.

6. How do I motivate my employees to deliver the results I want?

When communication improves, so does motivation. Employees are not mind readers. The more clarity, direction, information, guidance, instruction, training, and support you give employees, the more likely you are to get the results you want.

7. How do I get an employee to take responsibility for his or her own performance?

Managers create the environments that foster motivation and responsibility. In such an environment, communication is open and safe; employees know the work they do is meaningful; they know how their specific contribution supports other teams; and they know why it's critical for them to produce quality work. Also in this environment, risk-taking is encouraged, goal-setting is ongoing, and both managers and employees are involved in problem-solving and making decisions. In addition, managers provide feedback, resources, and growth opportunities; communicate encouragement and acknowledgment; and provide recognition, rewards, increased levels of responsibility, and job advancement. Employees experience the benefits of taking responsibility for their performance.

> Encourage employees to take responsibility for their performance through open communication and realistic goal-setting.

8. **Two of my employees are constantly bickering about work tasks and responsibilities. How do I motivate them to be more productive and less disruptive in the workplace?**
Employees generally bicker over work tasks because their manager has not clearly defined their roles and responsibilities. Meet with each employee individually to discuss the problem and clarify any uncertainties in roles and responsibilities. If the problem persists, ask each employee to provide two solutions to the problem, and work to come to agreement. If the bickering continues, it's likely that job tasks are not the real issue, and I would strongly suggest the use of a conflict mediator to get to the real source of the problem.

9. **How do I motivate my employees to take initiative rather than rely on me for continuous direction?**
Taking initiative is a risk. If you want your employees to make decisions and not rely on you for continuous direction, you have to create a work atmosphere that encourages risk-taking. That means when an employee makes a mistake, he or she is guided, not chided! When you, as the manager, allow and encourage initiative without backlash, it will happen.

10. **How do I motivate myself when I feel overwhelmed, criticized, and unappreciated?**
Focus on your past successes. Remember times when you were highly motivated, and look for what pushed you and gave you that internal drive. Break down your work into manageable tasks, and delegate. Let go. Look at criticism to see if there are legitimate points. Face your critics, and ask them for suggestions. Appreciate yourself by acknowledging your personal effort. Use your strengths to move forward, and seek to improve in areas where you are weak. Put things in perspective. Take a vacation day, and do something you enjoy. Just remember, when you are motivated, your employees will be more motivated.

Use constructive criticism to improve your own performance.

STREETWISE
advice

◆ **Motivation comes from caring, not scaring.**

Fear should never be used as a motivation strategy. It may get you what you want now, but it will set you up for what you don't want in the future in the form of employee anger, resentment, and lack of enthusiasm and commitment. When employees feel that managers care about them and that they are perceived as respected and valuable members of the organization, they are more cooperative, enthusiastic, and committed to organizational goals, both in the present and in the future.

◆ **Employee motivation grows and blossoms in the right environment.**

When employees feel nurtured, appreciated, acknowledged, and respected, they'll give 100 percent of their time, effort, and commitment in return. The job of the manager is to create a work environment that provides employees with the opportunity to attain their goals and experience what they value most in their professional lives. In this environment, communication is open and honest, coaching for success is ongoing, training for performance improvement is continuous, and creative problem-solving is a way of life. Managers also need to provide sincere expressions of recognition, appreciation, and acknowledgment to nourish their employees' feelings of self-worth.

◆ **Walk your talk.**

Modeling the behavior you want from your employees is the most effective way to change any behavior. If you want your employees to arrive on time, you should be in early or at least arrive at an accepted time. If you want motivated employees, you need to become a role model for motivation. In addition, becoming more aware of what motivates you will increase your understanding of what motivates other people.

◆ **Make work fun!**

The research is clear: Laughter is not only good for the soul but also is good for the mind and body. Having fun is a basic human need, and when it's met in the workplace, productivity goes up. Appoint a "fun" committee, and come up with ways to bring enjoyment into your department. Bringing fun into the workplace lowers stress levels and provides opportunities for employees to build rapport with each other, which is the foundation for successful team-building.

◆ **Use the law of attraction.**

The law of attraction states that whatever we focus on we bring to ourselves. If you focus on the lack of motivation in your employees, you'll find more and more examples of it. When you seek to learn more about motivation and create an atmosphere that fosters it, you'll find more examples of motivation in the workplace.

◆ **Foster an ongoing commitment.**

Motivating employees is an ongoing process because people are continually growing and changing. As they achieve something they want or value, they then seek to achieve more of the same. If motivation is not kept on your managerial front burner, you'll see the fires in your employees slowly fade and die out.

CHAPTER

4

LEADERSHIP

Today's worker wants to know that they are an important part of an organization that is going someplace! As a leader you need to paint a specific vision of where your organzation or group is headed that will get people to follow you there! And you've got to let people know that they are an important part of your organization by sharing information with them; showing them respect; and involving them in decision-making and other important work.

WHAT DOES A GOOD LEADER DO?

Leadership emerges when a person is intolerant of the status quo and is committed to change. Leaders are creative and quick-witted. People are often sought out for leadership positions because of their intelligence as well as their organizational "common sense." Leaders are also able to present a vision of the future that stimulates, excites, and motivates their followers. They provide an environment where learning is rewarded and the organization becomes self-renewing. Leaders are motivated by a drive that focuses their actions and inter-actions on what is right with respect to ethical, legal, human, and financial considerations. Leaders are flexible—they take what the pre-vailing situation offers and work with it. They are not bound by con-vention just because it is convenient or traditional. Leaders have an ego strength in the face of adversity and demonstrate a sense of reli-ability and integrity, which they offer and share with their employ-ees, customers, outside vendors, and industry colleagues.

> Leaders are able to present a vision of the future that stimulates, excites, and motivates their followers.

STARTING A NEW DIVISION

Setup

In this scenario, the CEO of a market research firm that serves the computer and biotechnology industries has decided to start a new division of his company that will repackage his company's information into products that can be sold as stand-alone CD-ROMs or download-ed from the Internet to a wider marketplace. He must sell his vision to his employees, who will assume control of this division under the CEO's guidance even though they have little or no formal training in this area. The CEO will attempt to convince his employees that they have certain skills he feels will transfer very well into this area.

CEO: I've called you together today to discuss my plans for a new division. As you know, our growth in research consult-ing services has been stagnant and I do not see any expan-sion possibilities in the near future. As such, I want to cre-ate a new division that focuses on repackaging our

LEADERSHIP

Leaders seek new opportunities for company growth and improvement.

information on CD-ROM and creating files that will be available for downloading off of our new Web site.

James: What types of products are you considering Walter?

CEO: I want to take our existing information and create CD-ROMs that would focus on three aspects of our consulting expertise that could be packaged and sold to other industries such as pharmaceuticals and financial services. I also see tremendous growth in the Internet, and we are going to create our own site where we can sell this information to a wider audience.

Jane: None of us has any retail marketing experience. How will we know if we are reaching our target market with these products?

CEO: We are not looking at the retail market because our information is too specialized and doesn't appeal to that audience. What I see here is an opportunity to take the information we have gathered and create a CD or a program that can reside on our Web site and that will demonstrate two or three business models that other industries can use in their business to improve their efficiency and productivity.

Cliff: So, in effect, we become information brokers for companies in other industries?

CEO: Something like that, but I wouldn't necessarily use that term. I want this division to act as a profit-and-loss center and build products that will get companies in these industries to come back to us to take advantage of our other services. It is one way to leverage the information resources that already exist within our company.

James: Wouldn't it be easier and less expensive just to repackage in print format what we already have and sell it to these companies?

CEO: We are known as a market research firm for two specific industries: computers and biotechnology. To reach these other companies in different industries, I want to create this division as a departure from our existing business so that there will be no confusion as to who does what for whom.

Jane: How will we produce these CDs and create files for this Web site?

CEO: My plan is to lease space in the building down the street and outfit the space with computers and equipment needed to create the CDs and the Web site. Staffing needs will be filled internally as well as with external hires. We will sell these products through direct channels as well as value-added or boutique resellers, and our marketing needs will be filled from internal people.

Cliff: Where do we fit into this plan? None of us has the experience in CD-ROM production.

CEO: It will be a learning experience for all of us, Cliff. We each have a skill set that I believe will make this venture a success regardless of certain technical inexperience. Anything in the way of production capability that we don't have internally will be filled by outside hires. I want to make it clear that all of you have a stake in this new division, and I am counting on you to make this a value-added venture for the company.

James: What will your involvement be in this project?

CEO: Initially, I plan to have day-to-day involvement in starting the division, but as time goes on, I will be counting on all of you to take significant responsibility in managing and growing the division. I realize that there will be growing pains, especially since we have no formal product experience, but I know that the skills and abilities of everyone here will help us grow this division. For instance, James, your work on page layout and design of our research reports for our clients was first-rate. I know that you can use that skill in designing the box packaging for the CDs.

James: Thanks. I am very proud of my design capabilities.

Jane: When do you plan to launch this division?

> Good leaders have faith in both themselves and the people they work with.

LEADERSHIP

CEO: I want start-up and launch to take place at the beginning of the fall quarter. I want each of you to draw up a plan for staffing requirements and tell me what information resources we possess that you believe will translate effectively into new products. Financing will come from several sources, including internal funding as well as outside investment. This is a great opportunity for us to jump into a new type of market for our information services, and I have every confidence that we can do an outstanding job of extending the growth of this company.

TURNING AROUND A TROUBLED DIVISION
Setup

In this scenario, senior management has called a manager of the snack foods division of a food and beverage company that has been losing money for the past year and charged him and his fellow managers with the responsibility for turning around the division. The implication from the meeting is that if this manager fails to turn things around, he and the other managers in the division will lose their jobs. The manager's initial reaction is one of depression and anxiety wondering how this could have happened and what lies ahead. After thinking about it overnight, however, he decides to adopt a positive approach and rally the other managers to boost their energy and enthusiasm for turning around this tough situation. At the same time, he is realistic about the possibility of layoffs if things do not turn around in a reasonable period of time.

Realistic and positive goals are encouraged by good leaders.

Manager (alone in his office): I must not allow the other managers to see me in this state. I've got to be positive and proactive and convince them that we have what it takes to overcome this situation.

Later, at the meeting with the other managers:

Sharon: You wanted to see us?

Manager: As you all know, I met with senior management and they are unhappy about the division's performance over the past year. They want to see some positive changes and a turnaround very soon.

Sharon: You mean we're going to lose our jobs, don't you.

Manager: Not if we pull together and develop a plan to turn the division around. There is a lot of talent here, and I believe that everyone in this room has what it takes to make this work. Of course, there are no guarantees that even if we are moderately successful, senior management might decide to go ahead and make changes.

Jeff: That doesn't sound very promising. If we don't meet their timetable, I'm sure they'll close down the division or sell it off.

Manager: Sure, that could happen, but I want to focus on how we can meet this challenge and succeed. Look, I'm not saying it will be easy, but if we don't try to pull together, we will fail.

Carl: Even if we succeed in turning a profit next year, who is to say that upper management won't take advantage of our success and sell us off to the highest bidder? They'll line their pockets and we'll wind up losing our jobs.

Manager: If senior management really wanted to cut their losses, we would have been sold off long ago. We should look at the talent in this room and in this division. Each of us has within us the capability to create, develop, and implement elements of a strategy that will return us to profitability. We have a great opportunity here to prove to upper management that we have what it takes to be market leaders in our category once again.

Sharon: This seems like such a huge undertaking. How do we know where to start or what to focus on to develop a turnaround plan? I've never been in a situation like this before.

> Good leaders focus on the positive and the importance of "pulling together."

LEADERSHIP

Manager: None of us has been through anything like this, Sharon. Our success or failure will be directly related to everyone's efforts to work hard, pull together, and support one another during this difficult time. If I didn't think we could do it, I would have submitted my resignation to senior management this morning. That's how much confidence I have in all of you that I know we can succeed.

Jeff: Okay, so where do we start?

Manager: We need to put our heads together to identify strengths and weaknesses in the division. Each of us should make a list of what we do exceptionally well and where we are stumbling versus our competitors.

Carl: Are we talking about people, products, resources?

Manager: Everything. We need to examine our problem areas that have left us vulnerable to our competitors and how we can shore up those areas and turn them into strengths.

Sharon: How will we prioritize what areas need the most attention?

Manager: After we brainstorm our ideas, we'll see where we concur and where the disagreements lie. After listening to all arguments for areas where we disagree, we'll formulate our top three problem areas and create teams to work on solutions to these areas. I know all of you are apprehensive, but I am committed to turning this division around, and I am confident we can do the job together.

> Effective leaders empower others by involving them in critical decision-making and analysis.

EMPLOYEE DECISION-MAKING

In this scenario, a new manager has been hired to run a manufacturing division that has barely managed to meet its goals each quarter for the past five years. The division was formerly run by an autocratic manager who insisted on making all the decisions for the other managers in the division. This new manager believes in pushing the decision-making down the line so that employees take more responsibility for decisions such as purchasing materials and sales forecasting. The employees are uncomfortable with this change and do not know how to react to this new style of leadership and the new responsibilities that go with it.

Fred: Hi, Nancy. Have you made a decision yet on how many new metal fixtures we should order for next month's delivery of new swing sets?

Leader: I'm not sure I understand, Fred. Aren't you responsible for signing off on all material purchases?

Fred: The previous manager of this division always set monthly purchase requirements and gave us the quarterly sales forecasts. He told us what to order and when to order it.

Leader: Well, I expect my managers to make those decisions without my input. If you want to bounce some ideas off me, I'll be happy to listen, but you've got to think through the process and make your own purchasing decisions.

Fred: But I have no experience in this area! What if I under or overestimate demand or make a mistake and order the wrong part?

Leader: Fred, as long as you are thorough and pay attention to the details, I'm not going to hold a mistake over you. We all make mistakes from time to time. It only upsets me when I see someone who makes a mistake due to lack of effort.

Fred: Can you give me an idea as to how I should start the process?

Leader: I'd start with the past six to eight months of purchases and see whether you can detect a pattern that will serve as a guide for future materials purchases. Tell Purchasing that all purchase orders should go through you.

Fred: Okay, I'll get right on it.

Leader: Hi Susan. What's up?

Susan: Nancy, I was wondering whether you have decided on a new morning and afternoon break policy. Since the company was bought by Remtron, some of the employees are confused as to which policy should be enforced, since

> Good leaders delegate—but also continue to be available for coaching.

LEADERSHIP

Re-evaluating management style is essential for improvement and change.

Remtron's policy is different from our current policy. What should we do?

Leader: That really is something I would like you and the other managers to decide among yourselves. What do you think the policy should be?

Susan: I'm not sure. The previous manager of this division always set the company schedule including the break policy. I've never established any company policies.

Leader: Well, maybe now would be a good time to start. Why don't you gather the other employees together, talk this issue through, and decide what you collectively think should be the new policy. Formulate the language of the policy so that all I will have to do is sign off on what you think the new policy should be.

MANAGER SELF-ASSESSMENT

As a manager, you should be interested in understanding your management style so that you can use this knowledge to become a more effective leader. Take the following self-assessment quiz to help gain some insight into your approach.

Overview

This assessment is designed to provide you with a personal profile of your leadership competencies, attitudes, and behaviors. Since leadership only becomes "good" or "bad" in its execution, this assessment should not be considered in that way. You should frame the interpretation of this instrument as a continuum of skills, attitudes, and behaviors that can be developed over time.

Give yourself 4 points if you check "Frequently," 2 points if you check "Sometimes," and 0 points if you choose "Rarely or Never." Total your score when you finish the assessment to determine your leadership rating.

LEADERSHIP

	Frequently	Sometimes	Rarely or Never

A. Activism/Change

1. When I sense that something is "not right," I find a way to make it better.
2. I understand who in my organization can help me or my employer achieve our goals.
3. I have little tolerance when inertia overcomes a project or employee.
4. I respect the past and our company's legacy; however, I do not avoid rethinking "tradition."
5. I am committed to quality.
6. I am driven toward high performance.

B. Intelligence/Learning

1. I believe that I have the mental capacity to think through most complex situations.
2. I welcome the challenge of complex issues and problems.
3. I am committed to creating an environment where mistakes become learning experiences.
4. I encourage my staff to disagree with me.
5. I tend to hire people who have talents, knowledge, and skills I don't possess.
6. I believe I am more intelligent than lucky.
7. I'm not intimidated by ingenious people.
8. I like being around "smart" people.

C. Vision

1. I look at things around me and I am able to envision how they can and will be better.
2. I articulate abstract ideas to others quite easily.
3. I have a picture of the future that I am committed to fulfilling.
4. The vision I have for the company incorporates what is strongest about our firm.
5. I often utilize symbols and images to motivate my employees.

LEADERSHIP

6. I communicate and exemplify high standards of
performance.

D. Altruism/Caring

1. I generally respect the employees with whom I work.
2. I hold general conversations with my employees.
3. I genuinely admire and appreciate the people who
work with me.
4. Knowing about my employees' values is important to me.
5. Knowing about my employees' hobbies is important to me.
6. I encourage employees to help each other develop to
their full potential.
7. I communicate often with my employees about work.
8. I communicate often with my employees about
leisure activities.
9. I provide personal attention to people who may need it.

E. Communication

1. I am generous in my praise and recognition of my
employees who perform quality work.
2. I seek the opinions of my employees.

F. Flexibility

1. If plans go sour, I recover easily and without searching
for a scapegoat.
2. I have a high tolerance for ambiguity.
3. When an employee has a "bright idea" I try to find a way
to accommodate it.

G. Spirit/Soul

1. I have an inner sense of balance that allows me to
move through the day with serenity.
2. I know how to relax.
3. I take the time to enjoy the nonwork component of my life.
4. I have an emerging leadership style that is truly my own.
5. I know how to "play."
6. I allow my employees to see and experience all facets of
my personality.

7. In the office as well as outside the office, my spiritual foundation guides me.

H. Integrity/Ego Strength

1. I do my own "dirty work."
2. I don't disappear when an employee is in trouble.
3. I don't ask anyone to do something I would not do.
4. If I had to choose, I would treat employees better than bosses.
5. I admit or explain when I'm wrong.
6. I can and do take the heat.
7. I consider myself a symbol of achievement and success.
8. I am comfortable with who I am.

I. Creativity/Innovation

1. Ideas readily come to me.
2. I strive to have employees conceptualize old problems in new ways.
3. I provide new ways of looking at issues that may seem puzzling to employees.

J. Reliability

1. I ensure that my employees have the information and resources necessary to do the job.
2. If I say it's so, I make it so.
3. I don't avoid problems or sticky issues.
4. I make sure that there is congruence between what employees are asked to do and what they can expect from me in support of their efforts.

Total Score:_____

Scoring

200+:

You are well on your way to being a superior leader. The attributes and behaviors you exhibit tend to motivate, enrich, educate, and inspire others. When those abilities are matched with organizational knowledge and personal drive, they become the mettle for solid leadership.

LEADERSHIP

150-199:

You are working well toward the development of leadership "savvy." By examining the various factors of the assessment, you can see where you need to focus your attention and possibly even reflect on your assumptions about work, the people who work with you, and why you want to be a leader. You may find from this exercise that you will learn how you stimulate more accountability and independence in others by showing more vulnerability within yourself.

110-149:

The reasons for attaining the leadership positions you seek may be more self-centered than organizationally based. Trust is an essential component of leadership, and your score indicates that either you believe the people you work with are not trustworthy or you doubt your own ability to lead effectively. In either case, you may be holding on too closely or not delegating at all. Consequently, those around you may not be confident of your support. Examine each area of this assessment and reflect on why you are so dedicated to "control" and what you really have to lose by guiding rather than "forcing."

0-109:

The attitudes, behaviors, and talents you are bringing to a position of leadership are unseasoned. You may be holding on to some archaic notions of "boss/subordinate" relationships, or have been too long under the influence of managers, who do not or a climate that does not value individuals' fundamental objective to do well and need to be appreciated. Before you accept or seek a higher position of supervision, management, or leadership, you may want to pursue new mentoring relationships within the organization, take some management courses, read some of the newer writings on management, and consider objectively why you want to lead. The goal of leadership is not out of reach; you are just going to have to do lots of "homework" to be effective.

> You can stimulate more independence in others by revealing dependence in yourself.

LEADERSHIP

QUESTIONS AND ANSWERS

1. **What is a quick acid test to see if my leadership style is working?**

   Focus on your attitude and approach to working to see if it attracts or repels people. Think about how you treat peers and employees. Do you treat people like "mushrooms," or are you a dedicated gardener who creates an environment that allows people to build competence and confidence and flourish to their full potential?

2. **How would you characterize a person's leadership style?**

   Leadership is no longer being the "Lone Ranger," and followers won't be led by the nose on pure faith. You have to offer people something of value (intangible, such as a preferred vision, or tangible, such as improved profitability) for them to muster the energy and dedication to support your leadership. The self-fulfilling prophecy is real; if you don't think much of others, you won't get much from them. Attitude has a lot to do with the altitude of accomplishment.

3. **What can I do to lead my team in a manner that gets the job done, and gets it done well?**

   An important part of the leader's responsibility is to ensure that the work team has something to work with. The leader must marshal the resources necessary, or illuminate the path or general direction for the workers to obtain the same means to get the task accomplished. All the while, the leader is also preparing followers for greater levels of responsibility and an independence of action and attitude that will stimulate higher levels of performance.

4. **What attributes distinguish me from others?**

   Think of the people in leadership positions whom you admire. What draws you to them? Make a list of those qualities, and then make a list of your own "leadership magnets." Do you have a winning attitude and a track record to back it up? Have you taken an unpopular or novel approach that reaped unforeseen benefits? Do you create a working envi-

> Good leaders not only give valuable guidance, but respect the value of others and guide themselves by it.

LEADERSHIP

> The attitude that you present to others will affect their performance, both positively and negatively.

ronment that encourages and supports others? How much do you need to be "the star"?

5. **What do I need to do to get my employees to follow me?**
Do people who work with you get anything other than tired? Are you too wrapped up in your own success? Do you forget about the development of others? Do you stimulate their minds? Allow for growth-inspiring mistakes? Greet crises as opportunities for innovation? Know and understand each individual's needs and aspirations and how you can promote them? Followers must be strong enough to support the leader, and they can become weary quickly if they're not fortified.

6. **What behaviors can I exhibit that will draw out my employees' commitment and that will stimulate their carrying the message of my vision?**
While you cannot be expected to always put on a happy face, you also should not assume the role of poster child for the end of the earth. Energy, confidence, competence, and a refuse-to-fail attitude will affect and infect others. And if you have taken the time to carefully draw up your vision and have presented it for all to see and examine and contribute to, you will have sown the seeds for a bumper crop of commitment and loyalty.

7. **What should I be willing to do or endure to achieve my vision?**
Leadership is not easy. It becomes easier after achievements accumulate; but the road is often not paved (or the path may not even be clear). As the leader, you are the "point." People up and down the hierarchy will be looking to you for answers, strategies, reasons, and positive outcomes.

8. **How do I respond when I am criticized or under pressure?**
Defensiveness breeds defensiveness and sets people apart from you. While certainly not all criticism is warranted, flying off the handle at most of it will be perceived as a sign of shallowness in your planning (or a weakness of the plan). Hear all critiques, ask for others to provide their assessments, and

utilize all the reactions and opinions as input for your response. If you want a team that will be honest and bring you the most relevant data, they must know that the bad news will be welcomed as easily as the good news.

9. **Am I still leading when I'm standing alone?**
Yes, you are. It is in those solitary moments and actions that the mettle of leadership is forged. So don't be seduced into thinking that you need a "bunch" of people behind you to lead. Leadership comes from having the courage, tenacity, foresight, and energy to blaze a trail, investigate a mystery, and take bold action.

10. **How do I communicate my vision so that it is _our_ vision?**
Of course, you are going to be committed and excited about the image you've sculpted for tomorrow because it is your idea. The challenge you'll have as a leader is to stimulate that same enthusiasm, dedication, and perspective in others. First, gently introduce the concept. Have ardor, but don't over-whelm them. Ask for critical impressions. Receive sugges-tions for changes. Recognize and try to minimize apprehen-sion. Talk to your people often, and provide them with occa-sions to articulate what their vision is and how yours sup-ports or conflicts with it. Over time, the group will be using the same language, similar images, and corresponding zeal. And if you are truly gifted in this process, they will actually believe that this vision was their idea.

> Share ideas and suggestions to encourage teamwork and positive feedback.

STREETWISE
advice

◆ **Take a stand.**
Robert Browning once wrote, "Ah, but a man's reach should exceed his grasp, or what's a heaven for?" Step out and stand for something. People are genuinely attracted to those who move in reasoned, affirmative, innovative, or intrepid directions.

◆ **Build and develop strong followers.**
One of the hallmarks of exemplary leaders is that they have surrounded themselves with intelligent, action-oriented, dedicated, and ardent followers. The mistake made by so many leader-aspirants is to shy away from or marginalize strong followers. This behavior is grounded in the mistaken notion that the follower may overshadow the leader. But in actuality, by showing confidence in the followers' abilities, providing challenging assignments, and being personally concerned about follower/colleague development, the leader is engendering respect, loyalty, and commitment while also stimulating high-quality performance. The collateral effect is that the leader is also making it easier to delegate and freeing herself or himself to devote more energy to novel and more strategic issues.

◆ **Communicate often.**
If you want people to follow you, they must know who you are, what you represent, what you can do, and what your vision is. To do that, you must tell them. Disseminate your ideas in meetings as well as in writing. Participate in formal and informal groups that address relevant issues of your firm. Have frequent meetings with your colleagues and coworkers. Inform those around you of what your priorities, dreams, and values are, and let your talents be known. Take advantage of opportunities to

feature and utilize your skills. Cultivate relationships outside of your area, so that when there is a task to be done, you will be considered for it.

◆ **Be a keen listener.**
For your workers as well as for yourself, it is important to "keep your ear to the ground." It builds your sensitivity to and knowledge of the organization, and it helps you to know how you can influence the organization.

◆ **Play to your strengths.**
This also means that you should understand and be committed to working on your personal weaknesses. As a leader, you must do those things that will make others want to be around you, and you must demonstrate that you are a competent and confident person. For example, if you are not a strong or inspiring public speaker, then do the background research, write the report or the speech, or introduce the subject at the meeting for someone else to present. But also put yourself into situations where new skills and competencies can be developed. Utilize your colleagues', mentors', and followers' expertise to complement and enhance your own. Work with someone—model his or her behavior, or have that person constructively critique your performance. Take classes, within the company or at a local college.

◆ **Leadership is everywhere; don't look for it just "at the top."**
Some leadership-aspirants wallow in despair because they are not "in charge." They think that just because they don't hold a designated position of leadership, they cannot exercise leadership (or they cannot have models for leadership who are

peers). Think of how you can effect change or promote the vision of the designated leader from where you are in the hierarchy. By becoming recognized for making things happen in one context, the opportunities for larger, more significant, more strategic influence will come your way. Search for leadership opportunities; volunteer for tough assignments. Find solutions to problems that your manager doesn't know exist. Then inform him or her about your findings.

◆ Be yourself and believe in yourself.

A positive self-image will help you project an aura of confidence that will inspire others. You are human—your leadership style should be a natural extension of who you are. If you find that it isn't, then your leadership venue is inappropriate, you are living out someone else's vision of you, or what you are working for is contrary to your values. While growing and changing, most leaders work very hard at developing skills and competencies. The thing that exemplary leaders do not do is to assume a mask that disavows essential anchors of their personalities. It is also important to be natural in your leadership endeavors, because in times of stress, an "act" or assumed character will disintegrate into your underlying essence, and the people who follow or work with you need to know just who will show up.

◆ Understand the "game"—be politically aware and learn how to effectively and appropriately utilize politics and the political subsystem.

No matter the level of expertise you possess, the confidence you exude, or the success you've amassed, if you are politically naive, your leadership acumen will never mature. So much of what leaders do involves negotiating the political environments of organizations. One of the best preparations an aspiring leader can have is to become intimately aware of the power players and political actors in an organization and understand the history and alliances of them. It also doesn't hurt if you are able to observe or work with any of these people.

◆ Make yourself visible.

There is an old adage that speaks of not hiding your candle under a basket. With leadership, that is very appropriate. There is nothing arrogant or inappropriate about letting others know what you have done or can do. When you have made a significant accomplishment or received recognition beyond your "home" base, be sure the word gets back home. Share a complimentary memo, or if the occasion warrants, see that a memo or letter gets back to your supervisor or mentor. Participate in activities that place you in the spotlight, and be well prepared to shine. Don't take on too much, but what you do take on, do it with quality and panache.

◆ Don't sell out; have and keep your integrity.

There will never be anything more important than your word, so keep it. Evaluate situations very carefully and communicate your position clearly. Followers will neither respect nor take risks for leaders who are unreliable. This does not mean that you cannot change your mind. However, that change needs to be conscientiously appraised, and you need to inform those closest to you, so they will not be surprised by you and will understand your decision. Be true to your values and what you think is right. Honesty must be your hallmark.

◆ Have genuine interest, concern, and passion for your followers and colleagues.

For people to follow, they must believe that you care for them. You must value them, not only for what they can do for you and the organization but also for who they are as individuals. Know who they are, what their strengths and developmental needs are, and design training assignments and offer opportunities for recognition that address each person's profile. Also, become familiar with their personal and avocational interests. In other words, always remember that the people who work with and for you have personalities and lives that go beyond the organization. Knowing them, treating them well, and understanding their needs and values will enhance your leadership.

◆ Teamwork is essential.

Simply stated, there is no leadership without followership. Be artful in your approaches for working with people. While you are the leader, never forget that there are many others who have contributed to your ascension. Provide them with relevant assignments, meaningful recognition and your confidence. You may be "on top," but others are supporting you; don't ever be so arrogant as to assume that you did it alone.

◆ Learn from mistakes.

Everyone makes them, so don't agonize over them but find ways to keep the same mistakes from happening again. If a mistake occurs on your watch, quickly debrief and regroup. Assignment of blame is not as important as construction of a recovery strategy. Leadership is about moving forward, not wallowing in the past.

◆ Be sure that people are really getting the message.

Ask people to be sure they are really getting the message you are delivering. At group meetings, ask people what they see as the key components of the company's strategy. At individual meetings or in questionnaires, ask questions like, "Do you feel that the company has a clear, future direction?" or "Do you feel the company is successful?" or "Do you think the company will prosper in the future?" If it turns out that the people aren't comprehending the message, give it again.

◆ Extend leadership to all parts of the organization.

In companywide meetings, or other large meetings, you can show leadership in a broad, visionary way. But you or your managers should have smaller meetings with people in each functional area. People want to feel that their department or function has a clearly defined role and direction within the overall plan.

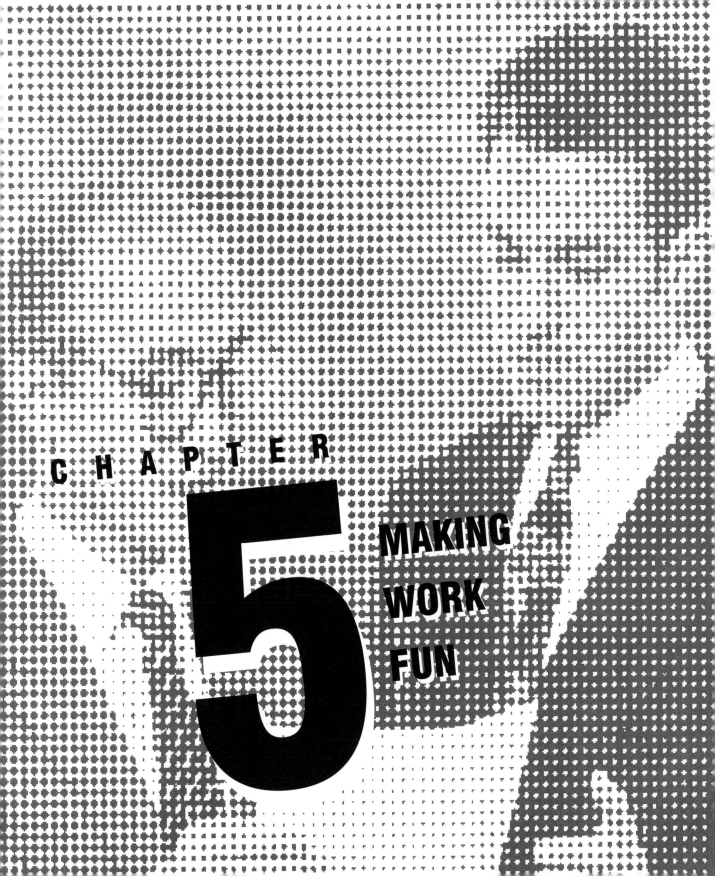

CHAPTER

5

MAKING
WORK
FUN

Creating a fun workplace means more than blowing up party balloons and serving birthday cake! Today's employees first want to feel respected, to feel that they matter, and to be kept informed. They expect to be treated fairly and consistently, and they expect to be challenged and heard. But a little time out for fun and games—especially celebrations—will help push your company to success!

MAKING WORK FUN

Just because other businesses are boring, stale, routine places to work doesn't mean that your business has to be, too.

Make work *FUN, EXCITING,* and *CHALLENGING* for your employees. You'll find you have *LESS TURNOVER, HAPPIER EMPLOYEES, GREATER PRODUCTIVITY* and *you* might have more fun, too!

If you can wear a sincere smile, you are on your way to making your workplace more enjoyable for everyone. Research has shown that people create a more positive perception of a situation when their first interaction includes a smiling face. Let your smile be the beginning of a strategy that will make your business a desired place to work for a diverse group of people.

IDENTIFY OBJECTIVES

Have you ever observed a child who was not motivated to learn, to explore? Have you ever observed a child who was not excited about a new addition to the environment or a new way of interacting with an object or person?

How many times have you gotten some highly creative idea after watching or playing with your child?

Creating an environment with the sheer energy, excitement, and creative enthusiasm of a child is something that business needs to understand and nurture.

Companies need to create vehicles to help blur the lines between work and play. They need to help employees feel that what they do at work is fun. The playful exchanges at work permit the development of enthusiasm, which breeds creative ideas that can easily be transformed into high levels of productivity.

The excitement that emanates from a playful work environment is directly linked to the ability of the work force to apply these creative ideas to solving problems and creating innovations in products, services, and commodities. These innovations generate profits because the marketplace is intrigued by and attracted to creative variations of the ordinary. The marketplace is eager to obtain new

> People who enjoy their work are more motivated and productive.

MAKING WORK FUN

and interesting products and services that address needs both real and imagined.

A case in point is the story of the Flat Cat Company. Some highly creative entrepreneurs decided that urban yuppies had strong desires for pets but were not always able to satisfy this need. Rental leases for apartments and condominiums oftentimes prohibited pets. The responsibilities of caring for a pet did not always mesh with the highly active and driven lifestyle of the yuppies of the 1980s. They decided that they could fill the need for a pet without any of the hassle. They decided that the market would support a line of Flat Cats and Flat Babies and Flat Plants. In effect, a totally off-the-wall idea was translated into a viable business that created a need that the marketplace didn't even know existed. Look around at your local gift and card stores. You are sure to find examples of this creative idea, now in its second-generation variation.

We can only imagine the highly creative environment in which this creative team worked. Lots of fun, lots of crazy antics all designed for the generation of some potentially strong business opportunities. The work environment was fun, and due to the fun the creative energy was allowed and encouraged to rise to the surface and emerge from the various players. People who have creative ideas will not always share their thoughts. It is very risky to expose yourself with the statement of a wild and crazy idea even in a supportive environment. But imagine the same wild and crazy idea expressed in a moment of shared corporate fun and insanity. The same idea that may have been respectfully listened to in a more formal setting will have the opportunity to get bounced around in a playful time within the company. This bouncing around is the key to developing new and creative solutions to problems.

Think about the creative process this way. Imagine an idea as a round ball thrown onto a table. In a highly structured, staid environment, the ball represents a new idea that may easily roll off the table because the people around the table are not easily engaged in commenting or building on the primary idea.

> A fun work environment breeds creativity that may not reveal itself otherwise.

In a fun work environment, where people are viewed in a more positive manner, the idea might get some immediate comments, funny in most cases, that will keep it on the table for a few minutes longer. Think about each comment as a small piece of clay attached to the ball. The addition of many pieces of clay will keep the ball from falling to the floor and keep the idea alive.

In a totally insane, highly charged fun environment, that same idea might get so many pieces of clay attached to it that it begins to actually take the form of a solid cube—something that out of a fun and totally crazy idea has become a valid, reasonable idea that is real and potentially a solution to a business problem.

Companies that encourage fun and encourage the child in each worker have a greater chance of capturing the golden ring of success.

EXPECTATIONS

People generally want to know what is expected of them in any given situation.

In any organization a sense of comfort and trust can be achieved when all members of the company know exactly what to expect regarding their authority and responsibility.

To achieve a level of enjoyment and fun at work, some basic expectations, for employees and the company, should be defined.

1. **Create a fair and consistent environment.** Make sure that every employee in the company is treated equally. Supervisors in particular should see to it that employees know where they stand at all times, and how things are going with the company as a whole.

   It is imperative that each employee knows and believes that he or she is equal to all other employees in the company. If there is the slightest sense of favoritism or bias toward a group, person, or situation, you and your company are headed for internal employee morale issues and in many cases legal challenges. You know that it is illegal to discriminate against classes of people, but be aware of the small

> Favoritism can compromise overall employee morale and create internal conflict.

MAKING WORK FUN

issues that might make someone feel discriminated against even if it is not an identified legal issue.

For example, the simple issue of letting one employee leave early without any obvious explanation and then having another employee ask to leave early and the second employee being asked a series of questions can give the appearance of discrimination. It seems like no big deal to you, but to the second employee it appears that employee one is getting preferential treatment. Your challenge is to be sure everyone believes and feels that you are fair and consistent in dealing with all issues. The development of policies and procedures is generally the way in which companies help to minimize problems with this issue.

2. **Challenge people.** Whenever possible, try to create jobs that minimize constant repetition with few variations. Be sure to include job responsibilities in which the employee is likely to encounter situations in which he or she will have to tackle new problems or devise new solutions for his or her tasks.

When you are designing the job descriptions for various positions, always include an expectation that will direct employees to learn the skills of other positions as part of their job description. For example, include a statement such as this:

Work with (name of other job position) whenever possible to become acquainted with the duties and responsibilities of this position.

This simple addition to your job description allows you to encourage an employee to learn new skills, become more valuable to the company, and to achieve a greater degree of self-gratification upon learning new information and new skills.

People want to learn and want to be challenged, but they also want to know what to expect, and it is important not to surprise them with the challenge. Make it part of the job they agreed to do and you agreed to pay them for. Don't forget to

> Employees who feel challenged are encouraged to learn more skills and to utilize the ones they already have.

MAKING WORK FUN

reward them with praise and positive feedback when they do stretch and learn new skills and abilities. As you apply this basic principle you will discover that your existing employees have the capacity to fill key positions within the organization, allowing you to save recruiting dollars and to retain your knowledge base within the company. Remember to keep the challenge positive; the results will be very positive.

3. **Be attentive to the people in your organization.** Listen to each and every employee. When employees know that you and/or their supervisors are taking them seriously, they are more likely to make positive contributions to the company. The contributions may be as basic as simple good work habits or as complex as the development of new products, procedures, or systems.

> Employees need to have their suggestions and ideas taken seriously.

Taking the time to listen to employees is the greatest weakness of poor managers and the greatest strength of good managers. Your people have most of the answers to the challenges that face your organization. How many times have you made a decision that has not achieved the results you desired and you subsequently find out that one of your own employees had made a suggestion that would have worked, and ultimately has worked, after you have expended a large sum of money and energy on a previously flawed solution? This happens all the time in organizations because the managers chose not to listen to the people who really know what is going on.

Consider what most consultants do when engaged to work with a client. The first order of business is usually interviewing and fact-finding within the organization. The consultant knows that the answers are in the company. The consultant knows that the best solutions to the problems identified by management will in many cases be solved with the input and support of the employees. A good consultant will help management to learn how to capture this information on their own for the future.

MAKING WORK FUN

> Being open and honest with employees affirms their worth as creative people and wins you their respect.

Save yourself some serious dollars. Listen to your people. You will be amazed at what you will learn.

4. **Communicate success and failure regularly**. Be direct and honest in communicating the successes of each employee. Show appreciation for your employees and you will generate enormous good will among your employees. When it is time to be critical and discuss failures or missed opportunities, be equally honest and sincere. When this is presented in a supportive, nonaccusatory manner, employees will benefit from recognizing how they could have transformed the negative situation into an exciting positive opportunity.

In reality, employees are people, and people want to know the truth. If you have been fair and consistent, if you have been offering people reasonable challenges, and if you have really been listening, then this step is very simple. When you have created a positive working environment, when you have created a sense of fun and trust within your organization, you are able to walk a much broader line in dealing with you employees. You are viewed as a person who respects the people who work with you. You are viewed as a reasonable person who needs to run a quality business that generates jobs and paychecks for many people. You are viewed as a person who has set clear expectations for, and has been attentive to the needs of the employees. You are perceived as a fair and reasonable boss to work for and with.

When you are at this point, your employees will respond favorably and positively to direct, clear communication of both their successes and their failures. They will look to you for approval and recognition when they succeed, as well as advice and support when they face failure. Be honest, be direct, be sincere ,and most importantly, be yourself.

THE BOTTOM LINE?

Never miss an opportunity to recognize employees for things they perceive as valuable and important. And after every third or fourth time you have dispensed sincere, deserving praise you will find your employees will be very receptive to your constructive criticism regarding how a failure could be transformed into a positive opportunity.

CREATE OUTLETS

Companies that encourage mistakes are encouraging people to try new ideas and are willing to allow them the fun of stretching their minds, pushing the envelope, and unzipping their brain, all leading to higher levels of creative productivity and higher levels of personal gratification.

People who work—and that is most of the adult population—spend more than ten thousand days of their lives at work. This is a very big chunk of one's life. Shouldn't we enjoy this time as much as possible?

To enjoy the work we do and the environment in which we work (read this to mean have fun), we must have a supportive and safe environment. Fun within the context of the business world means feeling comfortable to be oneself and to interact, even while working and accomplishing tasks, with other individuals you respect.

If a child felt that each new addition to the environment was a potential threat, his or her degree of enthusiasm and creativity would be greatly reduced. Companies that create a safe, supportive environment for employees have a higher incidence of fun and higher levels of creativity and productivity.

Here are some wild and crazy ideas to get you thinking about the kinds of outlets you can create for your employees and for yourself.

1. Create an annual apple pie bake off similar to old-time country fairs.
2. Organize a company Ping-Pong tournament.
3. Present quarterly tricycle races along the corridors of your office (have the final competition at your annual company outing).
4. Create a recipe exchange as part of a monthly bring-a-treat-for-lunch activity.

Fun work environments provide opportunities to interact with other creative people.

MAKING WORK FUN

Devise fun activities that involve everyone.

5. Determine your favorite food and plan to prepare this item for the entire staff as a surprise activity.
6. Create a Fabulous Friday program, with each department expected to plan and execute an activity that will create a positive outlet for employees.
7. Create a wild day. Once each month select one name at random (all names are placed in a hat) from your employee list who will be given an extra day off. By the next day the employee must designate the day he or she will be off, and that day will be called the wild day for that month. When 75 percent of the employees have had a wild day, all the names go back into the hat.
8. Plan dress-up or costume days on days other than Halloween.
9. Have community-based contests between departments. Link this to your charitable endeavors to get more of your employees involved.
10. Show cartoons or old TV sitcoms during the lunch break in the lunchroom. Bring employees back to their childhood.
11. Keep a box of puzzle toys that you can pass out whenever you sense things are getting a bit too tense in the office.
12. Keep some Nerf-type balls and items around to permit employees the opportunity to let off a little steam.
13. Set up a few days a year when employees are encouraged to bring their children to work.
14. Organize noontime basketball, softball, or tennis games.

CREATING EXCITING ENVIRONMENTS

There are many ways in which companies produce safe and supportive environments. Frequently the company will develop outlets that allow employees to feel comfortable and connected to the company while having "fun." These outlets increase the size and perception of the company and link all the company to a sense of fun and enjoyment.

MAKING WORK FUN

Company outings are a great example of expanding the environment and linking it to "fun."

Regularly scheduled outings as simple as monthly meetings at local restaurants or monthly meetings with pizza delivered to the office generate a sense of anticipation and a feeling that "we can get work done and still have fun at the same time." More extravagant family outings on an annual or semiannual basis allow the employees to include the family in a portion of life that oftentimes is so consuming. Interaction among family members helps to create a strong bond between work and home life that subsequently generates a higher degree of productivity and support of the work effort.

Additionally, the family outing allows all employees to see the managers, supervisors, and other management staff as people who have families very similar to their own.

A sense of parity is established when a group of coworkers gets to eat hamburgers and hot dogs at picnic tables with executives of the company. The residual impact of this event is long-lived.

For example:

Following the annual company outing, employee X has a problem with a project he has been managing. The numbers do not come in on target, and the client has taken some drastic measures to correct the problem. Employee X's supervisor brings all this information to employee X and is direct and blunt in regard to the problem that has been created. Employee X is very upset and angry at the supervisor for being so direct and blunt. He goes home in the evening and begins to fuss, fume, and complain about his supervisor and the entire scenario. His wife listens attentively to the description and then, comments: "Gee, I'm sorry to hear that the project has such problems. And I'm sorry to hear that your supervisor was so direct and blunt. When I met him at the company outing, we talked for quite a long time. He raved about you and what a great worker you are and how well your projects always turn out. Maybe he is getting pressure from above. He seems to really respect what you do and how well you do it. Do you think this may just be one of those crazy situations that got out of hand?"

> Family interaction creates bonds by merging work life with home life.

MAKING WORK FUN

> Celebrations are ways of affirming and recognizing the hard work of employees and encouraging further improved performances.

The knowledge the wife has of the organization is the result of what the husband brings home and what she has experienced. Without the company outing she can bring nothing to the table except what the husband has said. The simple company outing may create the opportunity to bring perspective to a situation that may occur months after the outing.

There is no guarantee that these situations will occur, but consider the potential benefit of these types of activities.

Celebrate—Celebrate—Celebrate

Take advantage of every opportunity to celebrate truly important moments within the organization. You'll want to make these celebrations fun for the right business reason. If you direct the celebrations toward birthdays, anniversaries, etc., you may not be encouraging improved productivity. If you celebrate project completions, reaching sales goals, new skill mastery, completion of training classes, quarterly profit reports, or anything that measures business performance, you will be creating an environment that equates fun with business success.

Celebrate these types of victories.

After a big sales initiative, after landing a new client, upon the wrap-up of a successful project or at the end of an exceptionally busy day that went flawlessly, gather everyone together for a celebration to mark this special event. Serve refreshments and use the opportunity to create an atmosphere of upbeat morale even if everyone is physically exhausted. You want everyone to go home and tell the family about how hard they worked, how much fun it was to complete the task (especially if it was very difficult), and how much they enjoyed being recognized for and celebrating the achievement.

This is very powerful and important dinner conversation.

For example:

A white-collar firm in its second year of existence is planning to distribute its first profit sharing. All the staff have been around during the insane start-up period, through all the hard knocks of the first year, and are now going to see the results of their hard work. Management had planned to pass out the success statements with

MAKING WORK FUN

the profit-sharing amount and leave it at that. The staff member responsible for administering the profit-sharing program suggested that the firm have a wine and cheese party after work hours to present this information. The staff member convinced management that everyone should celebrate the hard work and energy that went into generating the kind of profitability that would deliver this profit-sharing amount. At the announced ceremony, management gave a short presentation about the program and how well they had all worked to achieve the present status. Then with the opening of champagne bottles, management flashed the amount of money being placed into the profit-sharing program on a big screen for everyone to toast. The ceremony and the celebration made it clear to all the employees that their efforts were recognized and that they were also rewarded for this hard work. New employees were impressed with the enthusiasm and value placed on the work of the group. The senses of team and of being part of a larger group were felt by all.

> Office appearance can affect employee creativity.

Make the work environment interesting.

If your work environment is unattractive, spruce it up. No need to spend lots of money. A can of paint and some Spic and Span usually are all it takes to perk up an environment. Borrow artwork from your local library to create a constantly changing gallery in your office. Periodically ask local artists and musicians to visit your site at lunchtime to work or perform as a "diversion" for your employees. Create situations where the work environment becomes closely aligned with cultural and social endeavors, making work more like fun.

For example:

The Ajax Company works in relatively old office space that is not very attractive. Knowing that the shoddy condition of the offices may be affecting the productivity of the staff, the management plans a surprise for the staff. Working independently, the management team plans to have the main hallways and common areas painted over the weekend when no one will be in the offices. They have also arranged for the installation over the weekend of new name-plates for each employee to designate his or her workspace or office.

MAKING WORK FUN

> Organized sports outings are not only affective interaction techniques, but are also good outlets for stress.

Realizing that the employees will want some input into the cleanup program, management decides to create a schedule for the upcoming month that will allow for the painting of the individual offices and workspaces during the next four weekends. The schedule will accommodate everyone's input and also will show the allocation of a sum of money for each employee to use to decorate or enhance his or her office or workspace.

When the staff return on Monday they will be greeted by a newly painted office space and a table set with coffee and breakfast treats. Around the coffee and treats the management staff will explain the plan that is printed on the written information each staff member has on his or her desk along with the new nameplate.

Every employee is now part of the process to make the office more interesting and enjoyable. They also will know that their management team is really committed, since they have already taken the first step.

For the next month there will be a high degree of interest in the continual improvement of the office environment, with an increased sense of involvement and morale by the staff.

Get physical.

Whenever possible, support or organize ongoing programs of informal athletic competition. Encourage and support the efforts of employees who want to organize softball, bowling, tennis, basketball, volleyball, swimming, and boating activities. When supported by the company, more people will participate, creating another vehicle for work to be equated with fun.

Ultimately you want employees to think and behave in a fashion that always connects work with fun and enjoyment. You want everyone to say "Wow, what a day. I worked so hard and got so much done. It was great! I actually had fun today."

For example:

CCC Company operates out of a modern office in a suburban office park with an on-site dining room and convenience store. The office park is isolated from most commercial activities, making it

MAKING WORK FUN

difficult for staff members to do errands or other activities during the daily lunch break. The culture of the organization has created a highly charged work ethic, with staff members frequently working through lunch and staying late in the evening.

Productivity of the company is very high, but management is concerned that a limit will be reached and staff will begin to burn out, causing a decrease in productivity.

To address this potential concern, management designed a series of initiatives to create outlets for the highly productive staff to recharge their batteries. One of these initiatives was the Get Physical Program. The intent was to encourage employees to engage in some physical activity each day to keep them fit, alert, and stress-free.

The Get Physical Program included three components: the Breakfast Club, Lunchtime Walkers, and the P.M. Striders. Each component was set up to encourage a group of coworkers to engage in physical activity at a time that was most efficient for their lifestyle.

The employees who signed up for the Breakfast Club needed time to prepare for the hectic day of work. They appreciated the time to take care of themselves prior to jumping into the pressurized work environment of CCC Company. The Get Physical Program set up a schedule that allowed Breakfast Club employees to begin work later in the day as long as they engaged in the formal Breakfast Club regimen. The Breakfast Club regimen included a brisk walking tour of the suburban site followed by breakfast in the dining room.

The employees who signed up for Lunchtime Walkers needed a solid break in the middle of the day to restore their energy and to pull their act together. They appreciated the time to take care of themselves and regroup after a hectic morning of pressurized work.

The Lunchtime Walkers program included lunch in the dining room followed by a walking tour of the suburban site. This program also built in time for this group to make personal calls and get things done via telephone that might otherwise interfere with their staying focused on their job duties.

The employees who signed up for P.M. Striders needed a chance to totally unwind before heading home to the family. These

Fun, physical breaks help to rejuvenate employees and renew creativity.

MAKING WORK FUN

> Create a corporate moral system and well-defined strategy to create a sense of value and purpose.

employees wanted to be able to return home refreshed and ready to enjoy the family life they cherished. They appreciated the opportunity to start the day a bit earlier in order to unwind at the end of the day and still arrive home at a time that was family-friendly.

Consider creating your own version of the Get Physical Program.

DEFINE THE CULTURE

The culture of a company helps to define the level of support an employee will find within the organization. The day-to-day practice of this cultural sensibility is the ultimate driving force for the success of the company. A vivid example of a company that lives and breathes its culture is the Harley-Davidson company.

This motorcycle company has a culture defined by five formal values. These values are communicated to all employees as part of the recruiting , hiring, and orientation process and are promoted, reinforced, and used every day as part of the life of the company.

These values are:

- Tell the truth.
- Be fair.
- Keep your promises.
- Respect the individual.
- Encourage intellectual curiosity.

It almost reads like your mom wrote the list of formal values.

It is very clear what this says about an organization. Harley-Davidson values the basic human values that are part of the Judeo-Christian heritage of Western civilization.

Harley-Davidson goes further and supports these basic values by identifying issues that are always a concern to the organization. All members of the organization are reminded of these concerns via a simple statement that identifies these issues.

These continuing concerns are:

- Quality
- Participation

MAKING WORK FUN

- Productivity
- Flexibility
- Cash flow

Look again at these two lists. Notice how similar they are to the "Golden Rule" of times gone by. "Do unto others as you would have them do unto you." It seems corny but it still works, and it makes even more sense for the successful company of today.

Have you ever heard of a company where many of the employees actually tattoo the company logo on their body? Has Harley-Davidson a secret other companies should learn?

CASUAL DRESS CODES

Other companies have taken another approach to defining the culture. Many new entrepreneurial organizations have rejected the buttoned-down, white-collar dress code of the business world. These companies are making statements that say the facade of the person is not as important as the inner workings of the person. They want to create working cultures that respect and respond to the individual and not to the clothing the person wears. Although we all know that there are status symbols in all levels of clothing, the key to this point is that employees are allowed the opportunity to decide what clothing they feel is most appropriate to meet the needs of their position. This change in business thinking has had a profound impact on the business world.

Casual Fridays are the establishment's response to this concept. Almost every company in the United States now has casual Fridays as part of its policies and procedures. The rationale is that employees should be rewarded for working hard all week with a day to dress down and not be uptight.

You and your business must decide what you are trying to achieve and how best to achieve this objective. Will it make a difference if all your employees are in suits and ties or if they are in khakis and loafers? Whatever you decide to do, do it for clear reasons and be prepared to measure how well your decision has achieved your objectives.

> Casual dress codes encourage the shedding of inhibitions and help create a fun and stress-free environment.

MAKING WORK FUN

Create an emotional bond with employees to reaffirm their worth to both you and the company itself.

Still other companies create a culture of cross-trained employees wherein everyone can do major portions of other employees' work. The organization defines each job as critically important and expects that all employees have a working knowledge of the other positions within their department. This approach allows an organization to create a team-oriented culture that is exciting and charged with opportunity. Any one employee has the potential to move into a number of other positions. This situation allows individuals to recognize that not everyone likes to do what they do and not everyone wants someone else's position. Most importantly, this cross-training approach allows a company to respond to market changes more rapidly and without having to go outside the organization. Frequently companies will be challenged to achieve an objective in unreasonable time frames. With an employee population that is cross-trained and able to move into a variety of different functions easily, the company is able to respond to the need of the market and be more successful. Ultimately the employees are excited by a challenge that can be achieved due to the cross-training. They are able to translate this business challenge into a personal and team opportunity to work together and have a great time.

WARM FUZZIES

It's great to celebrate events and to promote activities and gatherings. But it's also very important to touch each employee directly and let him or her know that he or she is special and valued as a contributor to the organization.

How you choose to do this is a major challenge, and it frequently is a defining component in the culture you create for your company. This cannot be an idea you obtain from another company. This must be something that comes from inside you, something that is a direct connection to you and the kind of organization you wish to lead.

If you adore chocolate and can't get enough of the product, you may want to use chocolate as a personal way to say "thank you" to an employee. Just leaving your favorite candy bar on the desk of an employee may well become the defining statement within your

MAKING WORK FUN

organization of a job well done. This "warm and fuzzy" may be the key to creating a picture-perfect day for your employee, who in return will produce high-quality work for your company.

If you really enjoy coffee in all its modern variations, you may want to take an employee out for a cup of coffee. It might be the company coffee machine or you may go to one of the local coffee shops. This brief walk to the coffee station is a "warm and fuzzy" that will have significant impact on the employee and his or her productivity. Work is not just work, it is also fun!

Try to make your "warm and fuzzys" an extension of you. Don't make this too slick, or else it will turn into a "program" and will no longer be "warm and fuzzy."

As the boss you control the "fun pulse" of your company. Be aware, be alert, and have fun!

> Small gestures of thanks help the employee feel needed.

HOW TO MAKE WORK FUN! A SELF-HELP CHECKLIST

Use this simple checklist to determine if you are making your company a fun place to work with and for. If you are not, think about why not! If you are, how can you make it even more fun and productive for your people, your company, and you?

SMILE	Make a sincere smile a trademark of your company, starting with you.
COMMUNICATE	Offer all employees a variety of vehicles for communications, such as memos, voice mail, meetings, e-mail.
ALLOW MISTAKES	Translate mistakes into problem-solving activities.
MANDATE VACATIONS	Make sure all employees take vacations. Make it part of their performance review if necessary.
CREATE FAMILY EVENTS	Link work and family life in fun situations.
SUPPORT OUTSIDE INTERESTS	Offer company support for outside involvement.
ENCOURAGE HEALTHY LIFESTYLES	Promote exercise, healthy eating, no smoking, and well-being.
CELEBRATE	Take every opportunity to celebrate positive situations.

MAKING WORK FUN

To create a fun environment, you don't necessarily have to deplete company funds.

QUESTIONS AND ANSWERS

1. **How much money do I need to budget for these activities?**
   In many cases you can create dynamite fun activities for very little cost. A genuine smile doesn't cost a cent, and it goes farther than anything else to create a positive fun environment.

   Pull a group of your employees together and ask them for some no-cost ideas to make the work environment more fun. Within a few minutes this group will come up with a dozen free or inexpensive ideas.

2. **How do I know when I have gone too far into the fun zone?**
   If you listen to your employees they will be the first to tell you things have gotten out of control. If you are not listening you will begin to see the results in sales, productivity, and the general morale of the office or company. The key to any program is to monitor it and to constantly evaluate the program against your original objectives.

3. **How do I get started when I'm not a fun person?**
   You don't need to be a fun person, but you need to understand the importance of fun within the workplace. You will need to support the programs your create. Since you are not a fun person you will have a hard time coming up with ideas. Why not ask your management team how they would approach the situation? Let them know what your intentions are, and give them some clearly defined guidelines and a budget. Then let your management team come up with a plan of action for fun in your company. Review the plan with your management team. If the plan makes you feel comfortable, then you can get started implementing the plan.

4. **Is it appropriate for the fun to spill over into our customer interactions?**
   Most definitely yes! Your customers will appreciate the fact that your company still delivers the same quality service and product, but now they are actually having fun while they are doing business. The key is to be sure your quality service or product quality does not diminish due to the addition of

MAKING WORK FUN

fun to the work environment. Customers who are engaged by employees who are happy and in a good mood will be more satisfied customers. It's that simple.

5. **Should I plan fun events around the traditional holidays?**
In the big picture it would be better for you to plan your fun activities around nontraditional events. People have come to expect fun on traditional holidays such as Christmas, New Year's, Memorial Day, and Labor Day. Try creating new vehicles for fun that elevate other dates of the year to special days. Employees will appreciate the novelty and will begin to think about that new date as a special and fun day connected with work and your company.

> Create celebratory occasions on days other than the traditional holidays to create a fun work environment.

STREETWISE
advice

◆ **Don't be embarrassed by a fun environment.**
Remember, laughter is the best medicine.

◆ **Trust is one of the most important words for you to learn.**
You should learn to trust your employees.

◆ **Don't overdo the fun.**
Maintain a balance between fun and work. You do not want to lose the sense of urgency that all organizations need. Fun is critical for the success of your business, but it must always be connected to achieving the business objectives.

◆ **Bring your company into the community.**
Get your employees and yourself involved in charitable activities within your community. You will create another vehicle for employee interaction and fun and you will create a positive image for your company while doing something worthwhile for the community.

◆ **Be aware that what you consider fun may be offensive to members of your company.**
Tune in to the diversity of your workforce and think about how specific activities and events might offend a group or an individual. This doesn't mean you shouldn't plan fun activities; it just means that you need to think about and consider everything you do as part of your business. Building fun, into your business is important, so do it right.

◆ **Once you develop a plan to increase the fun factor in your company, you must keep it going.**
The worst thing you can do is start a program and then stop it. If you are not consistent in your implementation of your fun activities your employees will begin to doubt that you really support a fun company and you will begin to lose their trust. So be sure to design your plan for fun the same way you design a marketing strategy or the way you go about developing a new product.

◆ **Make having fun part of each manager's job description.**
Include a job responsibility that states "encourage a fun work environment by encouraging and participating in all activities promoted by the company."

C H A P T E R

6

BUILDING
A
TEAM

Teams can do wonders for pushing your company ahead! Members of teams can feel important and empowered. They can feel a particularly strong sense of belonging. And they can develop unusually strong and productive working relationships with their colleagues.

BUILDING A TEAM

WHY TEAMS?

With an increase in global competition, companies are placing an overwhelming emphasis on greater productivity from a smaller number of employees. To maximize this productivity, more and more companies are turning to team-building as an effective and efficient way to achieve their objectives in today's marketplace.

INDIVIDUAL CONTRIBUTION

Building a team is a simple concept when you recognize that teams are made up of individuals with diverse skills and talents. Each individual team member has a clearly defined skill set that needs to be identified and measured against the skill sets of other team members. Once the individual team member recognizes what he or she can best accomplish for the team, achieving the goal or objective becomes not only attainable but also eagerly anticipated. Companies that are committed to building a team recognize the value of bringing together a select group of employees to improve a particular aspect of their business.

TEAM LEADERS

Leaders who direct and influence teams are encouraged to consider the diverse strengths of each participant. The leader is responsible for tapping into the strengths and abilities of each team member and using those strengths to achieve an overall objective. He or she must also consider the need for balancing the personal agendas of each team member in favor of that overall objective.

WHAT TEAMS OFFER TO AN ORGANIZATION

Teams offer an organization the opportunity to achieve results in a more efficient manner. Because they are more flexible, teams leverage resources more effectively and can respond more rapidly to constantly changing market circumstances. Teams also allow individual employees to learn from each other, thus increasing their competence and broadening their experience.

> Personal agendas of team members must be balanced in favor of overall objectives.

BUILDING A TEAM

CHALLENGES TO BUILDING A SUCCESSFUL TEAM

- **Team Objective**
  Team members should share a clearly articulated objective. Without direction, the team cannot succeed. It's very easy for a team to spin its wheels and achieve the wrong outcome. The team must constantly check its progress against the defined objective.

- **Commitment to Team Guidelines**
  Team members must develop guidelines and procedures that all members commit to, even if some members are uncomfortable with the final mandate. If the team is to achieve its objectives, it must have clearly defined operating guidelines. Even if all members of the team do not agree with *all* of the operating guidelines, they *must* agree to follow these guidelines until the objective has been reached.

- **Time**
  You must have sufficient time allotted to create a supportive and responsive structure for allowing the team to operate. The members need sufficient time to create the procedures and strategies that will allow them to work efficiently.

- **Membership**
  You should ensure that members represent functional areas of the company that have a significant interest in the outcome of the team's work. More importantly, the members must have the authority to bring critical issues back to their departments and have input into decisions that affect these issues.

- **Skills**
  Don't forget that the skills and talents of each member must be clearly and accurately identified and assessed. The team needs to know who is the best equipped to deal with situations as they arise. An informed team has a greater potential for success.

> Clearly defined guidelines are essential to achieve team goals.

- **Advocacy**
  A team must always have a senior manager serving as an advocate, adviser, and supporter. The identification and assignment of this role immediately signals the value of this team to the rest of the organization.
- **Support**
  Senior management and other teams within the organization must consistently support and recognize the team's efforts. The company must demonstrate on a regular basis the value and importance of the team's work.

> Team leaders are responsible for guiding the team's work by delegating tasks and setting reasonable goals.

TEAM DIRECTION

LEADER-DIRECTED TEAMS

A team run by a team leader acts very differently from a self-directed team in that the team leader sets the agenda, runs all team meetings, and delegates tasks to team members. The team leader is usually a senior manager from within a particular department or an executive who runs a department. The team leader in this instance usually hand-picks team members from different departments based on expertise that will be relevant to a particular problem or issue within the company.

Setup

In this example, a team from a manufacturing company is trying to create a new employee orientation program. The ineffective team leader fails to keep her team focused on the objective, which is to create a new employee orientation program. The effective team leader never loses sight of the team's objective and keeps the team focused on each agenda item.

BUILDING A TEAM

> Organization is essential to encourage the best possible performance of a team.

Employee Orientation–Manufacturer

Ineffective Method

Team leader: We have to come up with a solution that gives new employees a complete picture of our company and gets them integrated into the culture right away.

Marsha: There is plenty of printed material from human resources but there does not seem to be a consistent theme that explains the company vision or strategy and the expectations for new hires.

Team leader: What are we doing about the new employee's first day at the company?

Tom: At this point it looks like a quick tour from a senior manager and then the employee is left to his or her own devices. It all seems to be patchwork.

Katie: I have an idea. Couldn't we put a videotape together that new hires could see on their first day, giving them an overall feel for the company?

Marsha: Well, that sounds okay, but who is going to produce it? We don't have the facilities in-house to create such a production.

Tom: Videos are just too expensive. What about a CD-ROM? Its small, portable, and offers a lot more flexibility for content development.

Marsha: Sorry Tom, but I think CDs are just as much if not more expensive. We should consider producing an audiotape that the employees can listen to on their way going home or coming to work.

Team leader: I've heard that CD-ROMs are difficult to install and almost never work the first time out of the box.

Katie: Why do we need to make a big production out of this? A simple video should not be that expensive to produce.

Team leader: Why don't we work on these ideas separately and reconvene next week to continue this discussion.

BUILDING A TEAM

Effective Method

Team leader: The agenda of this group meeting should be to discuss the following items in this order: (1) to focus on the message that we send to new employees about the company, its vision, and strategy, (2) the platform to deliver the message, and (3) any cost factors, including a budget and deadlines.

Marsha: Do we have enough money in the budget to afford a new program?"

Team leader: While money is certainly an important consideration, we need to stick to the agenda and focus on the company message. We will discuss costs and budgeting later on.

Katie: We have a lot of printed material, including the 401(k), annual reports, and the "Welcome" brochure, but it is pretty dry and boring stuff and not too inspiring for new employees. When I finally got through the material, I got the message that we are an entrepreneurial, forward-thinking, technology-driven consumer electronics company developing state-of-the-art home theater equipment.

Tom: I thought the material was pretty interesting myself, and I got the same impression, that we are a forward-thinking company with innovative consumer electronic technology.

Marsha: Yes, but are we customer-driven or technology-driven as a company?

Katie: The feeling I got from the material was that we are innovators and technology leaders.

Tom: That seems logical, especially since we just introduced that new home theater system.

Team leader: It sounds like we have a good handle on what our company message is all about. We should now decide what platform to deliver the message.

> The team leader must keep the team members focused on the task at hand and on the goal to be reached.

BUILDING A TEAM

> Skills of each member of the team should be utilized to their fullest in order to achieve the team goal.

Tom: Is there any way we could convert our printed material to a digital format?

Marsha: We have a number of computers with internal CD-ROM drives. How about creating a multimedia CD-ROM with our company logo, a picture of the company, and interviews with employees who work here?

Katie: Wouldn't it be easier just to synthesize the printed material into one booklet?

Tom: If we are going to spend the money, we should do four- instead of two-color printing.

Team leader: We should focus on the delivery platform and then discuss costs.

Katie: Well, if we are going to look for a new platform, why not videotape?

Tom: Our audiovisual work station with the VCR is tied up most of the time. I agree with Marsha. I think we should explore CD-ROM as a delivery platform.

Katie: Well, CDs are certainly easy to use and I like the fact that we can use them in our laptops as well as our desktop machines.

Team leader: Since we seem to agree on a platform, let's turn our attention to costs and budgeting.

Tom: My guess is that financially, a CD project probably won't cost much more than four-color printing of all the material we currently have in-house. In either case, we would have to outsource the job.

Marsha: The paper costs along with the costs of setup and color matching have to be prohibitive, given that we seem to be adding to company-printed material instead of reducing the paper flow.

Katie: Carol, since I work in finance, I'd like to volunteer to crunch some numbers and create a proposal for CD-ROM versus printing.

Team leader: That sounds fine. Why don't you plan on giving us a preliminary report at next Thursday's meeting?

BUILDING A TEAM

Commentary

The ineffective leader does little to either keep her team focused or to encourage brainstorming, establishing priorities, and most importantly, setting deadlines for key tasks to be accomplished by various team members. This is a team that while they are able to come up with ideas for creating an orientation program are unable to decide which idea is best and how it should be implemented. The effective team leader, on the other hand, sets priorities and continually works at keeping her team focused on the team's objective. She carefully considers input from different team members and always keeps them on track and focused on each agenda item.

Self-directed teams are reliant upon the roles of individuals to keep the team productive.

SELF DIRECTED TEAMS

Why Self-Directed Teams?

Self-directed teams are composed of members who may come from multiple areas of an organization, including finance, marketing, development, operations, sales, and administration. These teams are usually made up of a combination of staff and line managers with different skill levels and talents. Self-directed teams are built on the premise that the team will be driven by internal leadership and will not require senior management involvement on a daily or even weekly basis.

Teams in Action

Setup

There are many roles that individuals assume as part of a self-directed team. These roles include cheerleader, devil's advocate, creative spark, counselor, and facilitator. In this example, a self-directed team comprised of individuals who play these roles confronts the problem of steadily increasing workers' compensation claims and what can be done to reduce these claims.

BUILDING A TEAM

Team members play off each other to come to an agreement on strategy.

Cheerleader

"Look, I know we can reduce these claims. We need to focus on the past six months at least and sort out where the majority of claims are coming from. Before you know it, we'll have this problem licked."

"Come on, guys, there is no reason we need to argue about this. We know that Operations should be made aware of what is going on. Can't we settle on a method to communicate this information to them?"

"That sounds like a great idea! I'm sure that we can get them to buy in when they see the benefits."

Devil's Advocate

"Why stop at six months? And has anyone considered other departments in the company? Let's stop being so nice and attack the heart of the problem."

"Okay, what about this. Who will be responsible for setting up a reporting mechanism to track the claims? And who decides when management becomes involved?"

"I still think we need to focus on the root of the problem, namely what we can do to enhance safety and improve training procedures for all affected employees."

Creative Spark

"Here's an idea. Why not create a standardized form that all departments can use that can be scanned into a database that will track all essential data?"

"Let's use our groupware product and assign one individual who has responsibility for overseeing all claims and can alert management when the claims start to rise."

"Listen to this: Why don't we hire a financial analyst to tell us what these data mean. That way, we can make a more informed decision about reducing the claims."

Counselor

"This same problem came up with my last company. We got mired in red tape because no one took responsibility for the problem. Let's see if we can stick to fixing the core of the problem."

BUILDING A TEAM

"Instead of worrying about what management needs, we should worry about improving conditions at the plant. Management will be happy if they know that a workable plan is in place."

"We have a deadline to meet people, so let's continue the brainstorming process and prioritize the top three or four best ideas."

Facilitator

"There are two important tasks that need to be completed by next week. Kitty, could you gather all of the analysis we have done on the claims and create a report indicating our findings and any trends that jump out at you? Jim, please set up a meeting with the financial analyst to go over the numbers and review our recommendations for reducing compensation costs."

> Clearly defined objectives and goals help to focus the energies of the team members.

SELF-DIRECTED TEAM APPROACH

The objective of this team is to suggest methods to reduce claims to prevent an increase in premium charges. Consistent with this, the self-directed team should:

1. **Define team goals by identifying the details of the objective.**
   Be sure all aspects of the objective are identified. What has been the workers' compensation history at the company?

   - Identify the actual history of claims within the company during the past six months.
   - Identify the present premiums and the history of past premiums.
   - What sort of claims are you submitting?
   - Who is responsible for reporting claims?
   - Who is responsible for managing the workers' compensation administration?

BUILDING A TEAM

> All suggestions are valuable in determining the most viable solution to the problem at hand.

2. **Analyze the entire company situation with respect to the objective.**

   The team must determine the facts. Which departments are responsible for the greatest number of claims? Analyze all claims according to department, type of claim, and dollar value. When did you first notice a significant change in claim patterns? What event coincided with this change in claim patterns?

3. **Identify the necessary resources not available within the team.**

   The team may not have enough resources or the right people to address this specific issue and may need to bring in additional resources. For example: Is a financial analyst required to assist with calculations? Is there someone at the company who understands the specifics of setting workers' compensation insurance premiums? There may also be a need to obtain assistance from a safety expert.

4. **Create guidelines for communication, feedback, and support within the team.**

   The team needs to establish a clear set of guidelines for everyone to use. For the workers' compensation problem, the team should:

   - Set up a regular system for reporting claims data to the various departments.
   - Set up a mechanism for departments to input suggestions to reduce claims.
   - Create a schedule for officially informing the company of progress.
   - Create a master list of all available resources for this project, internal and external.

5. **Brainstorm creative solutions to achieve the objective.**

   The team will generate a large number of possible solutions to the problem. All options will be recorded and discussed. A crazy idea may even end up being the one that makes

BUILDING A TEAM

everything come together. When evaluating the workers'
compensation problem, the team should take the following
steps:

- Institute comprehensive safety measures.
- Upgrade equipment.
- Provide technical training for necessary personnel.
- Provide training to employees processing claims
  paperwork.
- Aggressively follow up on all claims.
- Hire an employee specifically to monitor claims activity.
- Self-insure claims under $100.
- Establish an incentive award for reduced claims in each
  department.

6. **Prioritize the possible solutions.**
   Once all the realistic options have been identified, the team
   must then measure the value of all the options. Once the
   most appropriate options have been selected, the team will
   have the beginning of a plan of action. It should select the
   ideas that have the greatest opportunity for success.

7. **Set timetables and deadlines.**
   By setting timetables and deadlines, the team begins to
   establish its work plan and strategy for dealing with the
   problem. Create a timetable based on the date the new premiums will be established, then work backward to develop a
   timetable for implementation. Include periodic times for evaluation, feedback, and confirmation that the project is moving
   along as designed. The plan should be adjusted as necessary
   based on new information.

8. **Communicate the selected plan of action to the entire
   organization.**
   When the plan of action and timetable are clear, the team
   should communicate these to the entire company so everyone will be able to support the effort. The plan of action and
   the timetable can be relayed through regular communication

BUILDING A TEAM

> Good team performance depends upon the proper delegation of responsibility.

vehicles. The team should also let the company know when it would like feedback and input.

9. **Execute the plan of action through delegation of tasks and responsibilities.**

   Within the plan of action and timetable, there will be numerous tasks and responsibilities. These duties must be distributed among the team members, taking advantage of the special skills and abilities of each member. Follow these steps:

   - Divide responsibility among team members.
   - Use each person's strengths in sharing responsibility.
   - Set due dates and clear levels of expectation so all members know what each is expected to accomplish.
   - Identify and reinforce the need to use each other and not to try to do everything alone.

10. **Evaluate the outcome of the plan of action.**

    Through the guidelines already established and the feedback from the company, the success of the team can be measured. Evaluate the plan as it progresses; modify the plan as necessary to achieve success; and measure the final outcome based on the information originally collected.

> Effective teams attempt to identify the problem and work to solve it rather than place blame.

TYPICAL SELF-DIRECTED TEAM SCENARIO

Setup

In this example, a self-directed team from a bank tackles the problem of customers who are discontinuing their accounts in favor of another bank. The issue revolves around a new bank credit card and its benefits to consumers. Notice how the ineffective team fails to identify the problem, instead focusing on internal difficulties, while the effective team focuses on the issue of losing customers and what action should be taken to bring those customers back to the bank.

BUILDING A TEAM

Losing Accounts–Banking

Ineffective Method

Kathy: It seems as if our bank is losing accounts at all branches as opposed to just one or two branches. Can we identify the cause?

Mark: I don't think marketing has their act together. Have you seen the new promotion lately? I can't figure out who they are targeting for the new check card.

Kristine: Maybe customers are unhappy about the interest penalties on the new card. Do we clearly explain why they are charged for purchases such as gasoline or food as opposed to drawing money out of their ATM?

Dave: The monthly statements take care of that. No, I agree with Mark. We don't know who we are after with this card. In fact, with this new card, we now offer three options with two different types of credit cards, and no one in management can seem to figure out a strategy for each card.

Kathy: But Dave, I thought the cards were supposed to be tied to new account promotions. You know, if you open a new account with us, you get a certain number of bonus points good for purchase dollars using one of the cards.

Mark: Kathy, you're missing the point. Customers do not seem to be taking advantage of the promotion. Either they are confused about the promotion or they fail to see the value in the bonus point system. I'm not sure I even understand the system.

Dave: I think it is pretty straightforward–the problem comes in trying to identify the right customer. We need better information about our customers.

Kristine: I don't agree, Dave. These new cards only add to customer confusion. If internal people at the bank can't figure out what the card benefits are, how can we expect customers to assimilate that information?

> Ineffective teams do not focus on the problem at hand, and lack the organization to properly analyze the problem.

BUILDING A TEAM

Effective Method

By clearly identifying the problem, an effective solution can be devised.

Kathy: Our bank seems to be losing customers left and right for the past six months, maybe longer. We have to find a way to reverse this situation.

Dave: If we are losing customers so fast, they must be taking their business elsewhere. Has a particular bank increased their presence in our area recently or rolled out new services?

Mark: I heard a rumor that Mid-States just acquired Newtown Bank and they are opening new branches with a special checking account promotion. Something about a new check card.

Kristine: I've heard that same rumor. You know, a couple of branch managers told me recently that our customers are unhappy and confused with all the charges tied to our checking accounts and our credit cards.

Mark: Marketing should be made aware of Mid-States' move into our area and start an aggressive program to promote the advantages of our services against those of Newtown.

Dave: We should try to clearly identify the reasons why customers are leaving the bank, as opposed to dwelling on the competition.

Kathy: Kris, have we done follow-up questionnaires with our dissatisfied customers to find out why they are leaving?

Kristine: I don't believe that any formal questionnaire was ever developed, but I would be more than happy to create one and get it into the hands of those customers who have recently closed their accounts with our bank.

Dave: We should be more proactive. I'd like to bring together a focus group of these dissatisfied customers to have them tell us what we can do to get them to come back to our bank.

Mark: As a follow-up to what Dave and Kris suggested, I'll take the data they gather and compare it to what Newtown is

BUILDING A TEAM

offering with their new check card to see how we can position ourselves to counteract their new promotion and keep our customers from leaving us.

Commentary

In the first case, which portrays an ineffective team, members are unable to stay with and focus on the objective. As such, they wind up wasting time arguing with each other instead of pinpointing the source of customer dissatisfaction that has led to a loss of business. Instead of working together as a team, members try to force their opinions on the group. The effective team, however, quickly addresses the problem and articulates a course of action, all the while working together rather than allowing a team member's personal agenda to dominate the group's efforts.

QUESTIONS AND ANSWERS

1. **What will be the biggest challenge I'll face in developing a team approach?**
   The biggest challenge will be the temptation to change the rules and expectations for performance once the team starts working. You cannot change the rules and still have a productive, efficient team. Only the team can change the rules. Don't interfere unnecessarily.

2. **Why should I develop self-directed teams?**
   Self-directed teams are a powerful management tool you can use to strengthen your company. These teams have the potential to improve the speed and accuracy of resolving problems within your organization. Ultimately they have the potential to make your company more profitable.

3. **What if the team doesn't succeed in solving the problem?**
   If a team does not succeed in solving the defined problem, use the situation as an opportunity to continue learning. Ask the team to analyze why it was unable to achieve the

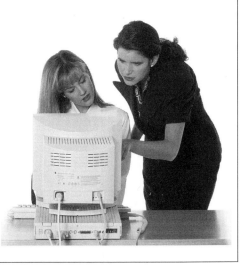

BUILDING A TEAM

objective. Ask it to evaluate the process so it is not repeated the same way. Redirect the team to move forward with a more clearly defined objective and plan of action.

4. What is the role of the company leader?

The CEO must be able to identify and articulate the team objective in a manner that will generate passion and commitment by team members. The CEO should serve as the mentor and work hard to advocate the team's efforts. He or she also serves to trumpet the cause of the team to external sources, should that be necessary for the team's success.

5. Why is it important for the team to create guidelines for a communication strategy?

To ensure optimum performance, each team member must feel comfortable working with the other members. They must have a clear sense that ideas and comments will be received and heard in an open, responsive, and respectful manner at all times. The team should identify the manner in which it will communicate its progress and successes to the organization to reinforce the value of the team to the organization as a whole.

6. What if there is conflict within the team?

Some conflict within the team is a good sign. It indicates that the creative process of problem-solving is taking place and that members are comfortable challenging each other. A well-developed team will have a communication strategy in place to resolve conflict. This strategy will serve as a model for the organization. Encourage positive, respectful disagreement.

7. How should I determine the size and makeup of the team?

The size and makeup of the team are determined by the size of your organization and the various areas that are impacted by the problem the team is charged with solving. Be sure all impacted areas are represented by a member who is authorized to make decisions. Any budgetary considerations should be resolved up-front and not made up as the team tackles its assignment. How much money you plan to spend on this team will help determine its size.

> Conflict between team members helps to define ideas and to challenge others to clarify assertions.

BUILDING A TEAM

8. **Which role is most important?**

   All the team roles are important. The ability of team members to assume different roles at various times during the process will help define the success of the team. This is why it is important to have a diverse group of people on the team. Be sure you include at least one person who demonstrates the traits of a strong facilitator.

9. **How do I celebrate the success of a team?**

   The success of a team can be celebrated in many ways. Announce the team's success in the company newsletter, at an informal awards ceremony, during a special event, or through any other tangible outlet that allows other company employees to know just how important the team was in terms of the overall success of the company. Make the celebration an extension of your company culture.

10. **What is a cross-functional team?**

    Cross-functional teams are teams that include representatives from various areas of the organization. In larger organizations cross-functional teams allow separate divisions of the organization to learn about other functions through personal interactions, thereby preventing the development of poorly designed solutions.

11. **How do I assess the strengths of team members?**

    Once the desired team objective is determined, ask a senior manager for feedback on a preliminary team list. Ask him or her to identify the one strength each suggested member brings to the table. Create your final team list based on strengths the person brings, not on his or her weaknesses. You want the team to reflect the best people have to offer so that when working together, any weaknesses are minimized and the team has a greater chance of success.

12. **Once we define the team objective and outcome, what should I do?**

    Your most important role will be to continually reinforce the objective, support team efforts, and follow up on requests,

> Assess a team according to its strengths, rather than its weaknesses.

> Trust in the skills of the individuals with a team to encourage the attainment of team goals.

BUILDING A TEAM

promises, and commitments to the process. Don't drop the ball, and don't interfere unnecessarily. Allow the team to do its job. Trust the skills and talents of the team to successfully achieve the desired objective.

13. **What if the team becomes isolated within the organization?** Without raising any concerns, ask the team to clarify its objective, outcome, and the process it created to achieve that goal. As the team replays this strategy, it will recognize that it has gone astray. Your simple question will serve as a sign-post to get the team back on the road to success. Don't tell the team what to do; ask it what it has been doing.

STREETWISE advice

◆ **Have a clear, concise, measurable objective.**

Your team must know exactly what goals it's shooting for and when it expects to achieve them. A clearly defined objective, describing the actual outcome, is critical for the success of a team. Without a clearly defined objective, the team will work hard to produce an outcome that may have no value to the organization.

> In order to effectively tackle a problem, the team must be equipped with the skills of individuals who are most able to work with themselves.

◆ **Create a diverse team from all impacted areas of the organization.**

Be sure you involve all areas that will be impacted. A small functional detail may be the key to successfully solving the problem. Although you may think a department cannot afford to be involved in the team, issues within the department might be the one detail the team forgets to address, so the objective is never achieved.

◆ **Allow sufficient time for the team to develop.**

Don't rush the process of team development. Allow for time during team development to ensure quality results. You should budget time appropriately, and more importantly, ensure that management supports the time needed for the team to get in gear.

◆ **Assess the skills and talent of the team members.**

Be sure all members bring unique skills to the table. Don't be concerned with their weaknesses of deficiencies. Look at bringing the best talent in your company together to solve a problem. The team will leverage each of these strengths for the benefit of the organization.

◆ **Encourage a clear, open, and responsive communication strategy.**

All team members must know they can contribute freely, be listened to and heard by other members of the team as well as by senior management. This will build trust. Trust builds confidence and strength. Do everything in your power to ensure that the team has developed a solid communication strategy.

◆ **Recognize the success of the team in a public manner.**

Celebrate the success. Support the efforts of the team and define specific ways to publicly celebrate its success. Teams will generally have deadlines and milestones upon which they measure their progress. Use these defined times to reinforce the value and success of the team.

> Open communication encourages trust and respect between team members.

CHAPTER

7

POWER
TO
THE
PEOPLE!

The more you can make your Temployees feel empowered—the more productive they are going to be. Unfortunately empowering employees doesn't always come naturally to managers, and it is going to take some self-discipline. You're going to have to work at developing a trust of employees' abilities; you're going to have to learn to "cut the cord" to employees; and you're going to have to work at instilling a sense of passion for the organization and the work with employees.

POWER TO THE PEOPLE!

EMPLOYEE EMPOWERMENT

The greatest challenge facing any company is achieving the highest degree of productivity at the lowest cost. One sure-fire way to achieve this objective is to maximize utilization of the skills of each employee. When a company defines a company objective "to support and encourage each employee to reach his or her potential" and when this objective is supported in every action and deed within the company, the organization is highly successful.

What exactly is "employee empowerment"? Let us begin by defining the word *empower*.

According to *Webster's New World Dictionary*, Third College Edition, empower means: to give power or authority to; to authorize; to give ability to; to enable; to permit. Translated into the world of business, this means:

- To give employees the power and authority to accomplish objectives independently
- To give employees the ability to accomplish objectives independently
- To give employees permission to accomplish objectives independently

Considering today's workforce, the companies that recognize and implement this concept will have the edge over the competition. The existing workforce in today's business world has been living and breathing the sensibility that exists in the management phrase "employee empowerment." They have grown up assuming the responsibility for making day-to-day decisions. Given the early learning curve of this workforce, they will outperform their parents in the ability to become "empowered"–if we allow them to do so.

To ensure the success of your business you must be able and willing to recognize the value each employee brings with him or her to the workplace. The potential of the workforce is enormous, but it must be tapped, and only you as the business leader can unleash this potential.

> To be successful, you must try to utilize the potential of each employee.

POWER TO THE PEOPLE!

Are you empowering your employees? Are you creating an environment where:

- People behave as though they owned their job and the company?
- People behave in a responsible fashion?
- People see the consequences of the work they do?
- People know how they are doing and how they are valued within the company?
- People are included in determining solutions to problems?
- People have direct input into the way in which the work they do gets done?
- People spend a good deal of time smiling?
- People are asking other people if they need any help?

If you have this kind of environment, you are clearly empowering your employees. If you do not have this kind of environment, then you should begin to carefully read every chapter of this book and try to modify your work environment. As you move toward a more empowered workforce you will need to do some very basic things. The words that follow almost seem like common sense, and they are, but frequently companies fail to practice what they know is correct and proper. Try your best to make the following concepts come alive in your own personal way:

- Create a communication process that is complete, consistent, and clearly understood by all members of the company.
- Ensure that all your employees understand what is expected of them in their respective job positions.
- Supply your employees with the appropriate training, information, and tools to successfully accomplish their job duties.
- Clearly define and establish measurement tools for the responsibilities for each job.
- Create controls that are guidelines that allow for flexibility.
- Encourage and practice behaviors that deliver encouragement, support, and clear feedback to employees.

Empowered employees attempt to work above and beyond their anticipated capabilities.

POWER TO THE PEOPLE!

- Encourage and promote a sense of responsibility in each employee.
- Create opportunities for people to work together in teams.
- Make it easy for people to give praise to each other. Make the company a company that recognizes and acknowledges praiseworthy actions.
- Listen to your employees all the time. Make the company's systems listen to the employees.
- Trust your employees.

RECOGNIZE THE INDIVIDUAL

Virtually every adult in America today has the responsibility for making decisions about investments, college tuition, purchasing a new home, refinancing the mortgage, or buying a car. These are all major decisions. The world has not collapsed because these everyday people didn't have the approval of a manager prior to making the decision. People are constantly evaluating choices available to them. Many of these people are also employees of a company. Yet the companies for the most part do not recognize and value the skills and abilities these people bring to the company daily. The existing workforce makes these critical decisions every day. These are life skills that everyone brings to the workplace.

The real question we are faced with is: What happens to this capability when employees get to the workplace? Why does it appear that highly functioning individuals who are capable of balancing budgets at home and making life decisions routinely, are not considered competent to make decisions about the kind of copy paper to buy or about the correct phone service to use? Generally companies are unwilling to *trust* employees. Companies are unable or unwilling to *trust* that the employee once shown or exposed to the desired outcome can achieve the objective. In many instances there is an enormous amount of distrust and arrogance by management. What impact does this lack of *trust* have on the workforce that drives our economy?

> By trusting employees you encourage them to work to their fullest potential.

POWER TO THE PEOPLE!

PRACTICE TRUST

To move beyond this limited, untrusting approach, we must first encourage, convince and help people to share the "power" they have. An employee who has the authority to control the circumstances of another person's work life also has the power to share this tool. When authority and responsibility are shared, trust builds. And as trust builds, confidence increases and productivity grows.

What is power?

- Power is the ability to do or to act.
- Power is the ability to control others; to have authority; to sway; to influence.
- Power is special authority assigned to or exercised by a person or group holding office.
- Power is legal ability or authority; also it is a document giving it.

It has been said that knowledge is power. When people are enriched with knowledge, they become more powerful by using this knowledge to shape their own destiny. Knowledge allows people to understand the factors that impact the various components of their world. The more they understand their world, the better able they are to deal with situations that arise in the day-to-day environment of work or home.

If we accept that knowledge is power, then the sharing of knowledge is equal to the sharing of power. With the sharing of power, everyone wins: the employee who now feels the gratification of participating in a job well done, the supervisor who had assistance in achieving the objective, and the company whose employee productivity and quality increase dramatically.

We frequently observe this sharing of power between skilled supervisors and employees. This positive interaction can also exist and survive within an organization even without upper management support. But there is a limit. As long as the interactions take place and stay within the parameters of the supervisor's area of responsibility, everything will work out well. Once they go beyond this area,

By sharing knowledge with employees, you empower them to take responsibility for their decisions and to make more responsible decisions as well.

POWER TO THE PEOPLE!

the wall of inflexible management is reached and everything stops dead. Therefore, senior management must also understand, believe in and support the idea that employees can and should be trusted and valued for the skills they bring to the workplace.

CUT THE CORD

To achieve this sense of "yes you can" and "everything is possible," managers must encourage and promote two basic ideas.

*If you're not part of the solution,
you are part of the problem.*

None of us is as smart as all of us

All members of the successful company of the twenty-first century must understand that each individual brings to the company the capacity to be responsible for the work assigned.

Employees who have the opportunity to share power and experience trust will successfully work together to figure out ways to increase productivity, reduce turnover, or solve any other problem facing an organization.

In many ways the potential relationship between a manager and an employee is very much like the relationship between a parent and a child.

- Enormous resources are invested in bringing the child to a level of maturity.
- Enormous resources are invested in bringing the employee to a level of competence and knowledge.
- The parent has raised the child to be a responsible citizen within the community.
- The company has oriented, trained, and supported the employee to be a highly productive member of the organization.
- The child has displayed skills and abilities in his or her developmental growth.

> Managers must guide and train employees to develop their skills and to use them effectively.

POWER TO THE PEOPLE!

> Managers should always encourage personal growth to help fully realize the potential employees.

- The employee has demonstrated skills and abilities in the various areas of responsibility.
- The child oftentimes learns additional information outside the scope of the traditional classroom or home environment.
- The employee often brings to the job complementary skills that were not formally required in the job description.
- Parents are not always aware of what the child really knows and understands.
- Companies do not always know the level of skill and knowledge for each employee.
- Parents seldom bother to discover what their child really knows and uses in his or her daily life.
- Companies seldom bother to discover what additional skills and abilities employees have.

This gap in awareness is frequently a critical factor affecting the efficient operation of the home or the workplace. The parent or company is perfectly happy with the skilled or knowledgeable employee or child and has no desire to upset the status quo. They would like everything to remain stable, normal, just the way it is.

But we all know how this story ends!!!!

Parents, like companies who do not recognize the need to cut the cord and permit children or employees to explore and grow beyond the defined structure, will eventually force the child or the employee to leave. At home, many children rebel and take extreme actions in response to a restrictive, controlling parental environment. In many companies the employees quit to move to "a better company" where they will be given the opportunity to continue growing and learning and to advance within the organization.

The innate desire of people to learn, grow, and successfully conquer challenges will make it impossible for employees to stay with a company that does not offer opportunities for personal growth and development. Companies, like parents, must learn to trust their employees and to allow them to become partners in solving larger and more complex business problems.

POWER TO THE PEOPLE!

NURTURE THE PROCESS

Even in the best companies, the economic conditions of the marketplace may demand varying degrees of downsizing, or in basic language, layoffs.

For the downsizing initiative to have positive impact on the company's bottom line, the plan must include an analysis not only of headcount, but also of the remaining employees who are "survivors." It is these survivors who ultimately will be responsible for making the stated goals and objectives of the downsizing initiative successful.

The survivors of downsizing have emerged from a highly traumatic experience. For weeks and maybe months they have waited for the ax to fall on their head. They watched colleagues lose their jobs. They saw entire functioning units of the organization dismantled. They survived.

As in any trauma, the impact frequently lingers for quite a time after the initial incident. Employees who have survived a downsizing or layoff are now faced with a redesigned work environment, increased work responsibilities, frequently a chaotic structure, and in many cases the personal guilt that accompanies being a survivor. Within this new environment they are expected to perform at peak efficiency.

It is no wonder that recent studies of companies who have downsized have shown that:

- Fewer than 30 percent of these companies met their profit objectives.
- Fewer than 50 percent of these companies met their expense reduction objectives.
- Fewer than 25 percent of these companies increased shareholder return on investment.

In most companies little or no planning goes into consideration of the employees who will stay (i.e. survive) after downsizing. The process of recognizing and respecting employees needs to be nurtured at every turn in the life of a company. Always keep the employ-

> Downsizing can crush the morale of remaining employees, and will not empower them to work to their fullest potential.

POWER TO THE PEOPLE!

ees as a major consideration in any and all decisions. How will employees help your company to achieve the stated objectives?

There are specific steps you can take to ensure that each employee who survives a downsizing is prepared and able to work toward achieving company goals and objectives. In the planning and implementation of a downsizing effort, be sure to include the following steps:

1. Present the future vision and encourage and support employees to work with you to implement this vision.
2. Communicate, communicate, communicate. You can never do too much.
3. Keep all employees involved. Be sure everyone knows that their input is welcome and respected.
4. Celebrate and reward performances that advance the goals of the company.

When you apply these simple principles to managing your department or running your business, you will reap enormous rewards, especially during critical periods.

In some cases you will encounter employees who don't have any desire to be empowered. They don't want any additional responsibility. They don't want to have control over their situation at work. They want things to be peaceful and stable.

Stop to think about this. Although this approach may be acceptable for some jobs, it may not be appropriate for your department and type of work. Is this really the kind of employee you want working for your company?

In every job there are basic duties and responsibilities. The individual hired to accomplish this job has clear duties and responsibilities. Employees, by the nature of the job duties they were hired to do, are "empowered" to carry out their assigned tasks. You as the manager need to be sure the job description indicates that the person is responsible for making the duties happen. There is no escaping this term "empowerment." It is a double-edged blade, working for both the company and the employee.

> Managers need to rebuild trust between management and employees through communication.

POWER TO THE PEOPLE!

Have faith in your human assets and in yourself. They will surprise you favorably if you allow them to.

. . . .

MEASURE

If you are curious about how you can determine the level of empowerment within your organization, begin by asking yourself some basic questions.

1. How frequently do I say " I should have done that myself"?
2. How many people do you have reporting to you directly?
3. How many people have been with you since the company started or for a long time?
4. How frequently are people absent from work when it is obvious they are not really very sick?
5. How many people have you directly supervised who still work with you?
6. How many people would follow you to another company if you were to leave?

In the final analysis it all comes down to you and how you choose to delegate at work. You have the power to make your work environment positive and supportive for everyone.

Which of the following scenarios best represents you?

Ineffective Method

Manager: John, I need to talk with you about your project, and I need to talk with you right now.

John: Bob, I'll be with you as soon as I finish this report; Sam needs it right away.

Manager: Sorry, Sam can wait. I want to talk with you now. I have a meeting in fifteen minutes.

John: Okay, Bob. What's up?

> Managers need to create a bond of loyalty and trust to empower employees.

POWER TO THE PEOPLE!

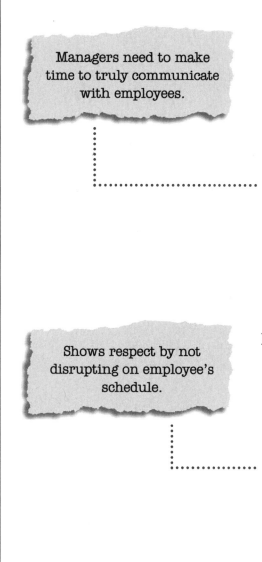

Managers need to make time to truly communicate with employees.

Shows respect by not disrupting on employee's schedule.

Manager: I am very concerned about how the XYZ project turned out and your part in the project.

John: What do you mean?

Manager: You were supposed to bring that project in on budget and it came in over budget by more than 20 percent. I can't have that happening in my department.

John: Bob, we knew things were off budget as we were finishing the project. We had a number of conversations about the problems and how best to resolve them. I thought we agreed to the plan we ultimately used.

Manager: I don't remember the specific conversations you are mentioning, and I don't have lots of time right now to go back rehashing this issue. I just need you to be able to bring projects in on budget, the way we are supposed to.

John: Bob, we really should talk about this. This is very confusing to me. I don't understand what your are saying.

Manager: Look, I don't have the time right now. We can talk some more later, but just remember you need to keep all your projects on budget. I'll see you later.

Effective Method

Manager: John, when will you have some time so we can talk about the XYZ project we just completed.

John: Bob, I'll can be with you as soon as I finish this report for Sam. He needs it right away.

Manager: Okay. When will we be able to set aside a good chunk of time to talk about this? I'd like to do it today, and I have meetings until 2:00 P.M.?

John: How about at 2:45 P.M.? I'm tied up in a team meeting until 2:30 PM.

Manager: Okay. Let's plan to meet in my office at 2:45 P.M. Why not bring the XYZ project folder with you so we will have it handy.

John: Okay, I'll see you at 2:45 P.M.

POWER TO THE PEOPLE!

Manager: John, thanks for making the time to meet with me today. I really wanted to take some time with you to understand, really understand why we were over budget 20 percent on this project. I know we talked during the process, but I don't know if I really understand everything.

John: Okay. Let me start at the beginning. When we took on this project, we knew we would have some problems. You basically told me to do the best I could with the situation because you were up to your eyeballs in alligators at the time.

Manager: Yes, that is true. That was quite a crazy time. So tell me more. Fill me in. What I really want to do is figure out a way in which we can prevent this from happening again. Do you have any ideas about how we could prevent this from happening again?

John: As a matter of fact, I do. I'm glad you asked. I was beginning to think you were going to blame me for the budget overage on this project. Thanks for setting my mind at ease. I recognize my responsibility as the manager of the XYZ project, but I also recognize that I am part of a team. Thanks for recognizing that.

Manager: You are right. We are a team, and I need your help to figure out how we can prevent this from happening again. Let's look at all the details. Maybe together we can identify where we went wrong and what we can do better next time. Are you prepared to stick it out with me so we can work this through tonight?

John: I think we have plans for the evening, but let me call home and tell my wife I'll be a bit late. She'll understand this is very important and will have an impact on all future work here. I'll be right back. Get the notepads ready.

Manager: Thanks, John, and tell your wife thank you also. I appreciate you taking the time now so we can work out this problem.

> Employees are more empowered when they feel that they have some influence on the problem at hand.

POWER TO THE PEOPLE!

Displays of managerial power only serve to discourage employee performance and creativity.

Commentary

In the **Ineffective Method** the manager is obviously getting heat from his boss. His immediate reaction is to put some of the heat on the person who led the project. His lack of respect for John is very obvious. He immediately lets John know who the boss was and who had the power to call the shots. Within a few moments it is clear that a solution to the real problems with the XYZ project will not emerge from this meeting. John is not going to really care how and why the project could be improved. He is only concerned about taking his punishment with the least amount of pain and aggravation. He is also starting to count the days to when he doesn't have to deal with Bob anymore. Not a very pretty picture. But a very common one.

The Effective Method illustrates a manager who recognizes that everyone's work is important and is respectful of that fact. Bob realizes that people need to know why they are engaged in a conversation and what the objective of the conversation is. Bob made sure that both his needs and John's needs were accommodated in the process of setting up the meeting. There was no one-sided power display. Bob was willing to share the power of determining the time of the meeting with John. Notice that John was then willing to offer his evening out with his wife as his offering to make this process work. Bob was able to present the issue of a 20 percent budget overage in a fashion that did not place the blame on John. John is now able to work with Bob and not feel as though he is defending himself. John can place all his energy into helping to solve the problem for the future. Although Bob really wants to get this problem-solving process accomplished today, he doesn't take advantage of his position as manager to force the issue. He allows John to determine how much time he wants to put into this process on this day.

POWER TO THE PEOPLE!

80-20

One way to allow employees to grow, develop, and achieve high levels of productivity is to employ the 80 percent—20 percent rule.

When you are speaking to an employee, monitor how much you say and how much the employee says. Monitor this for a week or so. Track your results. You can easily estimate the time via a simple "I talked 50 percent of the time, the employee talked 50 percent of the time."

In order to achieve a highly functional and productive employee workforce, you should do only 20 percent of the talking. Let the employee talk for 80 percent of the time, while you listen.

Listen!

You will be surprised at what you will learn about your own company when you take the time to listen.

Encourage Passion

"Where there is a will, there is a way!"

People who have clearly defined goals and objectives reach them, very successfully. A company that has clearly defined goals and objectives has a greater opportunity to achieve them than a company with poorly defined goals and objectives.

When a company finds individuals who share a passion for the product, service, or industry of the company, a dynamic synergy takes place. Synergy is the action whereby separate people, working together, have a greater total effect than the sum of their individual effects.

The employee with a passion for customer service and quality product discovers a company that promotes and supports high levels of customer service and quality. The blending of these two, employee and company, creates a powerful synergy whereby the individual passion is intensified and enriched by the company philosophy, mission statement, operational procedures, and objectives.

The company's vision is translated into real-life, real-time experiences that customers and other employees can hear, see, feel, and experience. The employee with passion helps a company to actualize its vision. A single passionate employee has the capacity to touch the

> Employers need to feel passionate about their work in order to reach company goals.

POWER TO THE PEOPLE!

soul of many others, both customers and employees, to promote, expand, extend, and demonstrate the passion of the company.

The story of the automotive assembly line worker from General Motors' Saturn division illustrates this concept. Saturn started out as an experiment in new design and new styles of management for manufacturing automobiles. The employees who decided to work for Saturn were selected because they shared an enthusiasm for a new idea and a new way of working. Part of this new idea was the fact that any employee on the assembly line could stop the assembly line at any time he or she discovered there was a problem with the assembly process or a defective part was identified. By allowing individual employees to stop the assembly line, Saturn was able to ensure that a problem would be identified early on in the manufacturing process, saving thousands of dollars. The exciting aspect of allowing employees to stop the assembly line is the power it gives to the employees. It helps Saturn employees feel totally connected and committed to the Saturn process. The positive impact on employees is immeasurable, but the positive impact on the Saturn division is clear—in saved time, reduced quality issues, and fewer recalls and defects.

To paraphrase Margaret Mead, "Never doubt that a small group of thoughtful, passionate employees can mobilize a company; indeed, it's the only thing that ever does."

> Making employees feel like an important part of the company encourages passion for their work.

QUESTIONS AND ANSWERS

1. **Why is the word *empowerment* used so much nowadays?**
   Like other management buzz words of previous years, *empowerment* is the buzz word of the '90s. It is a simple way of transmitting the idea that employees are valuable contributors to the success of any company. It is a simple way to get the point across that management should involve employees in the process of running the business, at all levels.

2. **What would I do to empower an employee?**
   Next time you receive a project from your boss, try this. Rather than deciding who within your subordinate staff will do the various steps as determined by you, meet with your

POWER TO THE PEOPLE!

staff and explain what you would like to do. Tell them you are very happy with the work everyone is doing, always aware that we all can improve and get better at what we do. Then tell them you would like to add some excitement and fun into the work environment by having them help you determine even better ways to get the projects done. In a group, ask for their assistance. Tell them this maybe the time when people will want to try different jobs or work together to get a portion of the project finished. Work with the group to plan the process for executing the project. You will need to be prepared to give the group the authority to make decisions about the project without having to go to you all the time. You may also need to share the project budget with the group. You are basically having the group work with you as a team so that more people are involved in the process of successfully accomplishing the project.

Generally, projects managed with a sense of employee empowerment are more efficient, more effective, and have greater lasting impact on the morale of the work group.

> Managers should both encourage employees and tell them how they could possibly improve.

3. **Do hourly workers really care what direction the company is headed in?**
Some lower-level employees may have little or no interest in what the company's plans for the future are, but they will want to know that they belong to a winning team. They want to be able to tell their families and friends that they work for a great company. If they feel they are working for a company that is going to succeed, they will feel more involved and thereby work harder and smarter.

4. **I tried this empowerment stuff and it didn't work. Should I continue, or am I going to waste more time?**
Let's start at the beginning. Empowerment is not a pill, it is not medicine, and it does not happen overnight. You and your employees need to work at making this notion of empowerment work. You need to be the driving force to make it work. So, for starters, you must dedicate a quality

> Empowerment is a slow process of showing responsibility and gaining trust.

POWER TO THE PEOPLE!

portion of time to this effort. You cannot plant the seeds and not nurture the process.

Just because employees don't jump on the bandwagon at first mention of empowerment doesn't mean they won't jump on board. Give them a chance. Maybe you'll need to bolster their confidence that they can do what you know they can do. Start with smaller, individual projects so each employee will have the opportunity to experience success before you put them in a group (team) with other employees.

Take time to explain what you really want them to accomplish, how long they have to do the job, what resources are available, and how they can get help from you without making it seem like they are not doing their job. You want them to feel comfortable with the process. Let them succeed.

If you take it slow and stay consistently focused on the need to share the responsibility and authority with your employees, you will be able to make this empowerment thing work.

5. **My company does nothing to empower me. Can I use empowerment only within my department?**
You can try, but you may be rowing upstream. For empowerment to really have an impact it must have the support of senior management and the policymakers. You will be able to increase the self-confidence of your employees and you will be able to have them assume more responsibilities and authority within your department, but it will be in an isolated environment. Be prepared for your employees who have gained self-confidence to be more resentful and negative about the circumstances that exist in the company once you have given them a taste of empowerment.

6. **Can you ever give too much authority to employees?**
Always keep in mind the reasons for any initiative. If you are empowering employees to help reduce defects or to improve quality, that should be the scope of empowerment. The term *empowerment* does not mean your employees will have the

> Though empowerment demands the sharing of power, the boundaries between management and staff should be made very clear.

POWER TO THE PEOPLE!

authority to change policy or to impact the company in every area. As part of your program you should define the guidelines and the parameters. All programs and initiatives need boundaries; it is your job to set these initial boundaries.

7. Will the concept of empowerment scare employees?

Most definitely it will scare some of your employees. Others will greet it with a sigh of relief. Still others will not know it is happening until they find themselves faced with making a decision at work. For those employees who are scared by the concept, team them with someone who understands and embraces the concept. You may even want to do some initial training to create a comfort level for all employees. The best training will be discussions of real-life situations.

8. Can I teach employees who have been with me for twenty years to be comfortable with empowerment?

Yes! Some of your more experienced employees will need your support in rising to the challenge of an empowered workforce. You will need to carefully explain to them the reasons for your taking this action and the thinking processes you went through. By explaining all this history to these employees you are demonstrating your respect and recognition for their commitment to you. Now you are demonstrating your commitment to them by explaining your thinking. You may need to hold their hands and you may have a longer learning curve for these employees, but if you are willing to put in the effort, you will teach these old dogs a new trick.

STREETWISE
advice

◆ **Establish baseline measurements to track the impact of your empowerment strategies.**
Include turnover rates, recruitment costs, sales increases or decreases, customer satisfaction surveys, and employee attitude surveys. You will want to know how successful your program has been so you can make adjustments to the program to improve its effectiveness.

◆ **Empowerment allows employees to learn from their mistakes.**
Each situation becomes a learning experience. If you design your empowerment strategy wisely, you will be able to lead your employees toward more successful experiences with fewer mistakes. Start off with projects or situations that have a small negative impact if a mistake is made. As employees become more comfortable and self-assured, move on to more complex situations with potentially greater impact due to mistakes. You will see a definite developmental pattern as your employees become more comfortable with the responsibilities and authority of empowerment.

◆ **Empowerment can work for all your employees, but you may need to bring people to the point were they will accept this new level of responsibility.**
Frequently resistance will emerge because some employees do not have enough confidence in their abilities. Your job is to develop the self-confidence of your employees. This process will not happen overnight, so be patient, and be consistent in your efforts.

◆ **You should implement training programs to help your managers learn how to empower employees and themselves.**
The best training is by your example followed by discussions of the outcomes. The real-life experiences you create in the work life of your managers will be the best training for them. They will then be able to transfer the same sensibilities to their employees. Be the best role model you can be to empower your employees.

◆ **Empowerment is a process that starts at the top.**
You must support and demonstrate your belief in empowerment by all your actions and deeds. If the leader doesn't believe, then no one else will.

◆ **Measure your success at empowerment by measuring the passion level of your employees.**

◆ **Once you set in motion the process of empowerment, you cannot turn back.**
You must continue with your plans. If you don't, your employees will lose faith in you and any future initiatives you try to implement. Additionally, once your employees get a taste of empowerment, they will recognize their own abilities and will want to participate at a higher level of involvement. If you start this, be prepared to continue and reap the benefits of an empowered workforce.

CHAPTER

8

COMMUNICATION

Misunderstood communication is one of the biggest problems facing businesses today. All too often people think they have effectively communicated, when in fact they have not, because each person heard something different. You need to employ "full cycle" communication—always confirming that effective communication has indeed taken place.

THE RULES OF SUCCESS

Everyone know the three rules of real estate. location, location, location!

In business the three rules of success are: communication, communication, communication!

1. Communication with employees
2. Communication with executive team
3. Communication with customers

Every chapter of this book is built on this basic need to communicate. A business needs to communicate all aspects of its business to all of the participating members.

Communicating with employees is the most difficult aspect of most organizations. The common feeling is, we hire them, they do what we want. To a point. Sometimes you don't know what you want, or maybe what you want is not really the best thing for the business. You must begin to encourage, support, and embrace communication with, to, and from your employees, who have the greatest knowledge of what is really happening. When you listen to the employees you will learn more than you ever imagined. When you listen, and when you communicate your understanding of what they have told you, they will see that they are recognized as valuable partners in the business. Your simple act of listening and communicating back to your employees will bring you more highly motivated employees as well as employees who will begin to think more creatively and more strategically.

Communicating with your executive team is critical for ensuring that they articulate and communicate the company's message and values to the employees. It is with your executive team that you develop your communication strategies and policy statements. When you clearly communicate your vision to your executive team and when they are able to understand and espouse your message, you are well on your way to a successful company. Now that your entire team shares a common language the team can and will speak with one voice. It is very important for customers and for all employees to

> By communicating with employees, you motivate them with trust and sincerity.

COMMUNICATION

hear the same words and meaning coming from all the members of the executive team.

An important component of communicating with your executive team is your ability to have the group reach consensus. You will depend on these key players to set policy and chart strategic directions. There will be times when you will have honest disagreements within your executive team. Your ability to foster honest dialogue and to reach consensus on the best course of action will be critical to your success as a leader and to the success of your business.

You will have reached consensus when all members of your executive team have been heard through meetings that are frank and honest. The dialogues must allow for all views to be presented and considered and all available information shared among all the members. All members of the executive team should feel as though they own the team's decision, and all members must agree to support the decision even if it is not exactly what a specific member wanted.

Communicating with customers is the ultimate challenge. The successful manager is able to serve as a positive role model for employees to learn how they can best deal with customers, both internal and external.

Many times managers fail to recognize their roles as coaches in the professional development of employees. Managers who are skilled at communicating with customers will, in most cases, be equally skilled at communicating with employees. Communicating with customers is an extension of good employee communication. The same habits and skills used in employee communication are needed to successfully communicate with customers. Companies who communicate with customers by listening to the customers are the most successful businesses. Customers have very simple needs. They want what they want when they want it.

When a business listens to the customer as part of the communication cycle, it is guaranteed success. When a business listens to what it *thinks* the customer is saying, it is gambling with success. The successful business is able to clearly understand the needs and expectations of the customer.

> Results are attained more readily when ideas and issues are communicated honestly.

COMMUNICATION

WHAT IS EFFECTIVE COMMUNICATION?

Effective communication is information that has been disseminated and understood by the targeted audience.

For communication to have impact or to be successful, there must be a complete cycle. The sender transmits the information to a receiver. The receiver should then confirm acceptance and comprehension of the message. The only one capable of verifying the comprehension is the sender. That's you!

Therefore, all communication should ensure a process for clarification and verification. There must be a way to ensure that the message was received and understood.

Misunderstood communication can be one of the largest problems facing business today. Businesses have lots of messages being sent, but not all of the information is received, and not all of the information is understood.

Without a complete communication cycle we don't have dialogue, we have monologues. Dialogue ensures that we are interacting with others to reach a shared meaning. Without the confirmation and verification of a message, all the sender has is a monologue of what was intended to be transmitted.

When you communicate in a positive, respectful manner and environment, the highest level of dialogue is reached.

Listening is the most important tool available to ensure that you are communicating completely to reach the shared meaning through dialogue. This shared meaning is the essence of communication and must be achieved if you are to be a successful manager. What kind of listener are you?

People listen in many different ways. The way in which you listen determines how much of the message you may be screening. Up to 70 percent of a message can be screened out due to your style of listening. When you recognize and understand what type of listener you are, you will then be able to modify your listening to capture an even larger percentage of the message.

Some people listen in an *appreciating* style. They are pleased to hear the information and are listening to identify the components

> To be a successful manager, you must be a good listener.

COMMUNICATION

that will allow them to hook on to or continue the dialogue. They are participating to relax and enjoy the interaction. They are looking to be entertained and inspired. Frequently these listeners may not catch a point if they are not totally engaged.

Empathizing listeners direct all their energy to identifying how the message being sent is similar to situations they have experienced. They are supporting the speaker as they express concerns. These listeners accept the message without judging, and oftentimes they learn from the speaker's experiences. They may sometimes miss an important component of the communication if they are too wrapped up in another aspect of the information.

Others listen in a *comprehending* fashion. They want to capture as much information as possible. They are looking to organize and make sense of the information being sent, to understand all the facts of the message. They like to make connections between or among personal experiences and attempt to find and understand the relationships between or among ideas. They frequently don't catch all the unspoken or subtextual messages being communicated.

Discerning listeners are taking the message in a very careful manner. They want to get complete, accurate information. They are driven to determine the main message and will then sift out what they consider to be the most important details. Each bit of information is carefully weighed and measured for accuracy, validity, and content. Needless to say, the discerning listener may miss some critical information as all the information is processed.

Evaluating listeners are motivated by a desire to figure out how this communication fits into the bigger picture. These listeners will question a speaker's motives and will accept or reject messages based on personal beliefs. Throughout the communication they will make decisions based on the information provided. Frequently these listeners will miss critical information if it doesn't fit into their belief system.

As you can clearly see, you must incorporate all types of listening styles to really receive a complete message. Think about how you

> Managers must be ready to listen to employees on many different levels.

generally listen. At your next opportunity, begin using all forms of listening to obtain the most comprehensive message from the sender.

For the success of your employee and business dealings, good listening is critical.

CONSISTENT APPLICATION

How does your company communicate to employees? Your company should be able to communicate information within the organization to employees in a clear and efficient manner.

Check all of the items below that you and your company use frequently.

____ written memo to employee bulletin board
____ written memo to individual employees
____ messages on payroll checks or inserted into pay envelope
____ voice mail
____ E-mail
____ company newsletter published weekly
____ company newsletter published monthly
____ company newsletter published quarterly
____ weekly meeting of all staff
____ monthly meetings of all staff
____ meetings as requested and necessary

Managers need to be able to communicate about company information effectively.

If you were unable to check specific items with certainty, you should seriously consider defining your communications strategy within your department or company.

Look at your department or company and consider the way your employees work. Which vehicles are best suited for your employees to receive communication, and which ensure that you have shared meaning?

Will the posted messages give you shared meaning and understanding? Will memos direct to employees do this? Will it be necessary to have meetings with all employees? How efficient is each of these approaches within your organization?

COMMUNICATION

What must you do to ensure that you have a message not only sent and received but also understood? This is the ultimate challenge of your communication strategy.

The successful communication strategy includes vehicles that have clearly defined systems to deliver the messages, allowing for clarification and verification while confirming receipt of the message by all employees. This type of system must be very efficient, with very few system problems.

For example:

A newsletter sent out monthly by the XYZ Company is attached to all payroll checks. This ensures that all employees receive a newsletter. Within the format of the newsletter is a statement that reads: "If you have any questions about the contents of this newsletter, especially in regard to policies and procedures, please call 1-888-XYZ-HELP. Leave your question on the machine and we will get back to you within forty-eight hours."

In another section of the newsletter is the following statement: "Policies and procedures published in this newsletter become effective the first day of the month following the publication date. Please be prepared to comply with any and all policies and procedures published in this newsletter."

This example of the XYZ Company newsletter, distributed as described, is capable of transmitting critical business information to all members of the organization in a fashion that places the responsibility on the employees. This newsletter vehicle can also carry traditional soft news and information and is a bona fide communications vehicle for the organization. You can be sure that every employee will read it knowing that business decisions and operational policies and procedures will be presented, explained, and introduced. The ability of the employees to operate within the policies and procedures of the company will be dependent on their faithful review of the company newsletter.

> Good communication ensures that the employee will work within the mandates of the company.

COMMUNICATION

QUALITY COMMUNICATION = POSITIVE INTERACTIONS

Successful managers want to achieve specific results due to the initiatives they employ within the company. A strong, quality communication strategy that reinforces these programs will reap many benefits, as we have mentioned in the preceding sections. An additional benefit is that quality communication increases the incidence of positive interaction among the members of the organization.

When an organization uniformly employees positive, constructive communication, it is sending a consistent message. The company is indicating that all communication within the company is based on respect for the individual and an honest appreciation of everyone's value and contribution to the efforts of the company.

Your communication strategy should support, encourage, and reinforce the mission and culture of the organization.

There are some very simple steps every member of every organization can do to ensure positive, healthy communication interactions:

- Help others to be right, not wrong.
- Whenever possible, have fun.
- Behave with enthusiasm.
- Figure out ways for new ideas to work, not reasons why they won't.
- Act with initiative.
- Be bold and courageous; take a chance.
- Help others be successful.
- Maintain a positive mental attitude.
- Don't believe gossip; check it out before you repeat what you hear.
- Speak positively about others whenever the opportunity arises.
- If you don't have anything positive to say, don't say anything.

> Good communication encourages creative interaction between employees.

COMMUNICATION

It really is very simple to begin demonstrating these basic principles within your organization. Why not try this tomorrow at work:

1. All day long, only verbally acknowledge actions and behaviors that are positive and productive for the company.
2. When speaking to individuals give brief, clear statements to capture their attention. Try not to engage in a conversation unless you really have something important to say.
3. Whenever possible, ask open-ended questions that allow your communication partner to talk with you. Once you have asked the questions, listen, listen, listen.
4. When someone mentions an idea that may sound a bit odd, ask, "Oh, how would that actually work?" rather than "Oh, we tried that years ago and it didn't work."
5. When you become engaged in conversation with another person, allow him or her to complete the full thought before responding. Listen to the total idea or statement of the person; don't jump onto one word, phrase, or statement. Hear the person out.
6. Whenever possible, rephrase the information you just heard to ensure that you are really communicating.
7. Allow yourself to recognize the importance of this topic or information to the speaker. Even if you think it is unimportant, demonstrate to the person that you value and respect his or her contribution.

If you try these simple yet profound tactics you will be amazed at the impact they have on your ability to learn and the impact they have on your organization. The key to all this is consistent application of these strategies.

OTHER COMMUNICATION IDEAS

There are numerous communication ideas that may help you create a strong and vibrant company. As mentioned previously, it is imperative that the ideas you utilize be reflective of you and your style. You should not adopt an idea from another company because it works for

> Be patient, open-minded, and receptive to the employee's ideas or problems.

COMMUNICATION

them. The idea must be tailored to fit your organization and to reflect your style.

Philip Crosby, the author of *Quality Without Tears: The Art of Hassle-Free Management*, has said, "Most communication blocks occur because people didn't know an information source was available to them."

The following are a variety of communication ideas that may fit into your management style and help to eliminate the problem Crosby mentioned.

MANAGEMENT BY WALKING AROUND

This communication style is wonderful for managers who are actively engaged in the day-to-day activities of the business. This approach works well when a manager has made a commitment to spend a dedicated amount of time on the floor with the employees or in various employee offices each day. This approach must be compatible with your style; it should not be forced or just a charade. Employees will see through you if you are "just doing this to do it."

In effect you are being yourself walking throughout the organization looking for opportunities to make positive comments and/or receive input and feedback. This approach allows you to see everything going on, and it allows you to listen directly to the employees. It is especially effective in an organization with many management layers. The approach permits all employees direct access to the boss and frequently generates high levels of spontaneous, creative synergy while employees and the boss exchange ideas.

BRAINSTORMING SESSIONS

When you are faced with a challenging opportunity or problem, you may wish to use brainstorming techniques to flesh out as many ideas as possible. The objective of brainstorming is to obtain as many wild and crazy ideas as possible to help formulate the few ideas that will emerge as possible solutions. During brainstorming, people will throw out as many ideas as possible without anyone critiquing, analyzing, or discussing the ideas. Once the group gets into the process, and no one is making fun of the ideas presented, even more ideas

> Management should make an effort to communicate with employees on a personal level to become engaged with the everyday workings of the company.

COMMUNICATION

> Create opportunities for creative exchanges of ideas and suggestions.

begin to flow. The opportunities for one idea to trigger another idea are increased dramatically with the comfort level of the group. When you begin to use the brainstorming strategy regularly you will see a larger number of ideas emerging. Some of these ideas will either be the solution to problems or will trigger the final creative solution.

SUGGESTION BOXES

Almost every company has tried a suggestion box at one time or another. Invariably the idea falls flat. The reason is simple: It was not part of a communication strategy that employees could and would trust.

In many cases the suggestion box emerged because management was frustrated about how to get things accomplished. Rather than meet directly with employees, management decides to create an anonymous vehicle to collect ideas.

Once the ideas are deposited, they are evaluated by whom? Generally management, who was originally unable to come up with successful solutions to the problems to begin with. Rather than having management actually meet with the people who make the suggestions to explore how they might work, the suggestion box system usually discards ideas for a variety of reasons.

Why not consider a suggestion box system that allows for exciting, creative exchanges for the discussion of all the ideas on a regular basis?

Even if only one idea emerges from the conversation, the employees who participated would know that their input was valued and respected and that they had the opportunity to engage in a highly creative and stimulating interaction with other employees and managers.

The net result of this approach is a higher level of communication and positive feeling about the organization.

MEETINGS

Meetings have the potential to be either the best or the worst. A meeting without an agenda is deadly. It is absolutely critical for

COMMUNICATION

everyone to know and understand why they are attending a meeting and what the outcome is intended to be. The meeting need not be a long, ponderous situation. It can be in a hallway, standing up. Frequently the best, most efficient meetings are short, direct, and very well planned.

Be sure to follow some simple guidelines:

1. Have you identified the objectives of the meeting?
2. Have you created a clear, written agenda?
3. Has everyone who will attend seen the agenda prior to the meeting?
4. Has everyone had an opportunity to modify the agenda?
5. Have all the necessary people been invited?
6. Have all the necessary data and materials been collected?
7. Are all participants able to attend at the designated time?
8. Is there a clear time for beginning and ending as well as a defined location?
9. Are people reminded to come to this meeting with a clear head, open mind and respectful attitude toward all other participants?

No matter how large or how small the meeting, no matter how long or how short the meeting, the same basic principles must apply if you wish to achieve high levels of productive communication.

- **Weekly Update Meetings**
  As a technique to communicate what is happening in various departments or in various teams, you may want to have update meetings wherein each member gives a brief update of the status of the project, workload, or activity. It allows all to be informed and it also keeps everyone focused on their objectives.
- **Creating a Visible Communication Device**
  If your company or department is contained in a single space with all members able to see or hear a message, try

> Communication keeps the employee informed about company objectives and focused upon them.

COMMUNICATION

something like this: Obtain a gong or a large bell and use this device to announce important information for everyone to hear. This would make it possible for an individual employee to announce the signing of a new contract or the completion of a particular project. Everyone would know about it immediately, and it would save a few forests in the process.

- **Memos and E-mail**

  Written and electronic mail messages are part of all organizations. To ensure quality communication, your organization must define the parameters of these tools and the ways in which they may and may not be used. As memos and E-mail can become evidence in legal matters, you should be clearly concerned that you have defined guidelines and procedures for their use. Whatever you decide, it must be clearly communicated, with a verification of understanding by all members of the organization. Then you must monitor compliance with this policy to reduce the potential of legal entanglements.

- **Monthly Managers' Breakfasts**

  Begin a tradition of inviting five to eight employees to join you for breakfast at a local restaurant. The opportunity to learn what is really going in the company is enormous. More important will be your ability to transfer information directly to the employees and nip any rumors in the bud.

Whenever possible, use these regular and routine vehicles of communication to reinforce the mission of your company. Consider including the mission statement for your company on the basic format for all memos. Use statements that reflect your desired behavioral objectives as a substitute for the mission statement, such as "None of us is as smart as all of us."

> Regular meetings or conferences within the company help keep everyone up-to-date on current issues, and also encourage a more open forum for discussion.

INEFFECTIVE COMMUNICATIONS SCENARIO

President of the company to the executive team:

I have called you all together today to tell you some bad news. We have gone through some very bad times. As you know, our sales are down, our expenses have not gotten any lower, and our cash flow is virtually nonexistent. There will be drastic steps taken to rectify this situation. I will keep you all informed through periodic meetings like this one. As much as I would like to answer questions, I don't have any more information for you at this time. I will need you to keep your departments working at peak productivity during this difficult time. I have faith that you will do just that. Thank you very much.

EFFECTIVE COMMUNICATIONS SCENARIO

President of the company to the executive team:

I have called you together today to ask for your assistance. You are the key managers in our organization. You are aware of some of our problems during these past few quarters. I would like to work with you to determine the most appropriate strategy to stem the tide that is pulling us down. This will take an enormous effort for all of us. I know we can turn the tide, but we will need to enlist the assistance of the entire organization.

I don't want to have layoffs or to have to cut service or quality to any of our customers. I want to work with you to figure out how we can emerge from this time stronger and more able to prevent this from ever happening again.

Let's begin by letting you ask any and all questions you might want to ask. I'm all yours until all the questions have been asked.

Commentary

In the first scenario the president left the executive team with nothing to hold on to except the fear that the company would close its doors at any time. It was not a very encouraging situation, and it is very unlikely that they will be able to keep their employees

> Effective managers communicate problems, while reinforcing the value of those working to solve the problems.

COMMUNICATION

motivated. He didn't even give them a chance to understand why this was happening. No questions were permitted.

In the second scenario the president engaged the group by asking for their assistance. He acknowledged their value and told them the truth about the existing circumstances. Then he validated their importance to him by asking them to work with him to come up with a plan of action. To help them get to this point, he is prepared to answer all questions posed.

It is very clear that the president in the second scenario has a better chance of making it through this difficult time than the president in the first scenario.

> Constantly seek more effective methods of communication.

QUESTIONS AND ANSWERS

1. **I started this business fifteen years ago and it has grown steadily ever since. We are profitable, and I don't have regular meetings with my employees. Why should I start now?**
   It is important to remember that every business is different and every manager is different. There is no one way to do everything, especially communication. Just because you don't have regular meetings with your employees doesn't mean you are not communicating. It appears that you are using other techniques to transfer information to your employees and for you to obtain information. Your are successful and profitable, an enviable position. Think for a moment or two about what you do and how that allows you to communicate your goals and objectives to your staff. You may be a skilled manager who is able to communicate volumes to people in a variety of ways, or you may be missing an opportunity to be more effective.

2. **I have weekly meetings of my staff, and no one ever talks. I do all the talking. What should I do?**
   Next time you have your meeting, be sure the agenda has been prepared and distributed ahead of time and that it

states clearly to come prepared with one idea on a particular timely topic. When the meeting begins, ask for someone to share the idea he or she brought to the meeting. Then just sit and listen. If no one speaks, sit and listen. Wait until someone speaks or until the time allotted for the meeting is over. If no one has spoken, call a meeting for the next day and set the same agenda. Your staff needs to know that you will listen to them. They need to trust that you will listen to them, so you may have to demonstrate that you can sit and listen to nothing first.

3. **We send out memos of all our policy changes, but people keep saying they never got the memo. How can we be sure that everyone gets the memo?**

   Each time you send a out a memo that includes a policy change, have a separate page that will serve as a receipt. When the memo is received, the individual must return the receipt to you for recording. If an old policy is being replaced, you may want them to send the old policy back so you will know only the most recent policy is being used.

4. **What kinds of things should I communicate?**

   You should communicate anything and everything that has a direct impact on the employees. Give them information. Information is knowledge, and knowledge is power. A powerful workforce is a critical tool in making your company successful.

5. **What kinds of things should I keep private?**

   There are many things that should be kept private. These include plans that have not yet been fully formed. Personnel issues pertaining to individuals should never be communicated to others. Facts and figures that are not solid and may change are best withheld until accurate information is available. Inaccurate information should never be communicated.

6. **How do I ensure that I am getting good communication from my staff?**

   The best way for you to be sure you are getting complete and accurate communication from your staff is to listen to them

> Listening actively and working to clarify views helps to make the most out of communication.

COMMUNICATION

and let them tell you everything they intend to tell you. Then you should ask for clarification, and if necessary ask as many questions as possible to fill in any gaps of information.

7. **When should I clarify communication?**
You should be clarifying all the time. You don't need to make a big deal of your clarification especially if the issue is not of critical importance. You may only need to use key words to confirm that you understand the key concept.

8. **Do I need to be a public speaker to be a good communicator?**
Not at all. What you need is a clear, consistent strategy for communicating what you want people to know. You should be able to communicate very effectively and only infrequently need to stand in front of a large group of people. Use other vehicles such as memos and e-mail, use other people whom you know understand your philosophy, but be sure that the meaning and content you are transmitting are yours. Also be sure you are always confirming and clarifying what is being communicated through this strategy.

9. **Why do people sometimes think I'm upset when I'm not?**
Maybe your tone of voice sends the wrong message. Sometimes we are totally unaware of our tone of voice. Ask people who work closely with you if your tone of voice conveys that you seem upset.

10. **I think I'm saying and doing all the correct things, but I don't feel that it is working. What could be wrong?**
Maybe you are communicating more messages than you think. People are not just hearing and listening to your words, they are also perceiving your body language. Sometime body language can be so strong that people don't hear the words. Think about how you present yourself and the settings in which you tend to talk to people.

11. **I'm so busy that I don't have time to communicate.**
Although you don't realize it, you are communicating by not communicating. By not talking to your staff or by not

> Non-verbal communication can be just as effective as verbal communication.

responding to your employees, you communicate volumes. You are sending them a message that they are not important enough or valuable enough for you to talk with them. By not responding to their memos or ideas you tell them that their ideas are not important. This behavior is very negative and counterproductive for any business.

STREETWISE
advice

◆ **Make quality and consistent communication a given responsibility for all management positions.**
This should be included in the job description for every manager.

◆ **Don't overreact to what you hear. Before you react, confirm and clarify what you think you have heard.**

◆ **Make sure you make listening a key part of your communication strategy. Practice, practice, practice.**

◆ **Recognize your style of listening and appreciate and respect the style of others with whom you work.**

◆ **Don't stay in your ivory tower. Interact in as many ways as possible.**
If you spend all your time in the office, you will never be able to fully communicate with your employees.

◆ **Every communication vehicle or tool you use should reflect your corporate mission and culture.**

◆ **Follow up each meeting with personal action steps that will communicate and demonstrate the value of the meeting everyone just attended.**
You need to let people know that they are valuable and that the time they spend with you in meetings has value to the company.

◆ **Don't forget to thank people for a job well done and for efforts expended.**
Don't miss any opportunity to reinforce positive behaviors and actions.

> Utilize communicated information to prove its worth to both you and the company.

CHAPTER

9 MANAGING CHANGE

As change becomes the only constant in today's workplace, managing change becomes a crucial skill. Managing change requires extremely careful attention to communication, to empathy, to building trust, to being positive, and to finding creative ways for employee input and empowerment. Today's workforce demands a clear and concise explanation of why change is happening—and it is necessary for managers to be able to articulate this.

MANAGING CHANGE

ELEMENTS OF CHANGE

Before discussing how managers can help their employees deal with change, it's important to establish some "common ground" regarding change and understand what's involved in the change process.

There are two main elements of change: (1) what exactly is changing and (2) how to deal with the emotional and psychological sense of loss of the old, familiar, or routine. The change may involve a job, a location, job responsibilities, a team, or a manager, and it can be very significant; however, the most vital part of change is the way in which we deal with it. The most successful change efforts carefully address both of these elements—in reverse order.

AWARENESS OF CHANGE

Managers can begin a successful change intervention by first realizing that employees have a "sixth sense" regarding changes about to happen, so whether anything is said or published, they can sense it. It's naive to believe that management can hide change until it's about to happen, and the air of uncertainty and suspicion among employees leads to counterproductivity, adverse morale, fear, and stress. The best decision managers can make (although our gut instinct is to try to hide "bad news") is to provide employees with as much detailed information about the upcoming change as possible and to be as open, honest, and up-front as early as possible when the need for change is recognized.

> Change should be addressed in an open and honest way to avoid problems later on.

CHANGE MANAGEMENT SCENARIOS

FIVE BARRIERS TO SUCCESSFUL CHANGE

- Fear, anger, and uncertainty (emotion)
- Failure to see the need for the change (perception)
- Feeling that all change must be negative (attitude)
- Lukewarm acceptance of change or a wait-and-see attitude (reluctance)

MANAGING CHANGE

- Failure or refusal to see the positive opportunities inherent in change (resistance)

When change occurs, employees are likely to put up several barriers to change, often without recognizing that they are forming these barriers. Emotion is always a part of change—both positive and negative change. For example, landing a new job and being transferred to another division are both exciting but incite very different emotions. We have to understand and allow for the letting go of the comfortable and familiar for a new experience or situation.

Failure to see the need for change (perception) may be a result of management's failure to fully explain the change and help people "buy into" the change. The attitude that all change must be negative is often a by-product of poorly handled previous change initiatives. Reluctance is a very natural reaction to proposed change because it signifies the loss of something familiar or comfortable. It takes time to work through this process, but it's also important to move people forward and get them involved in the new change and working toward positive goals for the future.

Outright resistance must be addressed head-on. If it shows in an employee at the very outset of change, work through the process and try to get the person to see the need for change, accept the change, and move forward. After all avenues have been exhausted, you must take whatever appropriate action is required to move the company forward, with or without this employee.

> Change is necessary to move people forward and to work toward positive goals for the future.

FIVE KEYS TO SUCCESSFUL CHANGE MANAGEMENT

- **Create an environment of openness.**
  Give people as much information as possible as early as possible to head off the "grapevine" proclamations of doom and to prevent employees from imagining the worst. Allow employees to ask questions, and give them straight answers. Employees worry because it's their lives and futures you're changing.

MANAGING CHANGE

- **Function as objectively as possible.**
  Be prepared with as many facts, figures, and examples that support the reasons why a change is necessary and beneficial, even if it is uncomfortable.
- **Be sensitive to subjectivity and emotion.**
  We live in our own comfort zones and almost automatically reject anything that violates our zone. Remember that, above all else, change always suggests losing or giving up something that may be very important and personal to the employee. You're dealing with human emotions and always need to be sensitive to that fact.
- **Encourage development of alternative perspectives.**
  Encourage employees to find positive ways to accept change. Minimize potential disruption. Evaluating as many options as possible is a valuable technique to open minds to the potential positive impacts of change.
- **Disconnect and reestablish.**
  It's important to allow a reasonable period of time for employees to adjust to the loss of the old and familiar. Afterward, it's equally important to get them focused on the new path, begin to generate excitement and attain positive goals, and reestablish the new comfort zone as another experience to be enjoyed and learned from as the company moves forward.

> By giving employees optional ways of dealing with change, you encourage them to keep an open mind about change.

REORGANIZATION

Setup

In this scenario, a manager has learned that his department is facing a reorganization because of poor operating results. He is meeting with an employee from his department to share what he knows at this point. This employee was out sick the day the manager held a group meeting for other department members, and the manager wants to make sure the employee hears the news from him rather than from other department members.

MANAGING CHANGE

> Work to make a negative change into a positive approach.

Manager: Hi Tim, have a seat. I wanted to meet with you this morning to apprise you of the current operating situation. I believe it's important for you to have as much information as is currently available.

Tim: I heard something about an organizational shift when I came in this morning. What's happening? Are we in trouble as a company?

Manager: I understand your reaction. That's why I wanted to talk with you in private. It's public knowledge that our company results haven't met with our forecast for either revenues or profits. While no definite decisions have been made, we're considering a company reorganization. That's why it's important that you have all the facts, and I wanted to make sure you heard them from me first.

Tim: What is going to happen?

Manager: Well, there are several things that we can do to prepare ourselves. One, we have to accept the fact that change is inevitable. My guess is that we'll lose one, maybe two, positions. While some situations are beyond our control, we at least can help the company by developing suggestions and ideas on ways to reduce costs and improve productivity. Let's brainstorm on how we can help the company through this transition.

Tim: What if we can't come up with anything constructive?

Manager: We have to be prepared for that reality; however, let's focus all our positive energies on creating alternative approaches. We may find some answers that will surprise us.

Commentary

This scenario works because the manager is proactively addressing expected reorganizational change (and possible job loss) prior to it actually happening. By doing this, he provides direct channels of accurate information, which helps derail the grapevine rumors. While he can't give an assurance of continued

MANAGING CHANGE

employment, he uses the situation to solicit ideas and suggestions for ways to solve the problem if possible and help the employee consider his options and take charge of his own future. He helps the employee prepare for uncertainty by examining strengths, developing possible career options, and keeping a positive focus during the session.

COMPANY BUYOUT

Setup

In this illustration, a manager who knows that his company is being bought out calls an employee into his office to apprise her of the buyout and its implications for her future with the company. There are expected to be a number of transfers and a shift of job responsibilities, but there is no concrete evidence to suggest job loss.

> Work with employees to find a positive focus in the face of an uncertain future.

Manager: Hi Jill, please come in. I wanted to share some information with you regarding the proposed buyout of our company and what the possible implications are for you.

Employee: Look, you don't have to sugar-coat this. I'm losing my job, right?

Manager: No, not necessarily. As you know, these situations often have a way of creating new opportunities either within our own company or the new company. I would rather we focus our energies on developing a strategy for you to take advantage of one of these opportunities. How do you think we should proceed?

Employee: Well, it is important for me to keep up with the latest technologies, so additional computer courses would be a good place to start. Can I get the company to fund night courses?

Manager: I think that is certainly a reasonable request. What else can I do to help you define your career goals either here, at the new company, or at another company?

Employee: Well, what would really be helpful for me is if you could give me a frank assessment of my strengths and weak-

MANAGING CHANGE

nesses as well as some ideas of new positions I should pursue given my background and experience.

Commentary

In this situation, there is no clear-cut decision on whether the employee's job is going to disappear. The manager states the situation up-front, which results in a negative, knee-jerk reaction from the employee. By using his listening skills, he is able to redirect the employee's thinking while being as frank and honest as possible. He skillfully takes a two-pronged approach of 1) what can we do for you as a company and 2) what can you do and what do you need to start assessing an alternative career plan. The manager demonstrates empathy balanced with reality.

> Managers must balance positive communication with a grasp on the realities of the situation.

TRANSFER TO A NEW DEPARTMENT

Setup

In this example, a manager informs an employee that she is being shifted to another department because that department requires her writing and phone skills. This employee does not want to make the transfer.

Manager: Hi, JoAnn, come on in. I wanted to talk to you today about a change in your responsibilities. This just came up yesterday, and I wanted to let you know immediately.

JoAnn: Okay, what's up?

Manager: I met with Tom Crowley in Public Relations this morning regarding the business needs in his department. Based on some specific skill sets required and the need for the best possible person to fill that position, I've selected you for the transfer.

JoAnn: But Ed, I love my job, and I feel that I make a positive contribution to the company as a whole by working in this department.

MANAGING CHANGE

Manager: I totally agree with you. It's because of your excellent achievement record that I have selected you for this transfer.

JoAnn: I hate PR! I have no interest in that department or in working for Tom Crowley.

Manager: I understand your feelings. I might feel the same way in your situation. However, as a manager, I have to balance the responsibility to the company with my responsibility to my employees.

JoAnn: Well, it seems like the company wins out in this case.

Manager: JoAnn, lets look at some of the positives that can come out of additional job responsibilities. Tell me: What do you see as some of the positives?

JoAnn: Well, you know I'm a solid writer with great phone skills. Our customers love talking with me!

Manager: That's great! This opportunity might bring you closer to our customers while giving you the opportunity to focus on what you're really good at.

Manager: JoAnn, I want you to understand that if I didn't believe that this could be a valuable career experience for you, I would not be recommending and supporting this transfer.

> Managers must use active listening and communication to outline the benefits of an awkward and unwanted change.

Commentary

This situation was particularly challenging because the manager was losing a good employee to another department at the request of his vice-president. It would have been easy to simply blame the vice-president, but instead the manager accepted his responsibility both to the company and the employee and dealt with it. The manager created the proper, supportive environment, outlined the situation for the employee, and used active listening skills and empathy to support the employee. He was firm in what he had to do but encouraged the employee to vent her negative reaction, listened openly and attentively, then refocused her into examining the positive opportunities for her personal growth and development.

MANAGING CHANGE

NEW METHODS IN CUSTOMER SERVICE
Setup

In this scenario, a manager discusses changes in handling customer service calls with an employee who is used to servicing one set of customers by himself. All calls to customer service will now be handled by an automated voice response system, and account information will be shared by several representatives. The manager must see to it that this employee successfully transitions into working on a broader range of accounts and shares information with other representatives.

Manager: Hi, Joseph, come in. Upper management has decided to implement a new system for handling customer service calls. Starting on Monday, we will use a voice reponse system to manage customer calls, and we will shift from having individual customer service reps handle twenty-five accounts each to a team-based approach where each rep will work on more than a thousand accounts with other representatives.

Joseph: What! I don't understand. I thought our customer service record was one of the best in the industry. Why the sudden change?

Manager: Customers have complained that they don't appreciate busy signals or being on hold. With this new system, customers will be routed to the next available representative for faster response. *[pause]* You seem distressed by this news. Do you have concerns about the new approach?

Joseph: Yes, I do. I'm used to giving high-quality, personalized service to my customers, and now I'm being asked to share my customers and their problems with other representatives.

Manager: I understand. Let's talk about this some more to see if we can come up with asolution that will help you adapt to this new way of handling customer calls. One of the immediate benefits that I see for you is that you no

The manager needs to both effectively communicate the focus of the change, and try to make a compromise with the affected employee.

MANAGING CHANGE

longer will be working in a vacuum but rather you will have the opportunity to share information and learn from your fellow representatives. Can you think of some other benefits?

Joseph: I suppose that by pooling our notes and comments on each customer, we could develop more effective customer profiles for upper management. But who takes charge of putting that together?

Manager: Change represents opportunity, Joseph. If you and your fellow customer service representatives can agree on effective reporting techniques, I see no reason why you can't assume responsibility for delivering those reports. Do you have other concerns?

Joseph: I am used to giving a high level of individual attention to our customers. How will my performance be measured as a result of this change to a team-based approach?

Manager: That has not been finalized as yet, but I assure you that every representative will know where he or she stands with respect to job performance.

> Managers should allow employees to have some kind of impact on the change itself.

Commentary

The manager has a difficult task in that he must convince the employee that the change in customer service operations will have an overall benefit for the company. The employee is shocked and dismayed to learn of the change, and the manager quickly reacts by encouraging the employee to put his concerns on the table. The manager continues by encouraging the employee to offer suggestions on how the company might benefit from this new approach to customer service. The employee recognizes an opportunity to contribute and offers suggestions on how to build on this new level of service. The employee is still concerned about how his performance will be measured in light of the new service, and the manager responds with a firm, honest, yet noncommittal answer.

MANAGING CHANGE

QUESTIONS AND ANSWERS

1. **Why is change necessary?**
   The concept of "staying in place" or "standing still" in business is little more than an illusion. You're either moving forward or falling behind. It may be slow, and you may not notice it on a daily basis, but it's happening. Change is the catalyst for moving ahead. Think what life would be like without change!

2. **Who is driving change in the workplace?**
   The global, competitive economy is fueled by incredible changes in technology. Change is dynamic and is usually initiated by external pressures to stay competitive. It "rolls downhill internally" and impacts employees. Businesses that don't keep up or take the lead go out of business.

3. **Why does change feel so different?**
   Change has always been present in business, but in the past the pace was much slower. We made a change, had time to adjust to it, did something the new way, and life rolled along. Today the pace has increased drastically: We are literally bombarded by one change after another, with little time to adjust and catch our breaths. And it is going to continue to increase, so we should devise ways to accept and welcome it rather than fight it.

4. **What do my employees really need to know?**
   When it comes to change, the more they know earlier on, the better your chances are to successfully get people on board. Change impacts their lives and is a disruption they must deal with. Think of a stack of dominoes. When you push the first one, many others follow. Change is similar: When you make the first change on the job, many others, often less visible, tend to follow.

5. **What can I do to accelerate the acceptance of change?**
   Very often your attitude, motivation, and behavior toward change is vital in setting the tone for others. If people under-

MANAGING CHANGE

stand that you also share their unknowns but approach them in a positive and trusting manner, they will find it easier to follow your way. No one wants to feel alone when a change that will alter his or her professional existence is about to take place.

6. **What are some of the danger signs that managers should watch out for in times of change?**

Be alert for negative and destructive, out-of-character behaviors such as arguments with other employees, missed deadlines, tardiness, expressed negativism, low energy levels, and a casual attitude toward the quality and quantity of work produced. This is also a time to be aware of employee defections to other companies, especially competitors.

7. **What should I do if I see these danger signs?**

Speak privately with the employee and let him or her know what you're seeing and that you are available if he or she is experiencing difficulties or would like to talk. Often just knowing someone cares and is available to talk with is helpful to an employee.

8. **What if I sense that a problem is more severe than I thought?**

If you have an employee assistance program, refer the employee or suggest that he or she speak with someone outside of work about the current situation. Depending on the type and amount of change, professional help also may be required.

9. **What else can my employees do to help themselves cope with change?**

It's helpful to understand that we are all "self-fulfilling prophecies." The things we say to ourselves in the privacy of our own minds, our "self-talk," largely governs our success in life. By making sure that our self-talk is a positive, supportive, I-can-do-it type of language, we dramatically increase our potential for success with change and enjoy our lives more at the same time.

> Managers need to work to maintain a positive outlook, and to change any negative feelings within the company.

MANAGING CHANGE

Open communication may help to avoid negative change by revealing alternatives to change

10. Is all change necessarily good?

In a word, no! That's why it's so important for managers to establish a trusting and open environment in which people can ask questions and get straight answers. The harsh light of the scrutiny of change before the process takes place often exposes incomplete thinking, poor judgment, or the need to review other options before moving ahead. This route will help avoid ill-conceived change initiatives and let people feel more of a sense of ownership of the change.

11. Is helping employees feel a sense of ownership of the change important?

Yes. People tend to give more enthusiastic support to ideas and changes that they helped to engineer; therefore their participation is recommended whenever possible. People don't mind change as much as they resent someone else trying to force change on them without any input from them.

12. In terms of employee attitudes, should I be more concerned about resistance or apathy?

In almost every instance, resistance is easier to deal with because it's out in the open and can be addressed. Even though it's not what you want, resistance shows that the employees at least care enough to take a stand. Apathy is more difficult to deal with because you can see it, but you have a harder time attributing it directly to change.

STREETWISE advice

◆ **Watch out for the internal "grapevine."**
Never underestimate the power of the internal "grapevine." News of impending change travels fast, and while its essence is often in the ballpark, the accuracy can be questionable. Employees' trust and confidence in you will be stronger when they hear about change from you rather than through the rumor mill.

> Managers need to be patient with employees to allow time for adjustment to change.

◆ **Give employees time to accept change.**
Remember that since you have been privy to the change before your employees, you have had time to develop acceptance and direction. Your employees need the same opportunity to understand, accept, and adjust. Be patient with them, within a reasonable period of time. Change involves old habits and the development of new ones.

◆ **Display empathy.**
Change is emotional. By its very nature it involves letting go of something one has become attached to. It involves a grieving, acceptance, and readjustment period. By showing empathy and understanding, you will help your employees understand why change is taking place and start building support for your change efforts.

◆ **Share the facts.**
Provide employees with all the facts you have. Show them why the change is being made. Share with them the dangers or repercussions of maintaining the status quo, and ask them for their input on the dangers as the employees see them.

◆ **Demonstrate the possible benefits of change.**
Enthusiastically show people the benefits once you've successfully implemented the changes. Admit that pain, anger, and disillusionment accompany change. The process is not always popular, and its wisdom is even questionable, but there has to be a reason and a benefit. Losing jobs and coworkers hurts, but the loss can provide stability and competitiveness that can protect many other jobs.

◆ **Communicate with your employees on a regular basis**
Hold weekly meetings to keep your employees updated as to the nature of all ongoing changes at the company. Any change, big or small, is bound to affect at least one or more employees, and you should have a regular forum to discuss these changes and encourage your employees to share their ideas and suggestions.

> Be honest about the impact change will have, but make the positive results apparent.

CHAPTER

10

CONFLICT RESOLUTION

Any workplace, no matter how well-managed is going to have some conflict. How effectively conflicts are handled, will greatly determine how productive your workplace is going to be. As a manager, you want to identify conflicts as early as possible. Determine what kind of conflict is involved. Determine any underlying causes of the conflict. Then actively involve the affected employees in finding solutions.

RESOLVING CONFLICT

In almost any type of business situation, conflict between a manager and employee is inevitable. If conflict is addressed effectively, it can benefit individuals and organizations by producing stronger, more resilient working relationships, improving creative output, and generating innovative solutions to problems.

PROBLEM-SOLVING APPROACH

Many of us naturally both prevent and resolve conflicts in everyday situations through avoiding, accommodating, and compromising behaviors. These approaches are effective in many cases; however, *problem-solving* is a better approach. It is a more conscious approach that seeks input from everyone involved and often results in a creative, lasting resolution. Also called a "win/win" approach because everyone gains or "wins" something, this approach is often necessary so employees can maintain good working relationships.

WHY DOESN'T EVERYONE USE IT?

Using a problem-solving approach requires confronting the issues. In fact, for some, a fear of conflict is what gets in the way of resolving it. That fear can be merely a lack of experience, skills, or tools for resolving conflict. Managers particularly need these tools because they must resolve their own conflicts with their staff, other managers, and outside clients and vendors as well as help others resolve conflicts.

TWO TYPES OF CONFLICT

It is critical that managers differentiate between two types of conflict with which they might be involved: unnecessary conflict and resolvable conflict. Unnecessary conflict occurs when individuals have differing perceptions, lack of information, or hostile feelings that can appear unexpectedly, cause disagreements, and build up into a full-blown conflict if signs are not noticed early enough. Resolvable conflict occurs when two individuals' viewpoints on an issue are initially seen as opposing fixed positions but are actually based on different needs, goals, values, or interests that first need to be understood and then worked out to their mutual satisfaction. In this section you will

> Our natural tendency is to avoid facing problems head-on.

CONFLICT RESOLUTION

see how managers utilize effective communication and listening skills to identify and prevent unnecessary conflict and use a ten-step problem-solving approach to work out resolvable conflict.

. . . .

UNNECESSARY CONFLICT

OVERVIEW

Unnecessary conflict occurs most often when an individual feels that his or her personal agenda is not being addressed by another individual. Unnecessary conflict can be the result of: (1) strong negative feelings such as anxiety, stress, or anger, (2) unclear communication such as misunderstandings or a lack of information, or (3) disagreements caused by differing perceptions and attitudes such as prejudice, resistance to change, or a bias toward "the way things have always been done."

Unnecessary conflict can escalate needlessly, especially when a manager inadvertently causes the conflict or adds to it. At times, managers don't even have the control to resolve these conflicts, which can be caused by organizational constraints. Therefore managers must discover ways in which they can prevent, reduce, or control such conflicts by defusing the emotion, then preventing the conflict from building. After identifying the conflict, they must decide whether to become involved, then determine how to ameliorate the situation. Thus they save time and energy for resolving resolvable conflicts.

The following three examples demonstrate unnecessary conflicts that the manager has either engaged in, fed into, or inadvertently exacerbated by conflict-promotional behaviors.

WEAK APPROACH: CUSTOMER SERVICE

Setup

In this scenario, a customer service rep, who has been overburdened with work, is called into the manager's office, whereupon the

> Unnecessary conflict can be diffused by isolating the conflict and preventing it from spreading.

CONFLICT RESOLUTION

manager informs her that her request for a day off is denied. Notice the manager's cool behavior toward the customer service rep and her singular focus on getting her work done versus the representative's need for time off.

Chris, a customer service rep *(a bit anxious and agitated):* You wanted to see me, Wendy?

Manager *(without making eye contact):* Yes, Chris, have a seat. Because of an increase in unit volume sales, I have to deny your request for a day off.

Chris: What! I can't believe this! I gave you plenty of notice. What gives?

Manager *(in a matter-of-fact tone):* We've seen a dramatic increase in our business, and it's just not possible to give you the time off. We all have to pitch in and help out.

Chris: I more than pull my weight around here. I just don't get it. I make only one request a year for time off, and this is the thanks I get. I really need this time off. I'm under a great deal of stress.

Manager: Stress comes with the territory. The decision is final, and I don't want to hear any more about this matter.

Chris: This is so typical of this company. Stiff the person who works the hardest and give her the least in return for her efforts.

> Managers can make a conflict worse by refusing to make a compromise.

Solutions: Identify which conflicts you could either prevent, reduce, or control so they don't get bigger.

STRONG APPROACH: CUSTOMER SERVICE

Setup

Here, the manager tries to prevent a potential conflict by expressing an understanding of the pressure felt by the customer service representative. At the same time, the manager remains firm in her decision to deny a day off for the rep. But the manager concludes

CONFLICT RESOLUTION

> In order to diffuse a conflict, a manager needs to seek the true source of the conflict and address it.

by showing empathy for the employee and by offering to help in a specific way—in this case, by trying to arrange an alternate day off.

Manager: Hi, Chris, thanks for stopping by. I'd like to discuss your recent request for time off.

Chris *(somewhat nervously):* What about my request?

Manager: Chris, as you're probably aware, our business has picked up dramatically, and in the process, the number of calls that come through to customer service has also increased.

Chris *(sighing):* Yeah, it's been stressful. What does this have to do with my request?

Manager: Unfortunately, because of the increase, I have to cancel your day off. I understand that this is very difficult for you. You've done a wonderful job in customer service, and your contributions are vital to our success. Is there anything I can do to help you decrease your stress?

Chris *(acting agitated):* You can't be serious. I made plans for my day off. I need the time.

Manager: I'd really like to give you the time, but because of the increase, it's just not possible at this time. I'll try to see if I can schedule you for a day off at a later date, and I would like to work with you to help you make your workload more manageable.

WEAK APPROACH: LACK OF SUPPORT

Setup

In this illustration, an employee complains to her manager about several team members whom she feels do not pull their weight. The manager doesn't get enough information about the source of the problem and thus can't determine the true nature of the conflict. This leads to an escalating conflict between the manager and the employee. The manager ends up judging the employee and prematurely adopts a defensive posture toward the employee's complaint.

CONFLICT RESOLUTION

Pat *(visibly upset):* Kathy, I'm really upset that Sandy and Paul aren't pulling their weight on this new project. I've had to cover for them three times this week.

Manager *(slightly condescending):* You can't compare yourself to them. You have more experience and have been here longer.

Pat *(looking downcast):* I don't see that as a reason for my having to cover for incompetent employees.

Manager *(acting surprised):* You asked me for more responsibility, and I gave it to you. This sort of thing comes with the territory.

Pat *(acting defensive):* Well, when I ask for help, they act like I am imposing on their time. Gimme a break—I thought we were a team.

Manager *(dismissive and slightly disgusted):* Look, if you want, I'll speak to Sandy and Paul, but I would rather you handle this yourself.

Pat *(downcast and disgruntled):* Fine, I'll deal with it myself.

STRONG APPROACH: LACK OF SUPPORT

Setup

In this example, the manager tries to reduce or minimize conflict by listening and providing a sounding board to defuse the situation. The manager avoids judging or giving unsolicited advice and helps the employee solve the problem so as to ensure a continuing level of high productivity. Although she listens empathetically, the manager is careful neither to agree with the employee nor to react strongly but instead remains even-toned. The employee still has her dignity and retains ownership of the problem.

Pat *(visibly upset):* Kathy, I'm really upset that Sandy and Paul are not pulling their weight on this new project. I've had to cover for them three times this week.

> Good conflict resolution can be achieved through communication and open-mindedness.

CONFLICT RESOLUTION

> In order to resolve unnecessary conflict, the positions of both parties need to be expressed, and the essential problem addressed.

Manager *(calm, neutral tone):* Tell me more about it, Pat.

Pat *(looks manager in the eye):* Look, I realize that because of my experience I'm expected to give more than others.

Manager: You feel I expect more from you because of your experience?

Pat: Well, yes, but that's okay with me.

Manager: So that works for you?

Pat: Yes, except recently I've had to stay late, and when I ask for help, Sandy and Paul act as if I am bogging them down.

Manager: Well, I wanted to give you the challenging work you asked for in the form of new assignments.

Pat: I don't mind new challenges—I just need to know that the support is there when I need it.

Manager: Fair enough. Suppose we meet once a week to discuss your progress on these new assignments, and I can give you feedback on additional support possibilities within the company.

Pat: That would help. Thanks.

WEAK APPROACH: RUNNING MEETINGS

Setup

In this scenario, a new manager gives a veteran supervisor critical feedback on running meetings without agendas. The veteran supervisor deflects the feedback by bringing up tangential issues.

> Managers need to be open-minded and flexible in order to avoid unnecessary conflict.

Manager: Joe, I wanted to speak to you about running our staff meetings without an agenda.

Joe *(defensively):* I don't have time to write an agenda with all these new projects that suddenly fell into my lap.

Manager *(irritated):* You asked me for new and exciting projects to challenge you. You should have told me that the extra work would interfere with your ability to plan meetings.

CONFLICT RESOLUTION

Joe *(annoyed):* I don't have time for meetings. Why do we need the agendas in the first place? We never had them before you showed up. Seems like more work and a waste of time.

Manager *(short tone of voice):* I think it's important to have agendas. I don't care what was in place before I got here. We need better productivity and a change in procedures.

Joe *(defensively):* I don't see the results. Seems like we do the same amount of work with or without an agenda.

Manager *(Judging):* Maybe if you tried using one, you would see the difference!

Joe *(complaining):* Meetings are too long to begin with.

Manager *(closing the subject):* The meetings are more productive with agendas.

STRONG APPROACH: RUNNING MEETINGS

Setup

In this scenario, the manager attempts to control the conflict while giving critical feedback by helping the employee focus on the central issue that can be resolved. The employee will try to convince the manager that his point of view is correct; it is the manager's responsibility to resist the temptation to argue, and instead, try to diminish the employee's defensive attitude.

Manager: Joe, I'd like to talk with you about running our staff meetings. I appreciate the fact that you've taken on this responsibility–the staff seems to be responding very well to your guidance and leadership. I wanted to give you some feedback on how you can improve your running of meetings.

Joe *(friendly demeanor):* Sure, what's up?

Manager: I've noticed that at the past few meetings, you haven't used an agenda even though I asked you to use one. Staff members are finding it difficult to accomplish

CONFLICT RESOLUTION

anything during these meetings, and we eventually run out of time needed to cover important issues.

Joe *(defensively):* I really don't have time to write an agenda. I have my hands full tracking new projects.

Manager: You're feeling is that you don't have time to write an agenda?

Joe *(diminished defensiveness):* Yeah, I can't spare the time to attend meetings let alone prepare an agenda.

Manager: So you feel like you don't have the time to attend meetings?

Joe: That's right.

Manager *(neutral but assertive tone):* Joe, several staffers have told me that they feel comfortable using agendas and that our productivity at these meetings increases dramatically. I would like you to prepare and use an agenda when you run our meetings.

Joe: Why, all of sudden, do we need agendas? We never used them before, and we did fine without them. I think they're a waste of time.

Manager: We've decided to use agendas as a team to help us stay on track. Previously, we were all over the place and accomplishing nothing.

Joe *(complaining defensively):* Meetings are just too long either way. Agendas don't seem to improve anything.

Manager *(firmly assertive):* Agendas help us stay on track and increase productivity. I'm committed to using them. I'd be more than happy to sit down with you and show you a sample that works for me.

STREETWISE advice

◆ **Confront difficult issues early on.**
Intervening when it's too late to resolve the issue only builds bad feelings and resentment.

◆ **Don't promote conflict by causing defensiveness or counterattacks.**
You can induce this behavior when you order, judge, name-call, threaten, condescend, show impatience, or use a tone of voice that communicates intense dissatisfaction.

◆ **Observe nonverbal signals that people are upset or overwhelmed.**
Some of these signs are deep sighs, tense shoulders, lack of eye contact, and sarcasm.

◆ **Avoid using hot-button words or phrases.**
Don't exaggerate or use hot-button words or phrases such as "always," "constantly," "never," "I hate it when you . . .," and "it's useless." Instead, understate with words and phrases such as "often," "usually," "sometimes," "I'm uncomfortable when you . . .," and "it's not productive."

◆ **Treat people with respect.**
Give people the benefit of the doubt, and allow them to save face. People often justify their actions or blame others because they aren't given the benefit of the doubt.

◆ **Avoid arguments.**
Don't argue with them or take their comments personally; briefly acknowledge their comments or needs, then direct the discussion toward productive action or agreement.

◆ **Actively listen to people who express strong concerns or complaints.**
Avoid the temptation to "fix" or take on the problem as your own. Listening can help defuse strong emotions and help solve a minor problem that could develop into an escalating conflict.

◆ **Assert your needs, and explain the impact of others' actions.**
Use "I statements" to prevent tensions from building and causing unnecessary conflict. Consider this example: "I'll be working on the monthly report for the next couple of hours, so I'd appreciate it if you'd only interrupt me for emergencies or, better yet, go to each other for help first. Will that work for you?"

◆ **Release your own tension regularly, and gain support for your needs.**
Don't add to conflicts with your own stress. Exercising, venting to a friend, or deep breathing can help managers prevent, reduce, and control conflict; if you discharge your own negative emotions regularly, you can be mentally ready to listen and communicate about tough issues.

> The best way to resolve conflicts is to attempt to avoid them altogether.

CONFLICT RESOLUTION

RESOLVABLE CONFLICT

Resolvable conflict occurs when two individuals' viewpoints on an issue are based on opposing needs, goals, values, or interests. An example of resolvable conflict is when two employees from different departments (e.g., sales versus production) within one organization have different views regarding the source of a problem, believing that the other employee is responsible for the problem. This type of conflict should be within a manager's control and can be resolved with a simple problem-solving approach.

TEN-STEP CONFLICT-RESOLUTION PROCESS

1. *Present the issue without emotion, blame, or judgment.* Use "I language" to bring up the problem, then clearly convey what you know about it so you don't blame or create defensiveness. If you ask the employee for help in solving the issue, he or she will be more cooperative and won't feel accused or threatened.

2. *Ask for the other party's point of view, and listen actively so you fully understand his or her needs.* Ask the other person how he or she sees the situation and what he or she needs to resolve it. Listen nonjudgmentally, and don't justify your position or argue against his or hers. Make an effort to fully understand the other point of view, get clarification if necessary, and communicate what you have understood.

3. *Explain your point of view clearly, and make sure the other person understands it.* Using "I statements," communicate your position and needs clearly and simply without referring to his or hers if possible. Make a strong attempt to clarify what you mean, then ask the other person to review what you have said. In this way you can make sure that you have been clear and that he or she has understood.

4. *Clarify and define the issue in terms of both of your needs.* Simply restate the issue, and make sure your statement accurately reflects both of your needs.

By clearly addressing the problem, and evaluating both viewpoints, a conflict can be resolved through compromise.

5. *Jointly develop an objective or condition to which you both can agree.* Ask yourselves: "What result or outcome are we both looking for? The issue will be resolved when . . . ." It is important to define an objective before looking for solutions.

6. *Brainstorm possible alternative solutions.* The goal of brainstorming is to identify several possible solutions without actually evaluating them. If you generate many ideas, you should find more innovative or workable solutions than the ones people typically use. If time permits, hold off choosing a solution until after this process is complete and all alternatives have been listed and debated.

7. *Select the solution that has the best chance of meeting both of your needs.* Take the list of possible solutions and evaluate them. Some of the best solutions are often combinations of suggestions or reworkings of a "crazy" idea that seems implausible but leads to a new way of working together. Write down the most viable solution that you would both like to try. Keep in mind that revisions might be necessary later.

8. *Develop a realistic plan of action, and determine who will do what when, where, and how.* Take the written solution, and plan the actions that must be taken to ensure its success. Make a schedule, and give a copy to everyone involved. Schedule checkpoints to assess progress along the way. Decide how each party will know if the solution is working and what criteria will tell you the objective has been met.

9. *Implement the plan.* Implementation occurs after the problem-solving discussion. Each party must complete his or her action steps. Usually some follow-up is necessary, especially if potential obstacles had to be overcome.

10. *Evaluate the success of the solution based on the joint objective.* During the initial discussion, it is important that you schedule a time to meet after the solution has been implemented. Some revisions or even an alternative solution

> Effective resolutions to conflict are both mutually pleasing and realistic.

CONFLICT RESOLUTION

might be needed. Since those involved probably chose this conflict resolution process because they value their working relationships and want good results, it is critical that you determine its success.

- -

CONFLICT-RESOLUTION SCENARIOS

WEAK APPROACH: SOCIALIZING

Setup

In this example, an older manager sees himself in conflict with a younger employee who "socializes constantly" with coworkers during quiet time, a time when employees are supposed to focus on their work undisturbed. This younger employee is not afraid to speak her mind and is popular with her coworkers. The older manager is afraid that this employee is influencing others to be less productive.

Manager *(confronting):* Sue, You've got to stop socializing with your coworker. It's really not productive. My philosophy is that the workplace was designed for work, not recreation.

Employee *(indignant):* What do you mean, "socializing"! What's wrong with talking to my colleagues?

Manager: If it's business, that's one thing. I'm talking about chatting during quiet time.

Employee: What's wrong with that?

Manager: We're a dynamic, hardworking company, not a singles club. From now on, I expect you to focus on your projects and leave the talking for after hours.

Employee *(aggressively):* I'm the hardest worker on this team. You know when you're under the gun, I get the job done! Why don't you speak to the others — I don't force them to talk to me!

Manager *(firmly):* I'm talking to you now. I'll talk to them later.

> To solve a conflict, managers need to remain unbiased and fair in their treatment of the people involved in the conflict.

CONFLICT RESOLUTION

Employee *(with disgust)*: I didn't take this job to be a workaholic; it's only human to talk to your coworker. I can't work with someone over my shoulder all the time.

Manager: I want you to focus on your projects during quiet time and leave the socializing for after work.

STRONG APPROACH: SOCIALIZING

Setup

In this scenario, the older manager shows the younger employee that her socializing during "quiet time" is very disruptive for other employees. The older manager wants to make sure he does not demoralize an enthusiastic and influential member of his team. He decides to bring up the issue using a problem-solving approach so they can find a creative solution together.

Manager: Sue, I wanted to talk with you about using your "quiet" time in a new way. I've noticed that after putting in a lot of energy on a project, you tend to gather with certain employees to shoot the breeze. While I can understand the need to do this, you're infringing on quiet time for other employees. Let's put our heads together and see if you and the others could help me find a creative solution to this issue.

Sue *(tentative, not sure what manager is really getting at)*: Okay.

Manager: How do you see the situation?

Sue: Well, we work hard here, and I think I'm the hardest worker on the team. You know when the pressure is on, I get the job done! I want to enjoy my work and not have it be a grind with no opportunity to interact with my colleagues.

Manager: So you enjoy hard work and feel the need to share your efforts with your coworkers?

Sue: Yeah, that's how I see it.

> Rather than laying down an ultimatum, the manager takes a problem-solving approach.

CONFLICT RESOLUTION

> The position of both the management and the employee should be made clear in order to resolve conflict.

Manager: That's fine with me. I believe that enjoying your work often makes you more productive. I want to make sure we don't lose that. I also need to make sure that every staff member continues to make progress on projects, no matter how insignificant. That is why we have "quiet time." Just to be sure that I'm being clear—what do you see me driving at here?

Sue: You're afraid that my interacting with employees during "quiet time" adversely affects productivity.

Manager: Exactly. We need to find a way of working together that keeps things enjoyable and interactive without disrupting "quiet time." Do you have any ideas about ways we could do this?

Sue: Well, I'm not sure. I don't want to interfere with anyone's work, but I do enjoy being part of a team and sharing my ideas with my colleagues.

Manager: How about this. Suppose you and several of the project planners divide up routine tasks for common projects. Schedule fifteen minutes during quiet time to meet informally at the coffee machine to give yourselves a "brain break" and review notes. We'll meet on a weekly basis to see how its going. How does that sound?

Sue: I think it sounds pretty good.

WEAK APPROACH: CONFLICT WITH ANOTHER EMPLOYEE

Setup

In this scenario, the manager is approached by the employee who needs help in resolving a potential conflict with another employee. This employee's job requires her to collect data from several people on a higher level, who also report to her manager, in order to compile and produce critical monthly reports. One of the higher-level employees has been negligent in giving her the data on time.

Employee *(reluctantly and non-assertively)*: For months I've been trying everything—reminders, E-mail, checklists, and

CONFLICT RESOLUTION

nagging, but I've been unsuccessful at getting the data from Cindy on time. That's why I've been behind on the reports.

Manager: You've got to get those reports to me on time.

Employee: I know. She's friendly towards me but consistently unresponsive when I try to get the data from her. I'd like to be able to handle it better, but I don't know how to approach it because Cindy's on a higher level than I am. Maybe it would be better if you spoke with her about it?

Manager *(very clipped and business-like):* I've got too much going on to handle this matter. My philosophy is just to be straight with people about what you need and don't give them so much room. Do you want me to enroll you in an assertiveness course?

Employee *(looking away and speaking hesitantly):* That would be nice, but I'm not sure it would be enough in this case ...

Manager *(impatient to end discussion):* Look, it's up to you. Do whatever it takes to get the data—Cindy knows you've got to have it. Put the heat on, and let her know you need it now!

> Managers should encourage employees to speak up about their opinions in order to evaluate the conflict accurately.

STRONG APPROACH: CONFLICT WITH ANOTHER EMPLOYEE

Setup

In this example, the manager uses the problem-solving approach to coach the younger employee who is dealing with a potential conflict with a higher-level senior employee. This younger employee is having problems collecting data from the higher-level employee and is unassertive and lacking confidence in trying to resolve the conflict on her own.

Employee *(reluctantly and non-assertively):* For months I've been trying everything—reminders, E-mail, checklists, and nagging, but I've been unsuccessful at getting the data from Cindy on time. That's why I've been behind on the reports.

CONFLICT RESOLUTION

Manager: Why don't you present the issue to Cindy by telling her that you'd like to talk to her about a way to make both of your lives easier in gathering the data for the monthly reports. Explain that you need to have the data by a certain time each month, but you find yourself having difficulty getting it from her without pressing her, which you want to avoid. Ask her how she sees the situation, and really listen to what she says, making sure you reflect back her key points on why this is hard for her. Knowing Cindy, what do you think she'll say?

Employee: That she tries but she has so many more pressing projects.

Manager: Then tell her how you see it. What could you say then?

Employee: That I need to get the data because the whole unit's progress and incentives are based on the information. Maybe I haven't actually talked to her about this before!

Manager: Then you can ask if you've made it clear why it's so important to get the data and if she see the importance? Next, I'd figure out how to keep both your needs in mind.

Employee: That sounds reasonable and certainly something Cindy should respond to.

Manager: Do some brainstorming to see if you can come up with something new and creative that appeals to both of you. After you come up with some different possibilities, agree to try one, and memo it to her afterward. She reads and acts on memos faster than E-mail. You can evaluate it after the next month's report. But first get her to agree to meet one more time to see if it's working for both of you.

> By suggesting non-combative ways to the employee about solving the problem, the manager is removed from the conflict.

WEAK APPROACH: TAKING RESPONSIBILITY

Setup

The product marketing manager, new to the company, has the responsibility to forecast sales for the next two quarters.

CONFLICT RESOLUTION

Halfway through the first quarter, sales are running ahead of forecasts, and production is getting bogged down trying to meet demand. The product marketing manager needs the production manager to ramp up more quickly. The production manager is furious that the product marketing manager has once again botched his sales forecasts, which means more production overtime, lost sales, and an overall decrease in profitability for the company as a whole. The production manager wants the product marketing manager to take responsibility and devise a more accurate forecasting method so his own department is not burdened with overtime and schedule overruns.

Production manager: This is the third time you've missed a sales forecast, Mark! Can't you find some way to more accurately gauge the market?

Marketing manager: Look, you know that our market is fickle, and depending on economic conditions, it becomes a game of Russian roulette.

Production manager: That sounds like a weak excuse for planning to me. Other departments seem to have a handle on what they need from us on a quarterly basis.

Marketing manager: Selling product is a lot different from estimating production costs of packaging and the number of shipping containers required for emergency shipments.

Production manager: Next time I need you to come up with an alternate plan so that if this happens again, my department's schedules aren't disrupted. We're getting hell from the VP of sales!

Marketing manager: You got it backward. We make the money for the company by developing and closing sales leads. It is your responsibility to make sure that we have plenty of product available for sale.

CONFLICT RESOLUTION

STRONG APPROACH: TAKING RESPONSIBILITY
Setup

In this scenario, the production manager decides to approach the product marketing manager with a conflict that has occurred in trying to meet market demands. By bringing it up as a joint problem that he would like to solve together, he hopes to foster a cooperative working relationship with a fairly new colleague.

Production manager: Hi, Mark, I wanted to talk to you about last quarter's sales forecast. It seems that we, as a company, somehow fell short in our sales forecasting and, subsequently, our unit production run. I'd like to discuss ways in which we can work together to prevent this from happening in the future. From your point of view, what happened?

Marketing manager: Well, Greg, the market shifted unexpectedly in favor of our product, and we wanted to take advantage of the shift. We thought we communicated that to you and that you would ramp up production to meet demand.

Production manager: I'm not sure we fully understood your intentions at that time. On such short notice, it's really tough to schedule overtime and adjust to increase production. Sounds to me like you need to be able to take advantage of these marketing opportunities. I need some sort of communication system so I can provide you with the product you need.

Production manager: It sounds as though we both agree that we need to take advantage of these market opportunities before they become lost sales. We also should have product ready to go under reasonable time frames so that we do not disappoint the market. Let's talk about alternative solutions that make sense to both of us.

> By not alienating people in a conflict, the manager can work together with them to solve the problem.

CONFLICT RESOLUTION

Marketing manager: How about this: If we in marketing sense an increase in the market, I immediately call you for a meeting to prepare to ramp up and have product ready to go.

Production manager: Well, Mark, I think we need to figure out a way to differentiate between a "sense" and a sure thing with respect to the market. I would like to avoid ramping up to produce product unless I was absolutely sure that the need was there. If we can't sell the product, it sits in inventory, which adversely affects our bottom line.

Marketing manager: I see your point. It would help me to understand how the production process actually works at this company so I can let you know how many unit runs you should schedule. Would you be willing to go over your production operation with me?

Production manager: No problem. Let's meet next week and I'll take you on a tour of the plant. Then we can discuss the scheduling process, potential bottlenecks, and possible openings where it would be easy to fill orders within a forty-eight-hour period.

> An open-minded exploration of various alternatives is a powerful way to defuse tension.

QUESTIONS AND ANSWERS

1. **Shouldn't conflicts be avoided at all costs in business?**
   Confronting a conflict or tolerating the expression and resolution of differences can be very useful. However, it's critical that you "fight fairly" and ensure conditions are right for engaging in a conflict rather than react impulsively or emotionally.

CONFLICT RESOLUTION

Resolution of a conflict requires the participation of everyone involved in an open and fair manner.

Communication should be honest and productive, rather than negative and accusatory when trying to resolve conflict.

2. **How do those engaged in a conflict ensure it will be productive and won't cause damage?**
Everyone involved must agree to engage in the conflict and make an effort to resolve it. If one party holds back and decides not to participate, the conflict will escalate to the point of damaging a professional relationship or causing the company some harm.

3. **When is the optimal time to confront and resolve a conflict?**
Take into account energy levels based on factors such as the time of day and fatigue, the amount of time available to devote to the process based on workloads and meetings scheduled, and emotional readiness.

4. **Who should be involved in the conflict resolution?**
All parties should be aware of and agree on who will be involved in resolving the conflict. People involved in a conflict don't like to be observed by uninvolved parties unless they mutually decide on the help of a third party to facilitate or mediate the process.

5. **Where is the best place to meet?**
Discuss conflicts in a neutral space that is neither party's territory or maybe is common ground and, therefore, comfortable for everyone involved. People discuss conflicts with less tension when there are few distractions and listening is easy for everyone.

6. **What other considerations should be taken into account?**
Make sure the conflict resolution process is not a venting or an unexpected attack on one of the individuals. It's critical that people be prepared to air their differences for the most productive outcome, especially if they are not generally friendly or cooperative with each other.

7. **If I am the third party who is helping others resolve a conflict, what should I do?**
As long as all parties involved are cooperative, explain the ten-step process and emphasize that your role is to facilitate

CONFLICT RESOLUTION

their going through each step as they concentrate on listening to each other. Then you can help develop a solution that meets everyone's needs.

8. **As the facilitator, what do I do if the parties are not cooperative or friendly and emotions are running very high?**

   You help them resolve the conflict by taking them through the ten steps without explaining the steps ahead of time. As you get to each step, identify what you want each party to do, and ask clarifying questions to make sure they understand each other and agree throughout the process. This method is very effective, although it takes more work on your part; you must make sure they don't draw you into their sidetracking. They are likely to sidetrack because they haven't agreed upon a process and don't know your method for helping them.

9. **What are some signs that might tell me there is an underlying conflict in my group?**

   People feel safe bringing up certain issues that are, in fact, a mask for the real sources of conflict. At times they aren't aware of the real source of conflict or are not sure of how to bring it up. Typical signs are chronic complaining, increased levels of stress, unnecessary competitiveness, absenteeism, failure to accomplish much, retaliation, and undermining comments between or among team members.

10. **How, as a manager, do I learn about conflicts early on so I can help resolve them before they become full-blown arguments?**

    Managers who meet regularly with their staff—individually and as a team—tend to stay abreast of conflicts and also learn more about their employees' needs. It is important to develop an active listening style that encourages two-way communication, so differences are brought to the surface easily and quickly, seen as part of the normal process of working together, and, if possible, resolved as they arise.

> Open communication on a regular basis can help to avoid conflict altogether.

STREETWISE advice

◆ **Evaluate the consequences and cost of engaging in a conflict.**
Are you bringing up this issue as an opportunity to resolve differences productively, or do you need to resolve some of your feelings about it first so it doesn't turn into a venting session and harm your relationship?

◆ **Be aware of your own needs and trigger points.**
Being aware of your own needs and trigger points will help you *not* take things personally and stay calm and focused to facilitate the discussion toward resolution.

> Conflicts should be approached by the manager in a positive yet neutral manner to avoid an escalation.

◆ **Cultivate a neutral, warm tone of voice.**
People often react negatively or defensively just as much, if not more, to how a message is delivered as they do to what is actually said.

◆ **Encourage people to air their differences with you.**
Employees will not see you as a threat and will come to you at an earlier stage when you can be more helpful in resolving something positively.

◆ **Own your part of the conflict and help employees own their part.**
Evaluate the situation to diminish defensiveness if possible. People may not be able to fully agree at first. Be careful not to overstate the situation. When they begin to accept some ownership or understanding of the issue, acknowledge it respectfully.

◆ **Defuse emotions before pushing to resolve a conflict.**
People can think more rationally and will make a real commitment only after they have calmed down. Put your efforts into letting them express their feelings and fully hear them out before you move to solutions.

◆ **Stay open to a solution that comes from the other party.**
Even though you have prepared suggestions for solutions, don't force your ideas on the other person. Ask for theirs first, then bring up yours. Seek to build true understanding, cooperation, and involvement.

CHAPTER

11

PERFORMANCE REVIEWS

Performance evaluations can be positive experiences for both managers and employees i... conducted prope... he review ... he ... uld work with ... ree to set goals ... ning year provi... tive feed- ack, and analyze strengths nd weaknesses. If the

---

To make performance reviews work, you've got to have a true two-way dialogue—not just a chance for the employee to offer a rebuttal at the end of your summation of their shortcomings! You've got to hear *their* perception about *their* performance—and you've got to address their perceptions during the review. You also need to work with the employee in developing goals and objectives for future reviews.

PERFORMANCE REVIEWS

PERFORMANCE REVIEW OBJECTIVES

A performance review can be one of the most positive and proactive tools a manager has to communicate with employees. Yet most managers dread conducting reviews, and most employees fear receiving them. A major reason for these feelings is that many managers don't know how to give good reviews. As a manager, remember that evaluations are the times to provide feedback, direction, and leadership to your employees. Use these times wisely, and you'll reap the benefits a hundred times over.

When preparing for and giving the actual review, keep in mind that your role as a manager is to guide the employee. You must not only you encourage and support but also educate him or her in areas that need improvement. At the same time, you must ensure that he or she feels positive about his or her efforts and understands what must be done in the future. The employee should walk away from the review with a good feeling about his or her accomplishments and an understanding about what still must be done and how to do it.

Giving a good review is easy if you prepare for it throughout the year and put forth the effort to make it a positive experience. In this section we'll introduce the steps needed to prepare for and conduct a review and present both a positive and a negative approach to conducting a performance review.

PREPARATION FOR THE EVALUATION

Performance evaluations can be positive experiences for both managers and employees if they are conducted properly. During the review, the manager should work with the employee to set goals for the coming year, provide constructive feedback, and analyze strengths and weaknesses. If the review is objective and constructive, the employee will gain insight as to how his or her performance contributes to the company's mission, what the manager's expectations are, and what the areas are in which he or she excels and/or needs improvement.

> A performance review is necessary as both an encouragement of positive accomplishment, and as a suggestion for future improvement.

PERFORMANCE REVIEWS

REVIEW THE JOB DESCRIPTION

Since the purpose of a good performance review is for a manager to objectively evaluate an employee's ability to perform a specific job, managers must remember that the best evaluations focus on issues that are relevant to the job and not on personal factors such as length of service or personal biases. The manager must also avoid the "halo effect" (in other words, giving a favorable rating for the year based on performance during the previous month or so).

To ensure complete objectivity, managers must first understand the employee's job. A good way to gain this understanding is to review the job description with the employee before the evaluation. The manager can learn what the employee has actually been doing, what he or she likes and dislikes about the job, and what he or she wants to do in the future. This is also a good time to work with the employee to revise and update the job description to reflect current duties and responsibilities.

REVIEW PREVIOUS DOCUMENTATION

The second step in preparing for a proper appraisal is the gathering of information such as the prior year's appraisal, reports, letters of commendation, or complaints and warnings. Review previous evaluations to search for any dramatic changes in performance as well as to determine whether goals were achieved. Properly set goals should have had measurable criteria set with them, making it easy to determine if the goals have been fully, partially, or not achieved.

GATHER SUPPORT MATERIALS

The third step in the preparation includes a review of notes kept during the year to look for concrete examples that support statements you will make in the review (especially critical ones). Employees appreciate examples, particularly when you have critical comments. Consider the following:

> You did achieve your goal of revamping the process, but you stepped on a lot of toes along the way. For instance, you neglected to speak with Mary Ann in Operations and with

The evaluation should focus on the employee's job performance, not how the manager feels about him or her personally.

the sales manager about how the changes would affect them. It is critical that you get everyone's input when you make radical changes in the way we do business. Next time, it would probably be a good idea to have a meeting before you start, to make sure everyone is on track with you. Other than this issue, you did a good job changing the process; it's much more efficient now.

Of course, these types of issues should be discussed with the employee at the time they occur and not merely after the fact.

BE CONCISE BUT PRECISE

When writing the appraisal, limit comments on a specific item or objective to one or two short paragraphs, but be sure to use the examples you have gathered. Do not draw generalized conclusions about the employee. If you are critical of an employee or if the employee hasn't met his or her goals, offer specific recommendations as to how he or she can make corrections or what he or she can do to achieve the goal.

> Criticism of an employee should be balanced with viable suggestions for improvement.

INVOLVE THE EMPLOYEE IN THE APPRAISAL

To get the employee involved in the appraisal process, ask him or her to do a self-appraisal, using the same form you will use. This helps keep communication lines open and gives you valuable insight as to how the employee perceives himself or herself. If the perception is very different from yours, you have not been successful at communicating with the employee. Obviously, the areas of greatest difference are the ones you should focus on during the appraisal interview. Also, for more employee involvement, ask the employee to be prepared to answer questions like:

- What do you feel your major accomplishments have been during the year?
- What could you have done better?
- What could I have done to make your job easier?
- What would you like to see changed in your job?

PERFORMANCE REVIEWS

SET GOALS AND OBJECTIVES

Once the current year's performance is evaluated, you should set goals and objectives for the following year. As the manager, you must have a clear idea of what must be accomplished in your department before you can help the employee set his or her own goals. You must also be able to communicate your needs and the department's needs so the employee can see where his or her responsibilities fit into the whole picture.

Performance objectives and goals represent the results you would like the employee to accomplish within a specific time frame. Objectives should be easy to understand and measure; they should be challenging but should also be within the employee's ability to achieve. Objectives generally fall into four categories:

- **Innovations** are new results the employee will attempt to create as part of his or her job. For example, he or she might take on a new job function or responsibility for a specific program, such as opening a new sales territory.
- **Solutions** involve situations that require objective analysis to solve a problem, such as getting an item from manufacturing to the customer more efficiently and with less cost.
- **Routines** are improvements in existing job standards, such as increased turnaround time on purchase orders.
- **Learning opportunities** are objectives that give employees the chance to grow in their careers, increase their responsibilities, or learn new tasks. For instance, he or she might learn desktop publishing so marketing materials take on a more polished and professional look.

The manager must work with the employee to decide what will be achieved each year and to ensure that the employee phrases each goal as clearly as possible. This formula might help when writing goals:

Employee's Name (or I) + Verb + Key Results
+ Measurement Criteria

> Clearly-defined goals help employees determine their own responsibilities to the company and gives them a concrete ruler to judge themselves by.

PERFORMANCE REVIEWS

So the goal might sound like: "I will reduce the amount of time a customer must wait on the phone to speak with a representative from four minutes to two and a half minutes." By including the employee in the goal-setting process, you get his or her "buy-in"; therefore there is a far better chance of the goal being achieved.

After the goals have been decided on, take the following steps:

- Agree on the steps the employee must take to achieve the goals.
- Agree on the method to measure achievement of the goals.
- If appropriate, agree on a budget.
- Agree on benchmarks throughout the year to monitor progress toward achieving the goals.

DELIVER THE NEWS

At this point in the review process, communicate to the employee where he or she stands with respect to the prior year's performance. Was performance average, above average, superior, or weak? Depending on what measuring tools your company uses, it's critical that the employee knows not only his or her strengths and weaknesses but also how you, as the manager, feel he or she has performed in light of your expectations and measurable goals. Before you "deliver the news," the employee should have, at the very least, a sense of the scope of his or her contributions to the company's success.

Delivering the news also means discussing salary—often a sensitive and delicate area for managers who are not tied to a strict grade-level performance pay scale. Annual salary increases usually average between 3 and 5 percent for average performers, while those individuals who are above-average or even superior performers can expect increases between 7 and 12 percent or more.

> Include the employee in the formation of goals, and agree upon a plan of action together.

PERFORMANCE REVIEWS

SAMPLE RATING SYSTEM

This is a sample rating system with suggested pay range increase.

Rating	Increase
Unsatisfactory Employee's performance is below minimum acceptable levels in major areas. Employee's performance must improve quickly and dramatically to allow for continued employment.	0%
Below-average Employee's performance meets minimum requirements but is below the average expected performance for the position. Employee is expected to improve his or her performance.	0-3%
Satisfactory Employee's performance is either generally satisfactory or at least meets minimum requirements in all areas, Any less than satistfactory performance in one area is offest by a greater than satisfactory performance in another area.	4-5%
Good Employee's performance is at least satisfactory in all major aspects of the position and measurably higher in some areas.	6-7%
Excellent Employee's performance is measurably higher than satisfactory in all of the most important aspects of the position. In addition, the employee's performance was truly exceptional in one or more key areas.	8-10%
Exceptional/promotion Employee's performance was excellent in all major dimensions of his or her position. In addition, the employee achieved a major accomplishment above the scope of his or her job description.	+10%

PERFORMANCE REVIEWS

Because performance reviews can be highly emotional, especially for the employee, it is best to approach a review with a specific agenda in mind. Plan in advance what you are going to say during each part of the review. Be sure you can successfully deliver the message you intend regardless of the employee's response.

- **Greeting**
  Start the review with a warm greeting and perhaps some very brief small talk to help relax tensions and create an atmosphere more conducive to the review.
- **Summary**
  Be sure that the employee understands exactly how his or her overall performance ranks. Summarize the overall performance first and then explain what the rating means. Don't announce any salary changes at this point. If you don't give the summary at the beginning of the review, the employee will spend the rest of the review trying to figure out what his or her overall performance is, based on your comments.

  The employee may want to discuss the rating immediately after you offer it. Try to put this off until you have been able to thoroughly review the employee's strengths and weaknesses.
- **Strengths**
  Unless an employee's performance is unsatisfactory, compliment him or her on both major and minor strengths as they relate to their job. Avoid saying anything negative until you have reviewed his or her strengths. You can be either specific or general in describing strengths.
- **Weaknesses**
  Unless an employee's performance has been truly exceptional, you should provide feedback on areas of weakness, or at least suggest room for improvement. In reviewing weaknesses, be as specific as possible. For example, rather than saying "you have a poor attitude," cite a specific example of his or her behavior, such as "you are often late for company

> Try to focus on the employee's strengths first, and remain positive about the improvement needed to correct weaknesses.

PERFORMANCE REVIEWS

> It is essential that the manager be as candid as possible when reviewing employee performance, to avoid problems later on.

meetings and several times throughout the year you complained incessantly about company policies."

- **Feedback**

  After you have discussed an employee's weaknesses, you should give that person an opportunity to air his or her thoughts. Listen politely until the person is done. Avoid being argumentative, but do let the employee know that his or her feedback has not affected your review. For example, you may want to say, "I understand that you don't agree with what I have said, but my perception of your overall performance remains as I have stated it."

- **Salary**

  Recap the employee's overall performance rating. Announce the new salary, if any, and the date on which the new salary will be effective.

- **Closing**

  Unless the employee's performance is substantially less than satisfactory, try to end the review on a positive note. You might say, "The company and I very much appreciate your work, and we are glad to have you here!"

PERFORMANCE REVIEW LEGAL ISSUES

The biggest job-related legal problems are often a direct result of unrealistic employment reviews. Managers often avoid conflict by failing to appraise a poor employee performance accurately and truthfully. Later, if the company fires the employee, it is easier for that employee to claim discrimination and offer his or her performance reviews as evidence of adequacy to carry out the job requirements.

1. **First step**

   So, as a first step, you need to make sure that all managers give each member of their staff a realistic review. Additionally, all reviews should be issued in writing. The reviewed employee should receive a copy of his or her review.

2. **Develop consistent review criteria**

   Another potential legal pitfall may be encountered when an employee claims that he or she has been discriminated against in the review. This is particularly likely to occur if the employee has been passed up for a promotion. To avoid this, you need to develop consistent review criteria and be absolutely sure that your managers adhere to the performance criteria. Reviews should also contain specific examples of negative and positive performance, not just generalizations.

3. **Other steps**

   Other ways to avoid legal issues during reviews are as follows:

   - Establish grievance procedures.
   - Have more than one manager determine each employee's overall performance rating or at least provide input during the preappraisal process.
   - Give employees feedback during the year, as appropriate, to avoid performance review surprises.
   - Encourage managers to work with employees who are underachievers in an attempt to raise their performance to a satisfactory level.

Well-defined and consistent review criteria help avoid favoritism or the suspicion of discrimination.

EFFECTIVE PERFORMANCE REVIEW

The following is an example of an effective performance review. Pay close attention to how the employee responds to the manager's evaluation, including critical comments.

Manager: Hi, Tom, it's good to see you. How are things going?

Tom: Fine, thanks, Michelle. I'm really looking forward to next week's company picnic.

PERFORMANCE REVIEWS

Discussing positive and negative performance with employees reduces the risk of conflict by keeping the review open, honest, and fair.

Manager: That's great! As you know, Tom, this is our annual review of your performance. We've been over your job description, made some changes, and reviewed your self-evaluation. Today I'll go over my evaluation of your performance. You'll have plenty of opportunity to ask questions. Once we've done that, we'll talk about your goals for next year and set the criteria we want to use to measure achievement against. Do you have any questions so far?

Tom: Not at this point.

Manager: This year, you took on additional responsibility for improving the customer service department by reducing the time customers have to wait for a representative and by increasing the level of service. It appears that you've done a great job in both areas. Call waiting time has gone from four minutes to two and a half minutes, and the number of people who call back because we don't get it right the first time has decreased by 20 percent. I'm pleased with your efforts, but I would like to discuss your communication skills in this area.

Tom: Is there a problem?

Manager: Well, as I mentioned to you last month, several individuals who work for you complained that you dictated to them what had to be done rather than seeking their input and building consensus before going ahead. It doesn't serve you well to have half of your department grumbling before you even get started.

Tom: I'm surprised to hear that! I just got so excited about what I was doing that I assumed everyone would be on board with me. Actually, they were, but it seems that I went about it incorrectly. Since that time, I've taken your advice, and we're now having weekly meetings to iron out all issues and to make sure everyone understands the goals of the department.

Manager: Good. I'm glad you took something positive away from our discussions. Now, let's talk about your goals for

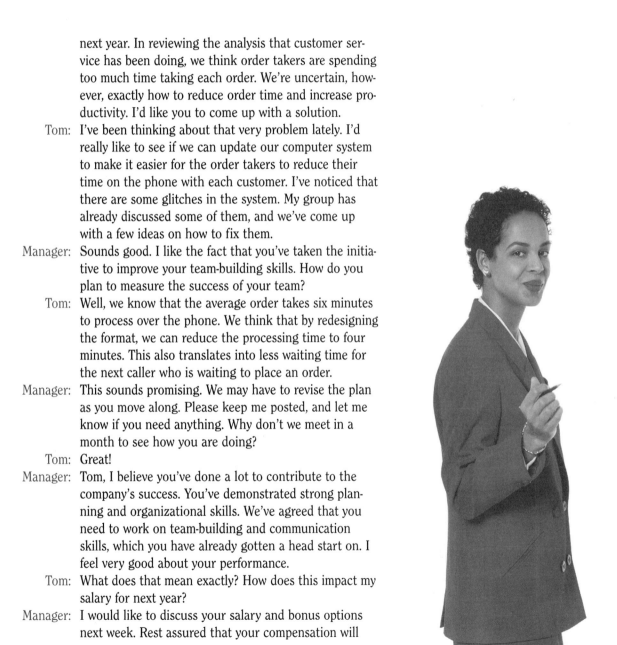

next year. In reviewing the analysis that customer service has been doing, we think order takers are spending too much time taking each order. We're uncertain, however, exactly how to reduce order time and increase productivity. I'd like you to come up with a solution.

Tom: I've been thinking about that very problem lately. I'd really like to see if we can update our computer system to make it easier for the order takers to reduce their time on the phone with each customer. I've noticed that there are some glitches in the system. My group has already discussed some of them, and we've come up with a few ideas on how to fix them.

Manager: Sounds good. I like the fact that you've taken the initiative to improve your team-building skills. How do you plan to measure the success of your team?

Tom: Well, we know that the average order takes six minutes to process over the phone. We think that by redesigning the format, we can reduce the processing time to four minutes. This also translates into less waiting time for the next caller who is waiting to place an order.

Manager: This sounds promising. We may have to revise the plan as you move along. Please keep me posted, and let me know if you need anything. Why don't we meet in a month to see how you are doing?

Tom: Great!

Manager: Tom, I believe you've done a lot to contribute to the company's success. You've demonstrated strong planning and organizational skills. We've agreed that you need to work on team-building and communication skills, which you have already gotten a head start on. I feel very good about your performance.

Tom: What does that mean exactly? How does this impact my salary for next year?

Manager: I would like to discuss your salary and bonus options next week. Rest assured that your compensation will

PERFORMANCE REVIEWS

accurately reflect your performance. You are an above-average performer, Tom.

Tom: Thanks, Michelle.

INEFFECTIVE PERFORMANCE REVIEW

The following illustrates an example of an ineffective performance review. Notice the way the manager is abrupt and curt. She doesn't give the appearance that she cares about the employee but instead merely wants to get the evaluation finished.

Manager: Hi, Tom. Listen, I know performance reviews are important to you, but I just don't have time to get into much detail, so let's get started.

Tom: Michelle, I'd like to talk about–

Manager: Tom, I really don't have time for questions or a discussion.

First, attendance–you got a 5 since you seem to be here on a regular basis.

Your technical skills–well, let's say a 3. Okay, but not great.

Productivity–I guess I'd say a 2 here. I'd like you to work faster.

Your communication skills also need some work. You never seem to clearly communicate your intentions to me. I'm giving you a 3 here.

You're very accurate and detail-oriented, so I'll give you a 4 in this area.

Overall, Tom, I see you as an average performer. You're good in some areas, but you need to work on those areas I mentioned. I'm giving you a 3 percent raise.

PERFORMANCE REVIEWS

Tom: Michelle, I have some questions about goals for next year and your expectations. Can't we talk for just a couple of minutes?

Manager: As I said, I really don't have the time. Why don't you write me a memo or E-mail me with your questions?

Tom: I suppose I have no choice. I'll send you something next week.

Manager: That'll be fine.

> Employees need to feel that they have some opportunity to affect your evaluation of their performance through open communication.

EVALUATION OF THE REVIEWS

EFFECTIVE PERFORMANCE REVIEW

In this review, you can see right from the start that the manager is friendly and interested in Tom's well-being. Chatting with the employee is always a good strategy to break the ice before an evaluation. The manager then gave an overview of the process and what Tom could expect during the evaluation. Taking time to give the overview gives the employee the opportunity to see where the conversation will be going and to mentally prepare for what will take place.

The next step was to begin the actual evaluation, with positive feedback and a discussion of the goal that Tom had achieved. During this discussion, the manager used feedback from other employees to bring something negative to Tom's attention. It was clear that she had already spoken to Tom about it, but this time it was to remind Tom the issue is important. She also wanted to give Tom an opportunity to discuss what action, if any, he has taken to correct the problem.

During the goal-setting portion of the review, the manager stated a problem that needed to be solved and asked Tom to come up with a way to solve it. Involving Tom in the process and having him identify a way to accomplish the goal as well as measure the accomplishment put the responsibility for achieving the goal on Tom's

> An organized and thorough evaluation delivered in a friendly and supportive way encourages the employee to improve.

PERFORMANCE REVIEWS

shoulders and make it far more likely that he will be able to succeed than if the manager had just told him what to do.

At the end of the review, the manager evaluated Tom as an above-average performer and indicated that his salary and bonus would be in line with his performance. Tom left the review knowing that he is important to the company and what he needs to work on for the coming year. His goals for the next twelve months were clearly articulated by the manager.

The success of this review is based on the interaction of both the manager and Tom as well as the thoroughness of the manager in preparing for the evaluation.

INEFFECTIVE PERFORMANCE REVIEW

The second evaluation did not get off to a very good start. The manager started out by indicating that she wanted to get the process over with quickly. She refused to answer questions or allow Tom to participate in the review.

The manager clearly took no time to think through the process or ways she could do it better. Her gratuitous suggestion to Tom to send his questions via memo or E-mail demonstrates a lack of commitment to work with him one-on-one to set goals and improve performance. She also didn't create a very good situation for the company because by conducting a review in such a poor manner, Tom has no incentive to improve his performance and will probably start looking for work elsewhere. If Tom does leave, the company incurs high costs in recruiting and training a replacement.

QUESTIONS AND ANSWERS

1. **Why should the employee complete a self-evaluation?**
   It helps open the lines of communication. If you've been consistent during the year with both praise and constructive criticism, you'll see that the employee has a fairly good idea of

PERFORMANCE REVIEWS

where he or she stands. By completing a self-evaluation prior to the review, the employee will have the opportunity to look at what he or she has accomplished in concrete terms. Your expectations should closely match and provide a solid basis to proceed with the review.

2. **Is it better to start out with the positives or the negatives?**
It depends on the employee's performance. A strong or even average performer should hear some positives at the start before you move to constructive criticism. A particularly weak or below-average employee, however, should not hear too many, if any, positive comments from the start because he or she will tend to filter out your criticisms and thus take issue with the lack of a raise or even a small increase.

3. **How can I find time for "mini reviews" throughout the year? I can barely get my other work done.**
A "minireview" is exactly how it sounds–quick and to the point. It can take fewer than five minutes and should be well worth the time spent; if you keep good notes, you'll be better prepared for the annual review.

4. **Employees always seem to complain about their raises after their reviews. What can I do to prevent constant complaining?**
Don't schedule the raise at the same time as the evaluation. Or make sure that if you give an above-average review, you give an above-average raise. We have a tendency to say only good things about an employee, then give what he or she perceives to be an average raise. By doing this, we send inconsistent messages.

5. **How do I ensure that the review is objective and not subjective?**
Document, document, document. You can't take too many notes. If you take the time to speak to your employees and to take notes on what actually happens, you are fast on your way to presenting an objective review. Also, keep personality conflicts and your personal biases out of the review. If you

> Documentation of reviews help present an objective view of the employee's performance.

PERFORMANCE REVIEWS

> Try to set mutually beneficial goals, with the suggestions of the employee.

set goals and criteria to evaluate employees, you'll be right on the mark.

6. **What legal issues must I consider when conducting a review?**

   Protect yourself and the company by evaluating performance as objectively as possible and by not evaluating the employee on a personal level. Be honest in your appraisal, but always use examples as supporting evidence.

7. **I tell my employees what they do wrong, but they don't seem to make improvements. What am I doing wrong?**

   When you criticize an employee, be sure to give a recommendation as to how the employee can fix the problem. It's important to remember that not everyone thinks the same way, and some people need more guidance. If you're patient and encouraging, most employees will catch on and learn how to solve problems on their own.

8. **How do I decide what goals to set for the employee?**

   If you don't have any specific goals in mind, ask the employee what he or she would like to accomplish. You'll be surprised by the problems employees see and want to work on but have been afraid to mention.

9. **Some of my own reviews have seemed so negative even though they actually haven't been too bad. How can I avoid this with my employees?**

   Discuss performance positively in terms of what the employee has accomplished. For example, explain, "I like your willingness to help when we are running behind schedule." But also explain what you would like him or her to do differently. For instance, state, "I would like you to volunteer to stay late when you notice that we're behind schedule." Avoid negatives such as "you didn't" or "you never."

10. **How do I get an employee to want to achieve goals?**

    It's imperative that goals be set *with* the employee and, preferably, *by* the employee. You can accomplish this by explaining the problem to the employee, then by working

PERFORMANCE REVIEWS

with him or her to develop a solution. This process helps him or her to "own" the goals and want to achieve them.

11. What are measurable criteria?

Measurable criteria are the methods you use to judge whether the employee has accomplished what you asked. The criteria can be expressed either as an objective that can be concretely measured—such as increase sales volume by 20 percent—or by desired behavior—such as maintain a friendly demeanor when answering the phone or follow orders without complaining.

12. How do I prevent an employee from arguing with me during a review?

Use concrete examples to support your statements. The employee can't argue with you when he or she knows you're right. Also, don't get side tracked. Stick to the point, refuse to argue, and don't let the employee take charge of the review. Make sure the employee clearly understands what your overall rating for the employee really means, especially with respect to salary increases.

13. What's the best way to get an employee to agree to what I request?

Get the employee involved in the process. Ask him or her what he or she is willing to do to solve the problem or what kind of milestones or checkpoints he or she would like to establish.

14. How can I ensure that an employee hears exactly what I say?

If you think there is a chance the employee didn't understand what you said, ask him or her to paraphrase it. You can do the same when he or she speaks to you by saying, "Let me see if I understood you correctly. You said . . ."

15. What can I say in an average-performance ranking other than "average" or "satisfactory"?

You can say something like "fully meets the job requirements with work of good quality." This type of response explains

> Support your conclusions with facts to avoid any conflict between you and the employee.

PERFORMANCE REVIEWS

> In a negative evaluation, work with the employee to try and discover the essence of the problem, and find viable solutions to the problem.

that the employee is meeting expectations. Be careful not to overhype whatever you say, as you may easily create a false set of expectations for the employee regarding salary and bonuses based on your statement.

16. **What percent of employees fall into the average category?**
Most of them. You probably have a few superachievers and rising stars; however, most employees do a good job and are satisfied with that. Your job is to make sure they maintain or improve their performance.

17. **What do I do about employees who are less than average?**
First, don't reward them with very high, or even average, raises. Second, if they don't meet your expectations, work with them to improve their performance. Include any warnings and advance notices as evidence of poor performance. If you must terminate the employee, follow the legal and accepted termination policy of your company; if you are unsure, ask your human resources department or manager.

18. **I think I might be part of my employees' "problem." What do I do?**
Ask them. Ask what you can do to make their jobs easier or better. They'll be honest as long as they feel they can trust you. If they give you an answer you don't like, take time away from them to reflect; they're probably right.

19. **Is there a formula for setting performance standards?**
There isn't a specific formula, but keep the following questions in mind:

- Do the employee and I agree on the wording and meaning of a particular standard?
- Is it as specific as possible so nothing is left to interpretation?
- Is it realistic and attainable?
- Will each of us know when the standard is met?
- Is it measurable by observation of behavior or by quantifiable methods?

- Does it focus on accomplishment rather than personality?

20. Why must the employee sign the evaluation?
The employee's signature indicates that the employee has received the evaluation, even though he or she may not agree with it. The signed appraisal protects you if he or she ever accuses you of not notifying him or her of a problem.

STREETWISE advice

◆ **Evaluate all year long.**
Have frequent conversations about what the employee is doing, even if they are informal. It makes a world of difference to the employee to know his or her manager is interested in his or her work. An informed manager is also a better manager because he or she has a greater knowledge of what's going on with employees as well as what's happening in the department.

> Frequent evaluations help to curb problems before they arise and encourage positive behavior.

◆ **Don't make the evaluation a surprise.**
If you evaluate performance on a regular basis, you have the opportunity to catch mistakes before they evolve into big problems. Also, an employee will feel more confident in coming forward with issues if he or she doesn't feel threatened by you and knows you are very interested in him or her and his or her work.

◆ **Document, document, document.**
Keep notes about performance issues, both good and bad. Don't rely on your memory to write the appraisal. Documenting performance, especially bad performance, also protects you from legal action should an employee have to be terminated.

◆ **Get the employee involved.**
Ask the employee for feedback during the year, ask the employee to do a self-evaluation, and work with the employee to develop goals and standards. Also establish commitments and agreements with the employee about what you want him or her to accomplish over the next year.

◆ **Evaluate performance, not the person.**
Measure behavior or output against prearranged, agreed-on standards. Don't write conclusions; give specific examples of where the employee succeeded or failed to meet goals and objectives.

◆ **End on an upbeat note.**
Spend time with the employee until you reach agreement on each point in the review. This is particularly important if the review is less than satisfactory and if the employee has failed to meet expectations. Be extremely careful with negative reviews; always document and have evidence on hand to substantiate the review, especially if you want to end the review with something hopeful to say about goals for the coming year.

> Evaluations should never judge an employee–they should support, guide, and encourage positive performance.

CHAPTER

12 ADVICE ON HIRING

If you're going to grow your company or achieve excellent levels of performance in your business unit, it's going to be a lot easier if you hire top performers to begin with, rather than if you have to be constantly pushing and pulling average performers to new levels. Hiring the right people requires a strategy, planning, and a good amount of time—but in the long run the extra work to hire great people will be one of, if not the very best, uses of your time!

ADVICE ON HIRING

HIRING EFFECTIVE PEOPLE

This book is about managing people. To manage, you must first hire the people. People are your human assets, as important as if not more important than the financial assets you have in the bank and in inventory.

The caliber of people who work for your company will arguably have more impact on the success of your company than any other factor. The easiest way to create a terrific work force is to hire terrific people in the first place.

Hiring terrific people who share your vision and your passion is the ultimate objective.

While you may never seem to have the time to hire people carefully, using the tools in this book will help you to continually improve on your hiring practices.

As in all endeavors, you should have a plan or a strategy for conducting your hiring. You will want to spend minimal time screening out the weakest candidates and maximum time comparing the more subtle differences between or among the strongest candidates.

DEVELOPING A HIRING STRATEGY

You as the manager of the department or the company must make some preliminary decisions about your hiring strategy. These decisions include the level of compensation and benefits as well as the basic level of skill and experience needed by candidates.

You will then determine the step-by-step procedures your company will use to recruit, interview, and hire new employees.

Following is a sample outline of a recruiting, interviewing and hiring strategy for a fictitious company called Company Q.

Company Q has a number of locations and has been experiencing significant growth over the past few years. Expansion has created a demand for additional employees. The mission of the company promotes high levels of customer service and employee involvement.

Company Q does not have a formal human resources department, so the CEO created a task force to help develop a strategy for recruiting new employees. The following documents represent the materials created by this task force. You may want to adapt these documents to fit the needs of your organization.

> The best way to insure the success of your company is to hire the right people.

TYPICAL ACTION PLAN OUTLINE

The typical action plan should outline the specific steps that will be undertaken to achieve the objective. The plan should indicate who will be doing which aspects of the plan; whenever possible, time frames should be included. For the purpose of this example, no time frames have been included.

RECRUITING PROJECT PLAN OF ACTION

I. Implementation support services

    A. Installation of 1-800 toll-free number

        1. Compose script for 800 number

        2. Compose telephone screening questions

    B. Letter to schools, colleges, etc.

        1. Create marketing packages for each location

        2. Follow up mailed information

        3. Identify a contact person

    C. Recruiting print advertising

        1. Resume response letter

    D. Overview of strategy to managers

II. Telephone screening of candidates

III. Interview of selected candidates

    A. Interview packet created for on-site interviews

        1. Welcome to Company Q

        2. Contents of packet

            a. Application

            b. Information about company and positions

            c. Summary of generic benefits

            d. How the interview process will happen

TYPICAL ACTION PLAN OUTLINE

    B. Appropriate candidates directed to designated manager for on-site interview

        1. Compose structured interview questions for recruiter

        2. Appropriate job description presented in interview for review

    C. Senior managers interview candidates following managers interview

    D. References are checked

IV. Selected candidates hired and oriented

    A. Manager makes final determination

    B. Manager makes hiring offer to candidate

    C. Manager completes all paperwork to hire new employees

    D. Manager orients new hires to company and operations

    E. Depending on number of new hires, group orientations may be planned

    F. Managers orient, train, and monitor performance and skill level while continually motivating and evaluating employees.

SAMPLE RECRUITMENT ACTION PLAN

COMPANY Q'S ACTION PLAN

Company Q has very specific reasons for developing a recruiting strategy. They want to maximize the return on their recruiting investment. By creating a structured, clearly defined process, they will have a greater incidence of continued success.

COMPANY Q RECRUITING PROJECT PLAN OF ACTION

I. Implementation of support services

  A. Installation of 1-800 toll-free number: an 800 number gives the company an opportunity to link intermittent recruiting into a regular internal referral program, which encourages employees to make candidate referrals for prizes and awards.

    1. Compose script for 800 number: When candidates call, a scripted interview is conducted on the telephone by a trained clerical person. This give Company Q the ability to screen the many calls that do not warrant further discussion.

    2. Compose telephone screening questions: The trained clerical person needs to have specific questions to ask, in the event the telephone screening generates a viable candidate.

  B. Letter to schools, colleges, etc.: Company Q wants to access as many free sources of potential labor as possible.

    1. Create marketing packages for each location: Each school needs to know something about Company Q prior to meeting a representative from the company.

    2. Follow up mailed information: A representative from Company Q will visit the various schools and universities to begin developing an ongoing relationship which will funnel potential candidates to Company Q.

    3. Identify a contact person: The name of contact person at the school and all other pertinent information will be entered into a database.

  C. Recruiting print advertising: An ad or series of ads will be developed to advertise for the positions needed. In some instances a generic ad will request all levels of resume to create a file of future possibilities.

  D. Resume response letter: Every resume submitted to Company Q will receive a reply. The reply creates a positive image for the company.

  E. Overview of strategy to managers: All management personnel are kept informed of the recruiting process in an ongoing manner.

II. Telephone screening of candidates: Once all resumes have been screened, selected resumes are first interviewed by telephone.

III. Interview of selected candidates

SAMPLE RECRUITMENT ACTION PLAN

A. Interview packet created for on-site interviews: Each candidate will receive a package explaining how the interview will be conducted and other information about the company.
   1. Welcome to Company Q: This is a welcome letter from the owner or CEO.
   2. Contents of packet: The package contains everything the candidate needs to know about the company and the interview process.
      a. Application
      b. Information about company and positions
      c. Summary of generic benefits
      d. How the interview process will happen
B. Appropriate candidates directed to designated manager for on-site interviews
   1. Compose structured interview questions for recruiter: Each manager is given specific questions to be used during the interview to ensure that all candidates are treated fairly and can be evaluated based on similar circumstances.
   2. Appropriate job description presented in interview for review: The actual job description is reviewed with the candidate to be sure the job responsibilities are clear.
C. Senior managers interview candidates following managers' interview. At least two people will interview each potential candidate for a position to ensure the best possible decision has been made.
D. References are checked: The candidate who is selected to be hired will have references checked prior to the offer being made. The intent of the reference checks is to determine if the candidate was truthful and to obtain any other information. Due to legal constraints it is difficult to obtain accurate information about employees.

IV. Selected candidates hired and oriented: The selected candidate is given an offer for employment. In certain cases the offer will be put in writing to ensure that nothing has been forgotten.

A. Manager makes final determination: The manager for whom the candidate will work makes the final determination about the hiring.
B. Manager makes hiring offer to candidate: The supervising manager is the one who makes the actual offer.
C. Manager completes all paperwork to hire new employees: The supervising manager is responsible for all payroll and other paperwork to enroll a new employee into the system.
D. Manager orients new hires to company and operations: The supervising manager arranges to orient the new employee, utilizing the company's new-employee orientation program.
   1. Depending on number of new hires, group orientations may be planned.
E. Managers orient, train, and monitor performance and skill level while continually motivating and evaluating employees. The supervising manager maintains a high level of interaction with the new employee.

ADVICE ON HIRING

SAMPLE LETTER TO SCHOOLS AND COLLEGES

This document will give you an idea of the type of letter that may help you develop a recruiting relationship with a school. With a bit of research you will be able to identify at least a dozen possible sources of potential labor. Once the relationship has been established, the school, college, agency, or organization will call you when they have a candidate perfect for your company.

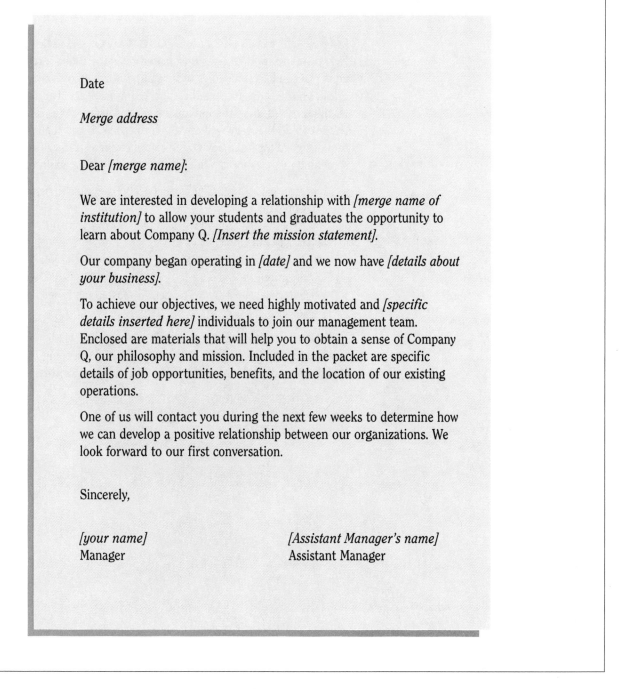

ADVICE ON HIRING

Date

Merge address

Dear *[merge name]*:

We are interested in developing a relationship with *[merge name of institution]* to allow your students and graduates the opportunity to learn about Company Q. *[Insert the mission statement]*.

Our company began operating in *[date]* and we now have *[details about your business]*.

To achieve our objectives, we need highly motivated and *[specific details inserted here]* individuals to join our management team. Enclosed are materials that will help you to obtain a sense of Company Q, our philosophy and mission. Included in the packet are specific details of job opportunities, benefits, and the location of our existing operations.

One of us will contact you during the next few weeks to determine how we can develop a positive relationship between our organizations. We look forward to our first conversation.

Sincerely,

[your name]   *[Assistant Manager's name]*
Manager   Assistant Manager

ADVICE ON HIRING

SIMPLE RESUME SCREENING TOOL

Every organization receives unsolicited resumes. When a recruiting ad is placed most companies receive large numbers of resumes. It doesn't make sense to have the supervising manager read through all the resumes to do the initial screening. A trained clerical administrator can do this very well are given the tools. Using the specific tool designed for Company Q, the clerical administrator will be screening resumes for candidates with the following qualifications:

- Five or more years of experience in the same industry as Company Q
- Experience working with retailers in the same quality category as Company Q
- Job responsibilities that are comparable to the job position in question
- Salary level within 20 percent of posted job range, higher or lower

Based on the training given this person, they will be able to review hundreds of resumes and conduct initial screening to capture those candidates who have the basic requirements for this position.

Specific qualifications help screen out unsolicited applicants.

SIMPLE RESUME SCREENING TOOL

COMPANY Q RESUME SCREENING

Last Name _____

Date Resume Received _____/_____/_____

Years of retail experience _____

Most recent employers _____

_____

_____

_____

Most recent job title _____

Salary requirement _____

Recommendations _____

_____

_____

Proceed with telephone interview _____

Send a "we are holding your resume" letter _____

Send a "sorry" letter _____

Person completing this form _____

Date form completed _____/_____/_____

ADVICE ON HIRING

"SORRY" LETTER

Many of the resumes you receive will not be appropriate for the position or for the company. Since every interaction with every person may be an interaction with a customer, we encourage you to respond to every resume received. Your response displays respect for the individual and lets him or her know that your company is sensitive to people. The following letter will serve as your rejection letter. Notice the tone of the letter.

ADVICE ON HIRING

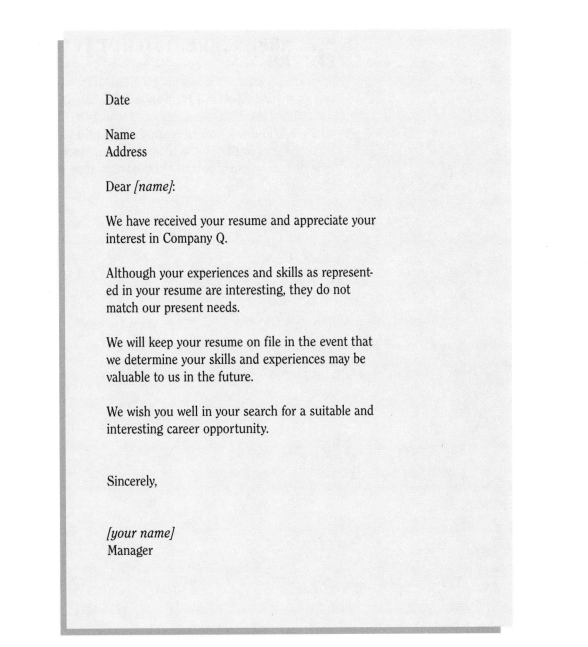

Date

Name
Address

Dear *[name]*:

We have received your resume and appreciate your interest in Company Q.

Although your experiences and skills as represented in your resume are interesting, they do not match our present needs.

We will keep your resume on file in the event that we determine your skills and experiences may be valuable to us in the future.

We wish you well in your search for a suitable and interesting career opportunity.

Sincerely,

[your name]
Manager

ADVICE ON HIRING

"WE ARE INTERESTED BUT VERY BUSY" LETTER

Frequently a company is swamped with so many resumes that it is impossible to deal with them all at once. In these cases we suggest you conduct the initial screening as previously mentioned and then send the following letters to candidates you plan to interview. This letter will explain that you would prefer to conduct a telephone interview first, to be sure it is worth both parties' time to have a formal interview.

ADVICE ON HIRING

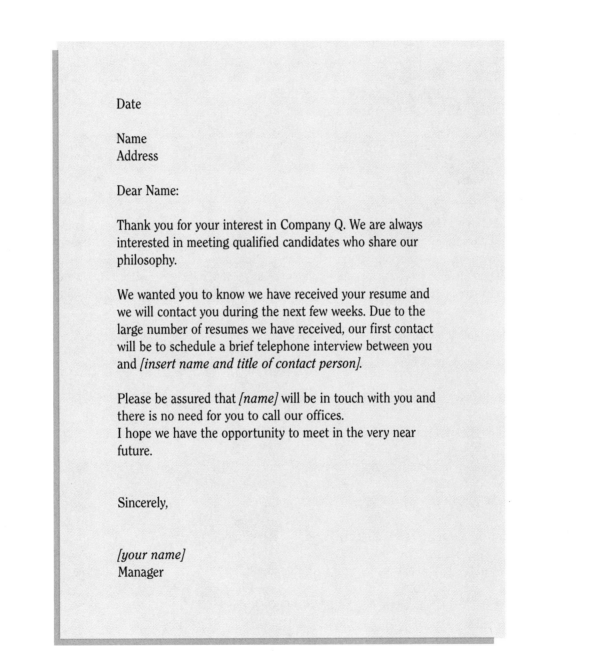

Date

Name
Address

Dear Name:

Thank you for your interest in Company Q. We are always interested in meeting qualified candidates who share our philosophy.

We wanted you to know we have received your resume and we will contact you during the next few weeks. Due to the large number of resumes we have received, our first contact will be to schedule a brief telephone interview between you and *[insert name and title of contact person]*.

Please be assured that *[name]* will be in touch with you and there is no need for you to call our offices.
I hope we have the opportunity to meet in the very near future.

Sincerely,

[your name]
Manager

THE TELEPHONE SCREENING INTERVIEW

To obtain the greatest productivity in screening potential candidates, you will want to reduce the amount of time your management staff spends in formal interviews. The time they spend should be dedicated to interviewing the best of the best. To determine the best of the best, a telephone screening tool such as this should be used. You will want to have a manager or assistant manager conduct these telephone screening interviews to ensure that a knowledge of specific operational information is available during the interview.

COMPANY Q RESUME SCREENING INTERVIEW

Hello, this is *[your name]* calling for _____.
At *[phone number]* _____

Thank you for submitting your resume to Company Q. Do you have ten minutes now? I would like to obtain some basic information from you and then ask you a few questions. Once I have asked you these questions I would be happy to answer any questions you may have about Company Q. The purpose of this telephone interview is to determine if you are interested in having a formal interview with a member of our staff. We are a growing company and are always interested in meeting highly motivated and skilled employees who can join us as we continue to grow.

Does this plan sound Okay? Fine, let's begin with some basic information.

1. Let me confirm your address on your resume:

2. Present employer:

3. Present job title/position:

4. Number of years/months with this company?

5. What is the volume of business that you are currently managing?

6. How many people do you have direct supervisory responsibility for?

7. What do you like best about the job you are doing now?

8. What was the best job you have ever had? What made it the best?

9. Who was the best person you ever worked for?

THE TELEPHONE SCREENING INTERVIEW

10. Explain to me how you were able to identify a person with good customer skills in your last job; What did you do or say to this person? How did the interaction end? What was the result of what you did?

11. Tell me about the greatest success you have had in exceeding sales goals/quotas. What did you do to achieve this success? How did your success impact you or the company?

12. Tell me about the most unpleasant time you had to "do what it takes to get the job done." How did you react to this situation? What was the result of your actions?

13. What is your rate of pay at this time? *[Don't ask this question until you are sure they are comfortable with you]*.

14. What prompted you to send us your resume?

15. What questions do you have for me?

Well! Based upon out conversation, I think:

A. You would *not* be happy working at Company Q. It dosen't seem like a good fit because of *[describe the statements the person made that indicate he or she would dislike the company work, the environment, the pace, etc.]*.
Do you agree with me?
[If so, then say, "I wish you luck with your next position and thank you for calling Company Q"].

B. You would enjoy working with Company Q. Am I reading our conversation accurately? Would you like me to arrange a formal interview for you? *[If so, tell them that you will have the manager schedule a time to meet, based on the dates and times they give you now. Collect the dates times and other pertinent information]*.
Which days of the week and times would be best for you to have a formal interview? The interview would take place at *[indicate the location at which the person would be interviewed]*. The manager will contact you to confirm the date, day and time for the interview.

Thank you for taking the time for this conversation. I hope we will have a chance to meet in person soon.

Good-bye.

ADVICE ON HIRING

THE INTERVIEW

The interview process is one of the most important tasks you have as a manager. Your ability to select the best possible candidate for a position will have a dramatic impact on your department or company. When you are skilled in the process and technique of interviewing candidates you will begin to notice a higher incidence of successful candidates. This is something you can learn to do, and do well.

Let's begin with the interview atmosphere.

An interview is a very traumatic time for the candidate, and it can be a very stressful time for the interviewer, especially if proper planning for the interview has not been completed.

Please don't interview a candidate unless all the following are in place and you are comfortable with the situation.

1. Pick an appropriate site for the interview.
2. Do not allow any interruptions.
3. Pick *your* best time, not the best time for the candidate.
4. Read the cover letter and resume carefully prior to the interview, but not as the candidate is waiting for you.
5. Allow enough time to do the job correctly.
6. Use a seating arrangement that makes the candidate feel comfortable and not at an interrogation.
7. Smile sincerely.
8. Take a few moments to build rapport and assess the nervousness of the candidate.
9. Don't rely on the resume sitting in front of you.
10. Take notes during the interview.
11. Tell the candidate how the interview process will proceed. Let the person know what to expect and how it all fits together.
12. Let the candidate do the talking. Listen and ask questions to collect the information you need.
13. Present Company Q in an honest and direct fashion to ensure that the candidate obtains an accurate picture of the company.

> With proper planning, the stress of an interview can be significantly reduced.

ADVICE ON HIRING

For the interview to achieve the objective of selecting a qualified candidate and ultimately the best-qualified candidate, you must
have a plan of action that will keep you in control of the situation.

All interviews should have four parts, each with a specific purpose.

- The opening of the interview is a chance to relax the nervous
  candidate and create an initial rapport.
- Describing the structure of the interview allows you to set
  the pace and keep the interview under your control.
- The body of the interview is when you do most of your
  research, asking questions, listening and taking notes.
- Closing the interview is when you clarify all issues presented
  and you inform the candidate about how the follow-up process will be handled.

An outline of this process follows.

THE INTERVIEW FORMAT OUTLINE

Prior to any interview review this format outline to be sure you are prepared to conduct a high-quality interview that reflects the values and philosophy of Company Q.

I. Open the interview
- Introduce yourself.
- Offer coffee or another beverage.
- Set the tone with small talk that is safe (e.g. the weather).

II. Describe the structure of the interview
- You will ask questions.
- You will describe the position and the company.
- You will review the actual job description with the candidate going over every task of the job description.
- You will answer the candidate's questions.
- You will take notes.

III. Conduct the body of the interview
- Begin with a request for a brief "oral resume."
- Lead with a very well-structured probing question about job related situations (these are three part questions).
- Highlight all the positive aspects of Company Q; be direct and honest.
- Answer questions from the candidate openly and honestly.

IV. Close the interview
- Maintain rapport to the end of the interview.
- Clearly explain the next steps that will be taken regarding the hiring process. Explain the role the manager and senior manager may play and the time frame in which a decision will be made.
- Be sure you follow through on promises made to the candidate even if the person is not selected for a position. Even people not hired can serve as ambassadors of goodwill if we offer them a high quality interview experience.

THE BODY OF THE INTERVIEW

The most important parts of the interview involve the questions you ask and the interaction between you and the candidate. There are a variety of different kinds of questions you can ask; your objective is to ask a mixture of questions that ellicit different information from the candidate.

When conducting an interview there are three basic kinds of interview question categories that will generate the greatest decision-making information.

Self-evaluations: These are questions that allow the candidate to make comments about himself or herself. The answers are not very reliable, since you have no way to measure accuracy.

What is your greatest strength? What trait or characteristic offers you the greatest opportunity for improvement? What motivates you the most? What is your opinion regarding the elimination of the blue laws in New England? What would you do if you were hired to be manager of this store beginning next week?

Experiences and activities: These are questions that let candidates tell you what they have done. Here they can tell you anything they think you want to hear; you don't have any way to verify until you check references.

What kinds of jobs have you had? Please give me a summary of what is listed on you resume. Which part of your job do you like the most? Which portion of your job do you dislike the most? What would you change about how your present company runs?

Behavior descriptions: These questions tell you how the person has behaved in situations in previous instances. These questions offer some insight into the way a person thinks and what drives the person to accomplish specific tasks.

Tell me about the last time you had a difficult customer service situation, what you did and what the final results were. When was the first time you ever had to confront an employee you supervised due to a major violation of company policy? What did you do? How did the person respond? What was the final outcome? What was the

> Questions during an interview should try to measure the personality and work performance of a candidate, using different techniques.

ADVICE ON HIRING

> Use probing questions to determine the behavior of the candidate in certain situations.

greatest disappointment you have every had? What did you do about the situation? How has this decision affected your life today?

To really make an interview effective, you must be skilled in the process of asking the right questions.

All questions are either *open* or *closed.*

Open-ended questions encourage wide-open conversation and allow the person to say whatever he or she considers to be appropriate to the question. You get to listen to lots of previuosly unspoken information when you ask an open-ended question.

Closed-ended questions encourage specific answers with simple yes, no, or otherwise concise replies. These questions do not allow for the person to do lots of talking. These questions allow you, the interviewer, to take back a conversation if the candidate is talking too much.

Open-ended questions can be even more valuable when they become probing questions.

Questions that probe into the behavior patterns of people are complex questions with three parts:

1. A description of a situation or a task the person has experienced
2. A description of the action or position the person took in that situation
3. A description of the results of the person's actions and the impact they have made

Try to form most of your questions into three-part probing questions, using adjectives such as best/worst, hardest/easiest, or longest/shortest, and time references such as first/last, or most recent/next.

As you consider the information captured in the interview, remember that the best predictor of future behavior is past behavior in similar circumstances.

Behavior is what a person says and does. It has a beginning and an end, and it can be measured, evaluated, and modified.

ADVICE ON HIRING

Attitude is what a person believes and thinks. It reflects perceptions, what is in the head and heart. They cannot be seen, cannot be evaluated, and are very difficult to change.

Don't interview for the proper attitude; interview for past behavior.

SAMPLE PROBING QUESTIONS

Here are some sample questions to illustrate the way an effective probing question can be constructed. The questions are constructed to address a defined need, or a skill or ability the candidate must demonstrate to be successful in the position.

EXPERIENCE

Tell me specifically about the store volume you were responsible for in your previous positions.

Who assisted you with the management of this volume? Describe the margins you achieved.

Tell me about the company you have worked for that had the most favorable company culture. What made it the best? How did this culture impact you in your job?

SYSTEMS AND CONTROLS

During your career, what was the best system or control you initiated? What prompted the new system, or control? How did you make it happen? Finally, what was the result of this new system or control?

HANDS-ON OPERATOR

In your present position, tell me about a typical week and how you plan the time you spend doing various functions of your job. How would you like to change this? What obstacles stand in your way?

UNDERSTANDING OF FAST-CHANGING INDUSTRY

What trends, strategies, or technology are driving you to modify the way you do things in your present position? How are you integrating this information in your world at this time? What would you do differently?

ADVICE ON HIRING

WORK ETHIC

In your entire career, what has been the most difficult situation you have ever been in? Describe the situation, and tell me what you did and what the outcome was.

Tell me about a time that you were virtually pushed to the edge by your bosses. What was it all about, and how did you deal with the situation? Tell me how it all ended.

INTERPERSONAL SKILLS

Describe the worst employee you have ever managed or supervised. What was the problem with this employee? How did you deal with it? What was the final resolution?

Tell me about the first time you were ever involved with a legal issue involving an employee at work. What were the circumstances? What did you do? How did it all end up?

COMMUNICATION

Tell me about a time when all your skills as a communicator failed you. What were the circumstances? How did you feel following this experience?

RECRUITING

Tell me how you recruited and hired staff at your former job? What was your role in the process? How well did the process work?

TRAINING

Tell me about the last time you developed a learning or training plan for an employee. What was the training need? How did you create and implement the program for the person? What was the result of your efforts? Who was the most difficult person you have ever had to train? What were you trying to teach that person? How did the whole process end up? How successful was the training?

PERFORMANCE REVIEWS

Describe the most recent time you conducted a performance review for an employee. How did you prepare yourself for this event? How well was the performance review received by the employee and your superior?

ADVICE ON HIRING

SCHEDULING

Tell me about the most creative schedule you ever had to implement: What did you do? How did your plan work?

CULTURE

Tell me about the most horrible environment you have ever worked in. What did you do to deal with the situation? How did the situation end?

PAYROLL

Tell me about the time you were most challenged to meet your labor budget for your operation. What steps did you take to meet your labor budget? What was the result of your efforts?

POLICIES AND PROCEDURES

When have you been most successful in following company policies and procedures? What did you do to make yourself successful? What was the result of your success?

WORK ETHIC

Tell me about the most unpleasant time you had to "do what it takes to get the job done." How did you react to this situation? What was the result of your actions?

BEFORE THE INTERVIEW

When the candidate arrives for the interview, he or she should be greeted by a receptionist or other staff member who will make him or her comfortable. The candidate should be given a packet of information that will explain how the process will proceed and some information about the company. The following sample materials are presented here as a possible template for designing your own interviewing package.

INTERVIEWING MATERIALS

Welcome to Company Q.

[Your mission statement]

Please read this page of instructions and follow it carefully, as it is part of the interview process here at Company Q.

Before you meet with *[Manager's Name]* we would like you to complete some important paperwork.

Complete the **Employment Application**. Be sure to answer all the information even if you have submitted a resume. Don't forget to sign the application.

Read the information regarding the **history of Company Q** and the materials we use to present our unique concept to our customers.

Review the **summary of benefits** offered by **Company Q**.

Review the **summary of job opportunities** available at Company Q

Formulate some **questions** you would like to ask *[manager's name]* during your interview.

Let *[manager's name]* know that you are ready to begin the **interview**.

Thank you for your interest in working with us at Company Q. I hope I have the opportunity to meet you soon.

Owner or President of Company Q

INTERVIEWING MATERIALS

Company Q.
[Your mission statement]

JOB OPPORTUNITIES

To ensure the highest-quality service to our customers, all Company Q locations are designed to maximize the ability of each employee to serve the customers. Although each staff person has very specific job duties, all staff are expected to deliver high-quality service and attention to all customers.

Following is a brief overview of the various staff opportunities within Company Q. Please keep in mind that it is the responsibility of each and every Company Q employee to deliver the highest level of customer service to every customer, all the time.

Sales Associate

The person in this position serves as our primary customer service resentative. There is an enormous amount of direct interaction with customers. Sales associates have the capacity to learn and retain information relating to a wide variety of products and procedures. This position requires a considerable amount of physical activity including, but not limited to, lifting, climbing ladders, and cleaning.

Merchandise Associate

This position serves as our primary stock handler and product availability handler. More than 70 percent of this job involves physical activity including lifting, bending, moving crates and cartons, cleaning, stocking, and climbing ladders. The merchandise associate is expected to have a keen eye to ensure the maintenance of the visual setup of the store.

Cashier

The cashier is our first and final checkpoint for the highest-quality customer service. Cashiers are generally the first contact a customer has on entering our stores. The cashier is are also the person who has the last contact with each customer. The cashier is the person who has the opportunity to have each customer depart with a smile and a positive attitude to return again.

Maintenance

Our maintenance staff are responsible for keeping our locations and the surrounding area spotless. Customers feel more comfortable in an environment that is clean and well maintained. Daily tasks include cleaning all glass surfaces, floors, bathrooms, high traffic areas, and all shelving and fixtures.

Manager and Assistant Manager

The people in these positions are responsible for all aspects of operation. Therefore, the manager or assistant manager may be required to fill in for any of the positions described above, at any time. The manager and to a limited degree the assistant manager is responsible for the supervision, motivation, training, and development of all employees. They are also responsible for successful compliance with all company policies.

ADVICE ON HIRING

FOLLOWING THE INTERVIEW

Candidates should be told when they can expect a decision based on the interview. If you know they will not be given a second interview, it is best to tell them at the close of the interview. Be honest and always try to have them walk away with dignity. Allow them to tell you why the position would not be in their best interest.

A person who does not get a job and is treated with respect and dignity will speak highly of the company that treated him or her so well. Your good interview technique will serve double duty as a marketing initiative for your company.

Following is a sample letter you may want to adapt for your company.

AFTER INTERVIEW LETTER

Date
Name
Address

Dear *[name]*

Thank you for taking the time to meet with *[insert the name of the person who did first official interview]* regarding employment opportunities with Company Q.

Although your experiences and skills as discussed in the interview are interesting, they do not match our present needs. Our recruiting and interviewing strategy is directed toward ensuring the individuals we hire are the most suitable candidates for the available positions.

We thank you for your interest in Company Q and wish you well in your search for a suitable and interesting career opportunity.

Sincerely,

[your name]
Manager

ADVICE ON HIRING

If the person conducting the interview is not the hiring manager, you will want a record of the interview to be sure the next interviewer has information to review prior to the second interview. The following form may be helpful as you create your own customized interview process.

INTERVIEW RECOMMENDATION FORM

(This form is completed if the candidate is interviewed by someone other than the manager)

Candidate name: _____

Candidate for the following position (circle one):
[A listing of the various positions in your organization will be placed in this space.]

The minimum rate of pay this person will accept is _____

Available date and time for an interview: _____

Additional suggestions, comments, and recommendations: _____

_____

_____

Completed by: *[signature of individual]* _____ Date:_____/_____/_____

****

ACTION TAKEN BY THE MANAGER

Candidate has been (circle one of the following)

Hired as a regular employee   Hired as a temporary employee

Returned to resume file for future openings   Returned to resume file for no further action

Comments _____

_____

Manager: _____ Date:_____/_____/_____

ADVICE ON HIRING

MAKING THE OFFER

Once a decision is reached based on the interview, reference checks, and conversations among the people who interviewed the candidate, an offer is made. Whenever possible, make the offer in person at a follow-up meeting. If that is not possible, call the candidate and make the offer.

In either case, be sure to send a letter confirming the offer so there is no misunderstanding. The offer letter should clearly explain that this in not a contract, nor does it represent any agreement beyond identifying the salary and benefits for the position.

Following is a sample offer letter.

ADVICE ON HIRING

Date

Name
Address

Dear *[Name]*

As you and I have discussed, it is with great pleasure that I provide you with additional details regarding our offer of employment to join *[name of department]* of *[name of company]*.

To summarize our understanding, discussed below are the details of our arrangements.

You will be joining the *[name of department]* as *[title]*.

You will receive *[amount]* on a biweekly basis.

You will receive benefits as a senior salaried exempt employee according to our benefits policy.

In addition, after completing one year of service with our company, you will be eligible to participate in the bonus program. Although the company does not guarantee that a bonus will be paid, and reserves the right to cancel the bonus payment at any time, the company has customarily paid a bonus in December. The bonus is based on individual performance.

On the first business day following the completion of three full months of service, you will become eligible for medical and insurance benefits.

It is important to note that employment at our company is at will, and is subject to termination at any time, by the company or yourself, with or without cause.

I understand that you will begin work on *[date]*. Please plan to report to my office at *[time]* so we can begin your orientation to our company. You will receive a formal orientation schedule in the mail in the next few days.

Assuming you begin work on *[date]* you will receive your first salary payment on *[date]*.

We look forward to having you join us at *[name of company]*

Sincerely,

cc: Payroll Department

ADVICE ON HIRING

A defined hiring plan will give you a consistent measure of all employees.

QUESTION AND ANSWERS

1. **What do I do when the candidate I want to hire indicates he or she has another offer and is on the fence?**

   The first thing you should do is ask the candidate what he or she would like to see happen. Use this situation to determine what the candidate is really thinking. You should have already decided what the salary range for the position is and what other flexible opportunities you may be able to offer. If money is the issue, you must be sure to stay within the guidelines you have set or risk throwing the entire compensation program off. In the final analysis you will need to determine how important it is to have this candidate join your company. If money is the only obstacle, and your compensation plan will not permit a larger salary, consider a sign-on bonus or some other one-time benefit.

2. **Why do I need a plan to hire a good person?**

   Without a plan you are not able to make midstream decisions quickly and with full information. Without a plan you will not be able to delegate portions of the interview and hiring process to others without being concerned about errors and inconsistency. A defined plan will allow you to have consistent hiring practices for all employees.

3. **What happens when I find a good candidate but I know he or she is not necessarily the best in the marketplace?**

   Before you begin any hiring process you should determine what skills and abilities are needed to successfully perform in this position. You need to create a list of characteristics for which you are hiring. Keep track of all the candidates and then make a decision. Also factor in the time you have allotted for this position. Sometimes you'll need to hire the individual who is good but not great and help develop that person to be supergreat. Remember, the second-place winner has incredible motivation to get to first place.

ADVICE ON HIRING

4. **What happens when I don't get a pool of qualified candidates from the recruiting ad?**

   First, review your recruiting ad to determine why it did not generate sufficient response. Was it written in a fashion to confuse people? Did you place it in the correct media?

   Then reconsider the job position. Is the position obsolete? Is the position too technical or obscure?

   If you have not discovered any answers, you can either pay a recruiting firm to do a search, or you can directly access other people in similar positions to ask them for assistance. Frequently, asking a person with a similar job if he or she knows anyone who is looking for a new position can generate interest by the person you called.

5. **How do I attract a diverse group of candidates that includes minorities to become part of the candidate pool?**

   It is always wise to advertise in a wide range of media. The range of media should include minority newspapers, radio, and TV as well as community groups. Be sure your advertisements include a statement about your corporate philosophy regarding diversity. It also helps to develop relationships with organizations that represent various minorities.

6. **What should I do when the candidate I offer a job to does not accept?**

   Never tell candidates they do not have a position until you are sure you have hired the person you want. In the event your choice does not want to work with you, you can still call the second choice and offer the position to that person. If you don't have a second candidate due to the available candidate pool, then you will need to begin the process all over again. It also will be helpful to know why she or he decided not to take the job. You can learn a great deal by asking questions and listening.

> Advertise positions in many different kinds of media in order to get the most diverse pool of candidates.

ADVICE ON HIRING

> Multiple interviews that use the same criteria help create a more well-rounded view of the candidate.

7. **Should I take the candidate out to dinner?**
   This depends on the company culture, and the level of the position for which you are hiring. It may be more appropriate to take a candidate out to dinner once you are sure you want to make an offer. You may use the dinner as an opportunity to confirm everything you determined in the interviews.

8. **How much effort should I put into references? How accurate will they be?**
   Due to potential legal ramifications, it may be difficult to obtain more than basic information from the references listed. Try to use references as a mechanism to confirm what the candidate has already told you. Most references will tell you if the information you mention is accurate but will not offer any other information.

9. **Should I see a candidate more than once or twice?**
   Every person you hire should have had at lease two interviews. You should be sure to have more than one person confirm that the candidate is a good selection for the company. Having multiple interviews using the same criteria ensures that all candidates are treated fairly, and you obtain more detailed and accurate information.

10. **Should I interview by committee?**
    Sometimes a committee works; it all depends on the job position. If a candidate is interviewing for a project manager position and will be working with a variety of different people, you would want to include these people in the hiring decision. If the interview committee is formed due to the function of the position, then it makes great sense.

11. **How do I attract candidates that are not all young white males?**
    Your organization needs to create an image as an employer of a diverse work force. Your company should also create an image of a successful company where being on your team is desired for a number of reasons, one of which is the diversity of the work force.

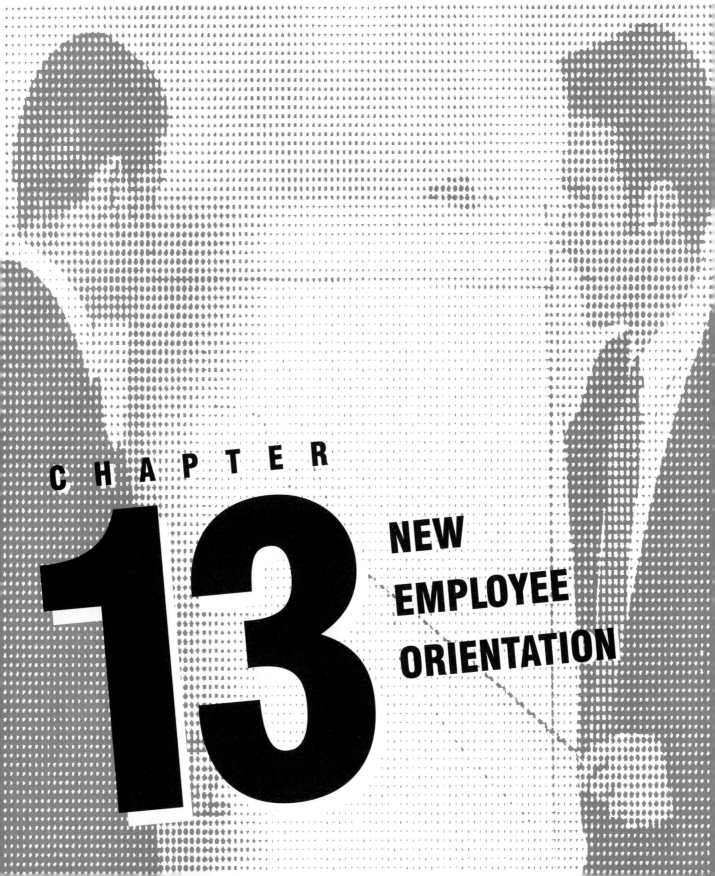

CHAPTER

13 NEW EMPLOYEE ORIENTATION

The new employee's first few days will go a long way to creating their long-term view of the company, and may very well impact how long they stay at the company, and how productive they will be at the company. This is a time when attention to a lot of small details can make a big difference in creating good morale and fostering a positive work environment.

NEW EMPLOYEE ORIENTATION

FIRST IMPRESSION

You have only one chance to make a good first impression.

When a new employee accepts an employment offer from your company, the real work begins.

To maximize all the investments you have made and will make in this new employee, you must begin the relationship in the best possible manner. Keep this objective in clear view as you design your orientation programs for new employees.

With a quality introduction to a new firm, the new employee is protected from the typical orientation scenario, which includes many of these comments and questions:

- Who is my boss or supervisor?
- Are we allowed to take a cigarette/coffee break? When?
- How should I dress?
- Can I eat lunch at my desk? When can I take lunch?
- When does the fiscal year begin?
- Who are our largest and/or biggest clients?
- Where are the rest rooms?
- Do I need a parking sticker for the parking lot?

New employees with a laundry list of questions have a difficult time "getting down to work" because there are so many distractions as they attempt to acquire the missing information. By anticipating as many questions as possible and incorporating these questions into the content of the new employee orientation, the new employee becomes assimilated more readily into the company.

> Anticipating initial questions helps integrate the new employee faster.

SMALL VS. LARGE COMPANY

New employee orientation is totally different in a small company as compared to a larger company. But the heart and soul of the program should be the same in both instances.

In a smaller company the quality new employee orientation program is managed and conducted by a person with direct authority over and responsibility for the new employee. Frequently it is the new employee's manager or supervisor. In companies that recognize the incredible value of a good first impression, the CEO/owner leads

NEW EMPLOYEE ORIENTATION

and directs the orientation. As you will discover, the person leading the orientation is not directly engaged the entire time. The lead person sets the tone and establishes the credibility and value of the orientation process while recognizing the new employee as a valuable new contributor to the organization. This person would most likely have lunch or dinner with the new employee to firmly establish the foundation on which this new professional relationship will be built.

In a larger company a leadership designee is usually the point person for the orientation process. A vice president, the director of human resources or a district manager may fill this role, depending on the position held by the new employee.

A quality orientation program delivers recognition, respect, and dignity to the new employee as part of his or her first impression of the new company.

Let's bring this concept a step farther. Although new office and management staff are often taken to lunch on the first day of work, should an hourly (nonexempt) employee also be taken to lunch? Think about the impact and cost of doing just that!

Imagine if a supervisor/manager were to take a new hourly (nonexempt) employee to lunch at the local restaurant. Can you imagine how "special," "important," "valued," and "respected," this new employee will feel? All for the cost of a modest lunch and a few hours of missed work.

The simple yet profound action of giving a new employee the time to interact with the "boss" is very powerful. The new employee will feel very important having a one-on-one conversation with the person who hired him or her and who is his or her boss. The location, the restaurant, and the food are not important. What is critical is that the "boss" took the time to recognize this new employee as a valued individual.

Consider the investment of time—an hour—and the potential return on the investment from this hour. Certainly the employee will be more motivated to perform at the highest level to please the person who took him or her to lunch. The "halo effect" will impact positively on the employee making them feel valued and respected. In

> By spending time with the new employee on the first day, the manager motivates the new employee through respect.

NEW EMPLOYEE ORIENTATION

turn, this feeling will permeate all actions of the employee. When a company "walks the talk" and consistently demonstrates these actions and deeds, the "halo effect" becomes real and part of the company culture. This same impact can be achieved in both large and small companies, but it takes a plan and the commitment to stick to the plan.

THE PLAN OF ACTION

Map out your orientation program with deliberate attention to detail. Here is a suggested step-by-step plan for you to use as a model for creating your own orientation program for new employees. The model is presented as three basic phases with suggested content. Keep in mind that this is only a model and is subject to the specific needs and circumstances of your department and company.

Phase I: A welcoming letter outlining orientation activities for the first day is sent to the home of new employee if time permits. If time is short, the information is presented to the new employee on the first day of work.

Phase II: The details of the letter are implemented on the first day of work.

Phase III: One month later, a simple questionnaire regarding the orientation is completed by the new employee.

Phase I: The welcome letter sent to the new employee outlines the specifics of the first day. No surprises! The new employee is informed of exactly what will happen on the first day and with whom it will happen. The schedule will include the following:

- Time and place to meet
- Name and title of the person to meet
- Description of any materials the new employee should bring
- Details of the schedule for the day, including who, when, where, what and why
- Meet the coach
- Complete basic paperwork, including
- Payroll enrollment

An organized orientation helps avoid problems and confusion on the part of the new employee.

NEW EMPLOYEE ORIENTATION

- Benefits enrollment
- Company policies
- Holidays
- Vacation
- Personal/sick
- Mandated regulations
- Departmental procedures
- The company culture
- The job and job description
- The work environment
- The coworkers
- The facilities
- Parking
- Rest rooms
- Cafeteria/lunch room
- Day care
- Health club
- Company resources
- Names of key people
- Organizational chart
- Important telephone numbers
- Close of the day
- Final meeting to review day
- General questions and answers

Important Note: A welcoming letter sent to a new employee will only work if the person referenced in the letter is prepared for and totally committed to the orientation process.

INVOLVE AS MANY DIFFERENT PEOPLE AS POSSIBLE

As you design your orientation, try to include as many different people as possible in the process. Let the new employee learn about the company through the existing employees. Be sure that one person, generally with authority, is the coordinator for the orientation. You do not want the process disrupted because an existing staff member decided he or she had more important issues to deal with.

> Employees can learn more about the company through other employees.

NEW EMPLOYEE ORIENTATION

Reinforce the critical nature of making a good first impression. Let it be known that new employee orientation is a hot button for the CEO/owner of the company. Because it is a hot button, existing staff should be held accountable for the quality of the work they complete in reference to the orientation.

DEDICATE SUFFICIENT TIME TO THIS EFFORT

To make this orientation a positive experience, the new employee must recognize and experience the sensibility of being respected as an individual who is considered a valuable member of the organization.

Don't keep this person waiting. Be prompt and set a good example. When you are working with this individual, put all calls on hold or ask your administrative person to hold all calls. A new employee on the receiving end of this behavior will immediately recognize your valuation of him or her as an individual. Invariable the new employee will replicate this behavior with others as they interact.

This is the beginning of quality training and learning.

During the orientation process, *listen* to what the new employee is saying. More importantly, *listen* to what he or she is not saying. Frequently an unspoken word, phrase, or sentence will tell you more about a person than the words he or she has articulated.

If you are scheduled to have lunch on the first day, *do not cancel*. This new individual is important to the success of the company. When a new person experiences a supervisor/manager/boss dedicating a full hour of time to a single person, the new employee sees a company "walking the talk," thereby making all the rhetoric believable.

People want to fit in; it's a natural tendency. People want to be accepted within a new organization. As you plan an orientation, don't skimp on time. Do this orientation properly the first time and productivity will increase rapidly while the incidence of employee turnover reduces dramatically.

Be sure each staff member participating in this orientation understands the need to dedicate sufficient time for this effort. It is useless if the CEO/human resources person does a wonderful job of

Make the new employee feel important by listening to them.

NEW EMPLOYEE ORIENTATION

orientation in the morning, only to have the supervisor/manager/boss cancel lunch or turn lunch at a local deli or restaurant into sandwiches and coffee at the manager's desk, retrieving messages while the new employee sits, eats and listens.

This is not the image you want to project. The only way a company can assure that all participants in the orientation will do a good job is to clearly inform them of the expectation and to hold them accountable for this action. Each manager/supervisor has a vested interest in the success of a new employee, but it may be necessary to force this connection to a higher level by linking it to their performance during new employee orientations.

INFORM EXISTING STAFF ABOUT ORIENTATIONS

The best way to ensure the new employee orientation program is comprehensive, informative, and interesting is to vary the format and include a variety of staff in the process.

The program must be organized in a step-by-step format that is communicated to the new employee as well as to the various staff members who will participate.

The most effective vehicle for communicating the program is via a letter to the staff members, with a copy sent to the new employee along with the welcoming letter.

A sample memo to the staff is supplied as a model of what your company may wish to include in your new employee orientation program. This sample is designed for larger organizations.

> Including the rest of the staff in the orientation of a new employee ensures the success of the orientation.

NEW EMPLOYEE ORIENTATION MEMO

To: All Staff

From: CEO (or HR/VP/DM)

Re: New Employee Orientation for Mary Jones

Mary Jones will be joining our company on *[date to begin]* as *[name of position]*. She is replacing *[or a new hire]* for *[division/department/function]*.

Please help us with Mary's orientation to *[name of company]* by reviewing the orientation schedule we have prepared for her. We are requesting your assistance with the areas that are highlighted.

As you know, we consider the new employee orientation program to be a valuable tool in the continual success of our company. If you have any questions, please speak with me as soon as possible.

8:30 A.M.   Arrival at address and building location

            Meet with human resources director to review schedule for the day

9:00 A.M.   With human resources director

            Complete all paperwork for enrollment into the payroll system

            Review company policies and procedures

            Identify company resources, partnerships, affiliations i.e. EAP, Junior

            Achievement, Community Groups, Charities, etc.

            Describe the company culture

10:00 A.M. Meet with supervisor/manager to:

- Review job description
- Review job duties
- Review job resources
- Identify critical deadlines
- Identify performance checkpoints
- Discuss project overview
- Explain strategic direction
- Collect baseline information

12:00 N   Lunch with supervisor/manager

NEW EMPLOYEE ORIENTATION

1:00 P.M.   Independent review of policies and procedures

Opportunity to reflect and evaluate privately

2:00 P.M.   Meet with supervisor/manager to:

- Introduce and meet coworkers
- Explore work station
- Have hands-on interactions with materials

4;00 P.M.   Meet with human resources director to

- Review key operating information (e.g., parking, payroll, rest rooms, vacations, sick days)
- Identify the company culture and where it was visible today
- Clarify the communication process within company
- Discuss questions and answers that emerged from the day

5:00 P.M.   Close the day and prepare for day two

Please remember the value of this orientation process to our company. People who understand our goals and objectives as a company and who understand the goals and objectives of their specific position have a higher incidence of success and productivity within our company.

Let's all work together to ensure that Mary Jones will be highly successful. Remember, your success is our success.

Thank you for your assistance in making Mary Jones's orientation a valuable starting point for everyone.

cc: Mary Jones

NEW EMPLOYEE ORIENTATION

COLLECT BASELINE DATA AND EVALUATE THE PROGRAM

How can you make your existing new employee orientation program better? The best way to improve a program is to evaluate and measure the success of the program. The program you design must be accountable to the objectives you have established.

The accountability can be as simple as a one-month survey of the new employee. Ask questions related to the information he or she should have acquired during the orientation. Here is a sample survey you may want to adapt for your company.

NEW EMPLOYEE ORIENTATION

To: New Employee
From: Human Resources Department
Re: One Month Anniversary

Congratulations!

You have been with XYZ Company for one month. We hope your transition to our company has been smooth and pleasant. In order to monitor the quality of our orientation program we request your assistance.

Please answer the following questions as accurately and completely as you can. When you have completed this survey, please send or deliver it to Mr. Smith, the director of human resources.

1. Who is your official supervisor/manager?
2. How and why do you communicate with your supervisor/manager after regular work hours?
3. When are you eligible to enroll in our health benefits programs? Please give an exact date.
4. What are the specific security procedures for entering the building after regular operating hours?
5. If you have a concern about any form of harassment, what should you do?
6. What procedures should be followed in the event of a natural disaster such as a blizzard, a hurricane or an earthquake?
7. What was the most valuable aspect of your orientation?
8. What do you wish we would have included in the orientation?
9. Any other comments?

The review and analysis of these surveys will help your organization to continually refine your new employee orientation program.

If you already have a program that delivers a high level of success, Congratulations!

To build on this success, you may wish to begin collecting baseline data about your new employees. Try this:

1. Identify five to ten specific skills you expect a person in this new employee position to have.

2. Identify an accurate way to measure these particular skills.

3. Administer a brief "new employee survey" to each new hire. Each new hire will have a specific set of questions based on the job position.

4. Track those data for new employees along with other members of the same department/division/function.

5. At the first performance review (six months or twelve months later), readminister the same set of questions to determine if the skill level has changed.

6. Compare the results for the new employee and compare to any data on existing employees.

7. Discuss the results of this survey with the employee, and utilize these data in addition to the performance review documentation to establish developmental opportunities for the employee.

NEW EMPLOYEE ORIENTATION

Respect the Input of the New Employee

The new employee orientation is a time to make a great first impression and present critical information, and it is also a time for the company to learn something about the new employee and the skills, attitudes, and behaviors that person brings to the company. To obtain the greatest value from this exchange, all company personnel involved in the new employee orientation must *listen* very carefully.

When all members of the orientation team are trained for active listening, they will learn a great deal about that person and what the new employee is bringing to the company. The results of good active listening is the icing on the cake for an orientation program.

IDENTIFY TASK/WORK EXPECTATIONS

It is very important for an organization to make each new employee keenly aware of the goals and objectives of the organization as a whole. But the big picture will be of no use to a new employee who does not understand what is expected to be achieved in the new position. Every orientation program must have a portion of time dedicated to the nitty-gritty of the actual job an employee will perform. The new employee must be clearly walked through the actual performance expectations for the position, with clearly established times and places for evaluation, using a clearly defined measurement tool or device. It seems so simple and so "commonsense," but the reality is that most new employees do not get clear information on what is expected of them.

Without clearly defined expectations, at best the employee will do the best possible job to achieve the objectives he or she believes are desired. Needless to say, this leaves an incredible opportunity for error, wasted time, and lost productivity, which invariably leads to lost revenue. Let's not forget the impact on the new employee who wants to be successful but who is now faced with a failure at the onset of his or her new career/position.

Let's look at a four-step plan to ensure that new employees are able to approach their new positions with the greatest amount of clarity and enthusiasm.

> Clearly defined goals and duties help the new employee settle in to work.

NEW EMPLOYEE ORIENTATION

> Allow the employee to set their own level of performance.

1. As part of the initial company orientation set aside a specific time to review the job description. During this time frame the supervisor and the new employee should review the details of the job description to ensure a clear understanding of the objectives of the position. The supervisor should encourage the new employee to explain he or she has successfully completed similar tasks in other companies. The supervisor wants to obtain a sense of how comfortable the new employee is with the tasks identified. This is a time for the supervisor and employee to establish a basic understanding of how each works, helping to improve the opportunities for accurate and clear communication.

   The supervisor should explain the level of productivity needed and expected and ask the employee, "How long will it take you to reach this level of productivity?" The supervisor should also ask the employee, "What will you need from me to help you reach this level of productivity?" With these simple questions the supervisor has given the employee the opportunity to set the level of performance at the onset. By giving the employee the power to make this decision, the supervisor has a greater chance of having the employee achieve the performance expectations desired.

   The supervisor should determine with the new employee what will be accomplished and when it will be accomplished. In some cases it is also very important to tell the employee how something must be accomplished, if there is a standard operating procedure within the organization. In effect the supervisor and the employee working together will establish a plan of action for performance that will be measured at specific times. It is best to set this for the first few weeks of employment. It is during this time that the critical work behavior will be evident, and if necessary, modified.

   Both the supervisor and the new employee should have a copy of a schedule that outlines the desired outcomes and the due dates for the outcomes. The schedule should also

NEW EMPLOYEE ORIENTATION

include the measurement tools used to evaluate the tasks due on these dates.

2. During these first few weeks the supervisor must place extra-special attention on the development and assimilation of this new employee into the company. If the supervisor is very busy, it will be necessary to include another worker in the orientation plan with the new employee. This other person must be included from the beginning. If this is not the case, the new employee will feel as though they have been abandoned and is not as valued as other employees. This is a very critical time, and supervisors must dedicate sufficient time, energy, and resources to orienting a new employee.

At the very first check-up point, the supervisor and the employee should be prepared to have an honest, up-front conversation. Start with something like "How has this first week been for you? What was the very best thing that happened all week for you? What did you do in this situation? How did this impact other parts of your job?"

By asking such probing questions the supervisor will have the opportunity to discover if the new employee is connected to the job in a big-picture way or in a narrow-details way. This will give the supervisor insight about how to communicate with the new employee.

The probing questions will also give the new employee a chance to say whatever he or she considers the most important aspect of the preceding week. Again, the supervisor can obtain a much better insight into how well the new employee will fit in and achieve the desired objectives.

Supervisors should be encouraged to give the new employee the opportunity to talk and should listen to what this person is saying. Don't be eager to reaffirm the details you mentioned previously. Let the person express himself or herself. Listen carefully, and the supervisor will begin to recognize the kind of questions that should be asked.

Managers should make a concerted effort to make the new employee feel a part of the company.

NEW EMPLOYEE ORIENTATION

Through pointed questioning, allow the employee to see areas of weakness, and ways to correct them.

The supervisor may discover that the new employee really doesn't have the degree of skill needed to complete a particular task. Rather than making this a negative issue, the supervisor can offer the new employee the support of a coworker or the direct assistance of the supervisor. By not allowing these conversations to turn negative, the supervisor is able to demonstrate a willingness to teach/train the new employee to accomplish the desired tasks.

Whenever possible, reinforce the positive aspects of what new employees are doing. Ask them what they need to keep doing their job better and more effectively. Ask them to identify the areas that need improvement. When new employees or any employees identify the areas they wish to improve, the potential for improvement increases dramatically.

Don't be afraid to criticize behaviors or performances that are incorrect or counterproductive. But be very wary of how you criticize. Offer the employee the opportunity to identify the situation you are concerned about. If the employee does not bring up the concern you wish to discuss, then be a bit more specific by asking a series of questions. The questions will get progressively more detailed until you are directly identifying the topic or issue you are worried about. By taking it step by step you give the new employee the opportunity to identify the issue first. Once you have exhausted all your questions, you are faced with insight about what the new employee might not want to acknowledge, although you must.

Here are some of the questions you might want to ask:

- "In the area of XYZ, are there any situations in which you may want some assistance or some explanation? Frequently new people have a hard time with this area." If the new employee doesn't respond, you will need to be even more specific. (Although this seems like too much work, consider how much more work it will be for you to start the entire recruiting , hiring, and

NEW EMPLOYEE ORIENTATION

orientation process all over again. Give each new employee the best possible chance to succeed.)

- "When I reviewed the information about the XYZ area I noticed some interesting information. I would like to take a few minutes to review this with you. Let me know if you have noticed the same information." (This question places the issue squarely in front of the new employee. This is a chance for him or her to say, "I need help.")

- "I want you to be very successful in this new position and I'd like to make your learning curve easier. Let me give you a real-life situation, and you tell me how you will handle it when it happens, because it will happen. Then I'll tell you, based on my experience, how your suggested approach will turn out. This should help you to be prepared for a problem I know you will have to face." (This question allows the supervisor to directly confront the employee with the real-life situation that has already happened but the new employee doesn't want to talk about. This question will offer the new employee the chance to finally get with the program. If the new employee doesn't respond in a positive manner, it's time for the direct statement.)

- "I was hoping to help you identify some areas for improving your performance, but I don't think we made any progress. I do have a concern, and it has to do with the XYZ area. I am not confident you understand the needs in this area nor am I confident that you will be able to learn what needs to be learned to take care of the XYZ area. What do you think?" (This question lays the issue squarely in front of the new employee.)

If the supervisor doesn't feel that the new employee gets it, this is the time to seriously consider letting the person go. The supervisor may want to give it another week, but the caution here is not to let this drag out. If the supervisor

─NEW EMPLOYEE ORIENTATION─

recognizes a problem now, and it does not respond to the type of interaction described above, it is best to terminate the new employee now.

If the new employee demonstrates the ability to work within the guidelines presented and shows a willingness to be up-front and willing to accept advice and criticism, then continue with this developmental process.

3. Continue to meet with the new employee to monitor this person's work and to ensure that he or she is producing what the organization needs and what is expected of the position. During this time the supervisor will be developing a strong relationship with the new employee. It will be very clear what the strengths and weaknesses of the new employee are. The supervisor should be able to identify meaningful opportunities for the increased development of this new employee. It is during these first ten weeks of employment that the supervisor should be expected to make a final decision regarding the long-term potential of this new employee. It is also important for the supervisor to identify all the areas in which the new employee is performing well. Always try to build on the strengths of the employee. Use the strengths as building blocks to improve in the weak areas.

It is at this stage that a supervisor will determine that an employee is no longer a probationary employee. He or she has been evaluated to be a valuable, contributing member of the organization. This person's status has or will change shortly from probationary employee to regular employee.

4. Once the supervisor has made a decision that this new employee is a good employee and now a regular employee, the process does not stop. Now the supervisor begins to train the new employee in skills and responsibilities that might be at a higher level or more complex. The communication and development processes go hand in hand. It is critically important for all organizations to have a regular and consistent process of feedback from supervisors to employees. Although

> Focus on the strengths of the new employee to help improve upon the weak areas.

NEW EMPLOYEE ORIENTATION

the company may have a yearly performance review system, the regular and consistent process of performance communication is critical for the success of the business and the individual.

. . . .

INEFFECTIVE ORIENTATION SCENARIO

Mary Jones has been hired as the new office manager for a growing food service management company with 250 employees in two states. She has more than ten years of experience as an executive assistant to the president of a similar organization in a different geographic region.

She reports to the CFO at the corporate offices. Hers is a brand-new position, as there has not been an office manager in the company before.

She interviewed with the CFO and the president of the company and after two interviews was offered the position. During the interview process she was shown around the offices and had the opportunity to visit the office manager's office and the administrative section of the office. She was given a job description by the CFO and was told she would be responsible for all duties listed on the job description and many other items that had not yet been recorded. She was also told she would supervise three other people.

She accepted the position and was told to arrive on Monday to begin work.

When she arrived on Monday, extra early to get a head start on the day, the office was not even open yet. The first person to arrive and open up was a member of the accounting staff who Mary introduced herself to at the front door.

Once inside, Mary went to her new office and started to explore. Shortly other members of the organization began arriving, and Mary made it a point to introduce herself to as many people as possible. The members of her staff arrived and she did the best she

> An ill-informed new employee can't feel comfortable in their position and can't perform to their best abilities.

NEW EMPLOYEE ORIENTATION

could to introduce herself and explain that the CFO was going to have a meeting that morning to introduce her.

At about 9:30 A.M. the CFO arrived and apologized for being late and for not having informed the group about Mary's arrival. He quickly introduced everyone and suggested they get together for a meeting at 11:30 A.M. in his office.

Mary then went to her office to figure out what to do next. She decided to take time to speak with each employee before the 11:30 A.M. meeting. In these conversations Mary asked lots of questions and tried to understand how things had been done at the company. Her main goal was to determine what the three employees needed and wanted from her to make the work responsibilities of the Administrative Department run as smoothly as possible.

At eleven-thirty the CFO told the staff the Mary would be their new supervisor and that he had high expectations for Mary and the department. He pointed out some of the critical issues the department had been facing and asked the existing employees to show Mary the ropes. He then asked anyone if they had anything to say and ended the twenty-minute minute meeting with a statement to Mary to come to him whenever she had a question or was not sure of a policy or procedure.

Mary left the meeting and returned to her office wondering if she had made the correct decision.

EFFECTIVE ORIENTATION SCENARIO

Mary Jones has been hired as the new office manager for a growing food service management company with 250 employees in two states. She has more than ten years experiences as an executive assistant to the president of a similar organization in a different geographic region.

She reports to the CFO at the corporate offices. Hers is a brand-new position as there has not been an office manager in the company before.

> The employee should not have to seek information about essential duties on his or her own.

NEW EMPLOYEE ORIENTATION

She interviewed with the CFO and the president of the company. She also interviewed with the staff she would be supervising. During the interview process she was shown the office she would occupy, and the administrative section of the office.

The CFO went over the newly written job description and explained that it would be a work in progress. He went through each item of the job description to be sure Mary understood the full scope of the position. He asked Mary if there were other issues that should be added or deleted from the job description. She was introduced again to the three people she would be supervising.

Mary was offered the position, and she accepted. She was told to arrive on Monday at 9:30 A.M. to begin work with an orientation.

Mary arrived at 9:15 A.M. on Monday morning. She was greeted by the CFO, who showed her to her office and arranged for coffee and breakfast treats. During coffee the CFO outlined his plans for the day for Mary. She would begin by taking a tour of the offices with the CFO and would be formally introduced to all the office staff. Then he and Mary would have a meeting with her new staff to outline some of the performance objectives the CFO had set for the department.

Based on a schedule he had created for Mary, she would then spend ten to twenty minutes with various members of the office, getting to know what they do and how her job will interface with theirs.

The CFO also explained that he and Mary would go to lunch at 1:00 P.M. so she would have time to speak with him about her first impressions. Following lunch Mary would continue with her visits and would end the day by meeting with her staff again, followed by a short wrap-up meeting with the CFO at 5:30 P.M.

As Mary moved through the hours of the day, she was impressed with how cooperative everyone was in sharing information about the company and the way things work in the organization.

Her lunch with the CFO was very pleasant and he made it clear to Mary that she should feel free to ask as many questions as necessary to reach a comfort level with the company and the job. He offered her some positive insights about the people she had already

> An organized orientation helps to integrate the new employee and present a positive appearance of the company.

NEW EMPLOYEE ORIENTATION

met, and he shared some company history with her. Mary's meeting with her staff at the end of the day was animated and positive because the staff knew that Mary was there to help make the organization run more efficiently.

She left the meeting with the CFO thinking how exciting an opportunity this would be.

Returning to her office to prepare to leave, she smiled to herself and realized she had made the correct decision in taking this job.

QUESTIONS AND ANSWERS

1. **Do I need to have a big, elaborate orientation program for new employees? Can't I just have the new person assigned to a new employee for the first day?**

   You don't need an elaborate program, but you do need a clear and consistent program that will operate all the time and in the same way for all new employees. If you want to incorporate a buddy system into the orientation program, do so. Be sure everyone involved knows what they are to do.

   It would be very wise for you to train the people who are going to be the buddies. The important part is to ensure your new job duties.

2. **Can I wait to do an employee orientation for a larger group of employees once per month?**

   Many companies do have monthly or weekly orientation programs for new employees. They are scheduled on a regular basis to ensure that new employees are not on the job working for any long period of time without a formal orientation. Frequently new hires will be asked to attend the orientation prior to their actual starting date to ensure that they get accurate and consistent information.

   Even with a large group orientation schedule done on a regular basis you will need a basic program to ensure that

> Keep employees aware of the new orientation program, and train those involved adequately.

NEW EMPLOYEE ORIENTATION

job expectations are clear to new employees when they begin. You must be sure that each new employee knows what is expected of him or her and how he or she should behave within the company.

3. **How do I know if new employee orientation will benefit my company?**

   How is your company doing now? What is your turnover rate? How much money do you spend on recruiting advertising? Are you getting the optimum productivity from your employees? You should figure out the answers to these questions and then ask yourself the first question again.

   If you are still not sure, try an orientation program you conduct on your own with new employees. Try it for six months to a year. Notice if you see a higher degree of performance and follow-through from the people you have personally oriented to the company.

4. **Can I delegate this process to others?**

   Yes. But you will need to stay involved and to maintain veto power over final decisions. You will want to get other people involved so you can slowly but surely have other people represent the mission and the culture of the organization as well as you can. Someone else may coordinate the program, but you still will be an integral component of the program.

5. **What should I do if after one month following orientation, the new employee has not transitioned into the corporate culture?**

   First you should speak directly to the employee's supervisor to determine how well the individual is doing in terms of job performance. If the performance on the job is good, then you may need to spend some time with the employee to reinforce the mission and culture of the company. You should let the employee know how important it is for you to have a complete team of people who share your philosophy and company mission. The only way to do this is to be honest and speak directly to the employee.

> Try to get as many people involved in the process as possible.

NEW EMPLOYEE ORIENTATION

If the employee's performance is not up to par, then be sure the supervisor does his or her job.

6. **If I really need a new person to get working right away, can I postpone or skip the orientation?**

You can do anything you want as the owner, but consider the impact. If the new employee is not given this important information how will he or she understand what you expect in terms of long-term goals and objectives? You have created a program to help integrate people into your company more efficiently. Skip the process and suffer the consequences.

7. **I already have an orientation program in place. How can I make it better?**

Congratulations! The best way to make your program better is to ask the people who have gone through the program. Invite the most recent new hires to a meeting with an agenda to get their feedback regarding the orientation program. You will be surprised at the amount of quality feedback you will receive. If you implement any of their suggestions, the next time you do the feedback session you will get even more information.

STREETWISE advice

◆ **A company without an official orientation program really has an unofficial program.**
This unofficial program is whatever may happen to a new employee when he or she first arrives. Actions experienced by a new employee on the first day may have a negative impact. If they are not part of a formal orientation program, they could become the image of the company to a newly hired person.

◆ **Your orientation program should be documented to ensure it happens on a consistent basis for all employees.**
You do not want a program that is conducted only when someone feels like doing it.

◆ **Don't let anyone, including yourself or the CEO, give an excuse for not participating in the orientation process.**
For the program to give you everything you want to receive, all parties built into the design must participate. The importance of having the key leadership person involved in this process is critical to the success of an orientation program.

◆ **Be sure to dedicate quality time, resources, and money to your orientation program.**
Invest in the initial intake of your new employees. You have spent considerable money recruiting and hiring this person. Now spend money to be sure they are welcomed and integrated into the company so they can begin to contribute as soon as possible.

◆ **Assign one person or a team of people to serve as orientation program coordinators to assure that the orientation program happens the way it was designed to happen.**
Make this duty part of the employee or the team's job description.

◆ **Prevent new hire rivalry by distributing the new hire's job description to appropriate members of the organization.**
It would be best to include this job description with the details of their involvement in the new hire's orientation.

Invest time and energy into the orientation of a new employee, as it can only benefit you in the future.

CHAPTER

14

RETENTION
AND
RECOGNITION

E mployee turnover is expensive—a lot more expensive than first meets the eye! So you need to do everything you can not just to retain people, but to recognize people and make them really feel appreciated. You also need to know what your turnover rate is; why people are leaving; and what you can do about it.

RETENTION & RECOGNITION

KEEPING EMPLOYEES

What's all the fuss about retaining employees? Does it really make a difference if you have employees coming and going on a regular basis?

If you are not sure of the answer, think back to the last time an employee left or was terminated. Can you recall the number of times you heard someone say, "Oh, Sally was the only one who knew how to contact that person" or " Sorry, I never learned how to complete that task, Sally left before I was totally trained?"

As you know, this is the day-to-day reality in many organizations.

Good managers should be concerned about the impact of losing not only employees, but also the information and the skills they take with them. It's not as if every employee can return all their knowledge along with their keys, uniforms, and materials. The information, knowledge, skills, and relationships they developed while working for you are also important assets—sometimes more important than you realize.

Have you ever thought to calculate the value of the information and knowledge you have supplied to your employees? Sometimes you might even think about charging a fee for all the training you have made available. How long did it take you to finally get a particular employee trained for that employee to perform at a high level of productivity? In some cases it may have been months. Consider the product knowledge you supply to your employees. Think about the customer service and sales training you have invested in your employees. Think about the team-building and supervisory training you have supplied. Think about the lost revenues for your company. Think about the impact on *you* as *you* support the slow, methodical process of training the replacement employee to be a fully contributing member of the organization.

There *is* an impact, and it is very important!

It is almost impossible to record and classify all the information each employee has accumulated. The good employee has developed relationships with customers and coworkers that may have a profound impact on the productivity of the group. As we all know, certain people make a greater difference than others when working

> In losing employees, you lose valuable experience and knowledge.

RETENTION & RECOGNITION

together in a team environment. Certain clients and customers also demand a level of skill, service, and consistency when doing business with your company. When individuals leave your company and these individuals have developed positive relationships with your customers, the potential for problems is very great.

In many cases clients and customers actively seek out former employees to replace your company for the delivery of the service or product your company had been supplying. The clients or customers likely have no allegiance to your company; their allegiance is to the employee.

Your potential loss is enormous.

When you lose an employee you are also losing a part of your company. But it's not as simple as just losing a part of your company. You are losing a portion of the company you cannot even identify. It is the ultimate paradox of business that the obvious individual contributions of employees are frequently enhanced by unknown and undefined contributions. Frequently it is the undefined contribution that makes an employee so valuable. In effect it is this long list of undefined and unknown contributions to the organizations that make the retention of employees so important.

> Losing an employee is losing, perhaps, an undefinable contribution to the company that is essential to your business.

WHAT IS TURNOVER?

Once you have an employee on the payroll, it is in your best interest to keep him or her working with you. Of course, you must ensure that this person is operating at a high level of productivity within the organization.

According to your department or company budget, how many employees should you have in any given year? In other words, what are your budgeted staffing requirements? What is the total number of employees or FTEs (full time equivalents) you have in your annual budget?

In the past year, how many employees left your department or company, for any reason, during the full twelve-month period?

When you take these two numbers and place them in the following equation you are able to calculate what is know as the *employee turnover rate* for your company.

RETENTION & RECOGNITION

$$\text{Employee turnover rate} = \frac{\text{Number of Employees who Left}}{\text{Number of Staff Budgeted}} \times 100$$

For example, at the WOW Company they have a budget that allows for 75 hourly nonexempt employees and 33 exempt employees. They are very interested in finding out the turnover rate for each classification of employee because they use different recruiting strategies and the groups receive different benefit packages.

During the past year 20 hourly nonexempt employees left the company for a variety of reasons, including resignations and terminations. To calculate the turnover rate for the nonexempt employees the WOW Company divides the total number of nonexempt employees who left by the number of bugeted nonexempt positions and multiplies by 100.

$$(20 \div 75) \times 100 = 27\%$$

The turnover rate for hourly nonexempt employees at WOW Company was 27 percent during the last year.

During the past year twelve exempt employees left for a variety of reasons, including resignations and terminations. To calculate the turnover rate for this group the WOW Company divides the total number of exempt employees who left by the number of budgeted exempt positions and multiplies by 100.

$$(12 \div 33) \times 100 = 36\%$$

The turnover rate for exempt employees at WOW Company was 36 percent for the past year.

The turnover rate for the *entire* WOW Company is determined by dividing the total number of employees who left by the total number of budgeted staffed positions.

$$((20 + 12) \div (75 + 33)) \times 100 = 30\%$$

The total employee turnover rate at WOW Company was 30 percent for the year.

This chapter will help you to make the most of your recruiting dollars and help your business to reduce the unnecessary expense of

RETENTION & RECOGNITION

restaffing chronic problem positions by helping you to create strategies to reduce your employee turnover.

CONDUCT RESEARCH

Before you can address issues regarding retention and recognition, you and your company must identify if you have a problem and what the problem might be.

Your company may already be doing such a good job of retaining and recognizing employees that very few people are leaving. Employees are feeling respected, valued, involved, and connected to an organization that is fun to work with.

So before you go any farther in this chapter, answer these questions:

> A high turnover rate is an indication of some problem within the company.

1. Is your turnover rate greater than 20 percent? (In a larger company you may want to calculate this rate by division or department.)
2. Have you had a large number of terminations for just cause during the past twelve months?
3. Did you exceed your recruiting advertising budget? How much over budget were you?
4. Are employees complaining about constantly having to train new employees?
5. Have you been experiencing excessive quality, accuracy, or customer service problems?

If you answered "yes" to most of these questions, your company may be suffering from employee retention problems.

Companies that have employee retention problems generally exhibit similar characteristics:

- Low productivity
- High turnover
- Low morale
- High incidence of illness
- Low enthusiasm
- High degree of cynicism

RETENTION & RECOGNITION

When investigated, this employee retention problem leads to discovering a number of critical issues that affect the company negatively. These tend to fall under one of four major categories:

- Unclear and poorly structured communication systems
- Unclear and poorly defined policies and procedures
- Unclear and poorly defined compensation programs
- Low levels of employee involvement

Unclear and poorly structured communication systems make it virtually impossible for members of the organization to know what you want to achieve. Without this communication road map your staff may decide to set their own course and achieve objectives that are not desired by you and the company. The well-designed communication strategy for both internal and external communication will help you to stay on top of your business objectives. These defined strategies will also make your employees, at all levels, better able to accomplish their job duties in the most efficient and effective manner possible.

Unclear and poorly defined policies and procedures create opportunities for error and potentially damaging situations. Operational policies and procedures ensure quality product, service, and follow-up. Administrative and personnel polices and procedures ensure a smooth-running business with a higher degree of quality assurance and fewer legal problems. Employees who work with clearly defined policies and procedures are able to manage the day-to-day activities without having to ask you every little question. They become better able to achieve the objectives you want them to achieve.

Unclear and poorly defined compensation programs invariably create interpersonal resentments and conflicts. New people are paid more than highly functioning senior employees because there is no clear compensation policy. The senior employee finds out and is sincerely hurt by the perceived lack of respect and compensation. The money is important, but more important is the perceived value they have within the organization. The time and energy needed to "fix"

> Well-defined communication strategies help keep employees involved and productive.

RETENTION & RECOGNITION

this type of problem are enormous. And, to make it worse, the problem is never really "fixed" because the senior employee will always resent the fact that he or she had to speak with you about it. It was embarrassing and humiliating that this person needed to demand recognition for the hard work he or she has been giving to the company. Watch this senior employee. He or she will soon be part of your turnover rate.

Low levels of employee involvement create a sense of unimportance and in turn create low levels of motivation and productivity. Employees want and need to be involved. They spend most of their time at work. They want the work to be interesting and challenging. Treat your employees as partners and as intelligent contributing members of the team. You will see an immediate change in the way they behave, perform, and respond to the challenges you present.

USING EXIT INTERVIEWS

One of the most effective ways to capture information about the reasons for your turnover rate or about your ability to retain employees is the use of exit interviews. These simple devices offer you great opportunities to learn why employees are leaving your company and what they plan to do in the future. Frequently a well-constructed and well-executed exit interview can create a bridge that will encourage an employee to return to your company at a future date with increased skills and knowledge. The benefits of conducting quality exit interviews are enormous.

Exit interviews can be conducted via formal interviews or via direct-mail questionnaires.

Following are some sample exit interviews you may want to adapt for your company:

EXIT INTERVIEW QUESTIONNAIRE, USED IN AN INTERVIEW FORMAT

The purpose of the exit interview is to obtain information that may assist the organization in improving the way in which business is conducted. The exit interview also allows the departing employee

> Exit interviews are useful in pinpointing possible problems within the company.

RETENTION & RECOGNITION

to obtain some advice and support as this person moves on to his or her next career opportunity.

Inform the individual that you will be taking notes and that the information shared during this session will be brought to the attention of the various people who have had an impact on them while employed by your company.

Impress on the individual that their honest and detailed comments will be very valuable to the company and to other employees remaining with the company.

RETENTION & RECOGNITION

Employee's name: _____ Unit: _____

Date of resignation or last date worked: _____ Job title: _____

Supervisor's name: _____

Why are you leaving our organization? _____

_____

_____

Why now? _____

_____

_____

Do you have a new job? _____ Where? _____

Title/position: _____

Is your new rate of pay lower than _____, equal to _____, or higher than _____

what you were paid at *[name of your company]*?

How much will you be earning? _____

What did you like best about your job or jobs at *[name of your company]*?

_____

_____

What did you like least about your job or jobs at *[name of your company]*?

_____

_____

What changes would you make to improve the department in which you worked?

_____

_____

RETENTION & RECOGNITION

What changes would you make to improve the company as a whole?

_____

_____

Did you receive your performance appraisals on time? _____

Explain how your performance appraisals were helpful or not helpful.

_____

_____

_____

When was your last performance appraisal? _____

What was the outcome of the last appraisal? _____

Mention the opportunities _[name of your company]_ has offered you for career advancement.

_____

_____

Describe how well informed you were kept regarding company policies, procedures, programs, and activities. _____

_____

Do you have any other advice, or suggestions that may help to make _[name or your company]_ a better company and a better place to work? _____

_____

_____

Interview conducted by _____

RETENTION & RECOGNITION

EXIT INTERVIEW QUESTIONNAIRE, USED IN A DIRECT MAIL FORMAT

To obtain reliable and consistent data you should routinely send an exit questionnaire to every employee who leaves your company. Even if a departing employee had a formal in-person exit interview you will want to send that person one of these surveys. You should plan to have a member of your staff keep track of the results in a data-base. The information captured will help you to make strategic decisions about policies, procedures, and employee relations issues.

As in all initiatives, the key to success is consistency. Be sure this form is sent to all exiting employees, all the time.

Dear *[former employee name]:*

We are sorry you have decided to leave *[name of your company]* and hope that this career move you have taken will be positive and productive. Because you helped to contribute to the success of *[name of your company]*, we would like to ask you a few questions that may help us to improve the manner in which we conduct our business.

Please take a moment to answer the following questions and then send this survey back to us in the stamped, self-addressed envelope supplied.

Again, thank you for your hard work at *[name of your company]* and good luck in your new position.

Sincerely,

[your name]
President

RETENTION & RECOGNITION

Please circle the dot that best expresses how you feel about:

The Job

VERY SATISFIED	SLIGHTLY SATISFIED	NEUTRAL	SLIGHTLY DISSATISFIED	VERY DISSATISFIED	
●	●	●	●	●	1. The training you received.
●	●	●	●	●	2. The opportunity to use your abilities and skills.
●	●	●	●	●	3. The opportunity to do challenging and interesting work
●	●	●	●	●	4. Your workload.
●	●	●	●	●	5. The recognition for the work you did.
●	●	●	●	●	6. The amount of responsibility you were given.
●	●	●	●	●	7. The opportunity to supervise other people.
●	●	●	●	●	8. Your pay.

If you have any additional comments, please write them in the space provided:

Communications, Policies, and Practices

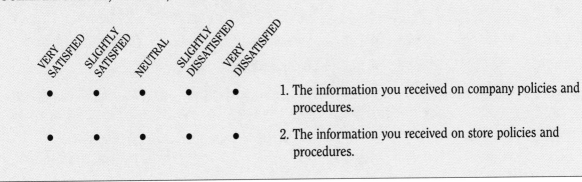

VERY SATISFIED	SLIGHTLY SATISFIED	NEUTRAL	SLIGHTLY DISSATISFIED	VERY DISSATISFIED	
●	●	●	●	●	1. The information you received on company policies and procedures.
●	●	●	●	●	2. The information you received on store policies and procedures.

RETENTION & RECOGNITION

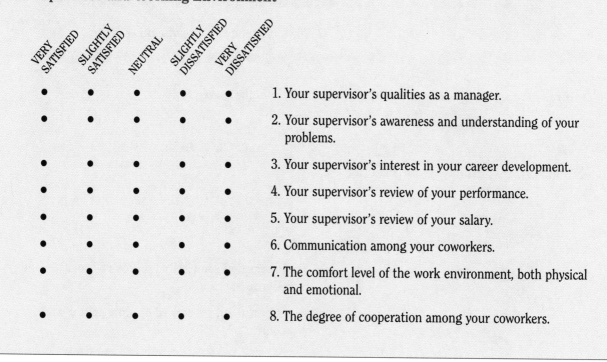

• • • • •   3. The overtime policies and procedures.

• • • • •   4. The policies regarding internal promotion and advancement.

• • • • •   5. The performance review policy and procedures.

• • • • •   6. The opportunities to participate in decision-making.

• • • • •   7. The reception of new ideas.

• • • • •   8. The speed with which information was communicated.

If you have any additional comments, please write them in the space provided:

Your Supervisor and Working Environment

VERY SATISFIED	SLIGHTLY SATISFIED	NEUTRAL	SLIGHTLY DISSATISFIED	VERY DISSATISFIED	
•	•	•	•	•	1. Your supervisor's qualities as a manager.
•	•	•	•	•	2. Your supervisor's awareness and understanding of your problems.
•	•	•	•	•	3. Your supervisor's interest in your career development.
•	•	•	•	•	4. Your supervisor's review of your performance.
•	•	•	•	•	5. Your supervisor's review of your salary.
•	•	•	•	•	6. Communication among your coworkers.
•	•	•	•	•	7. The comfort level of the work environment, both physical and emotional.
•	•	•	•	•	8. The degree of cooperation among your coworkers.

RETENTION & RECOGNITION

If you have any additional comments, please write them in the space provided:

Working Conditions and Benefits

VERY SATISFIED	SLIGHTLY SATISFIED	NEUTRAL	SLIGHTLY DISSATISFIED	VERY DISSATISFIED	
●	●	●	●	●	1. Physical working conditions.
●	●	●	●	●	2. Absence (sick) policy.
●	●	●	●	●	3. Lateness policy.
●	●	●	●	●	4. Vacation policy.
●	●	●	●	●	5. Medical coverage (individual).
●	●	●	●	●	6. Medical coverage (family).
●	●	●	●	●	7. Life insurance.
●	●	●	●	●	8. 401(k) program.
●	●	●	●	●	9. The Bonus program.
●	●	●	●	●	10. The 20 % discount.
●	●	●	●	●	11. The employee referral programs.

If you have any additional comments, please write them in the space provided:

RETENTION & RECOGNITION

Please keep in mind the need to be consistent with the use of all management tools. These exit interview tools work only when used properly and consistently. You must be sure that these direct-mail exit interviews are sent to all terminated employees, even the ones who have had the one-on-one personal interview. The data you collect from these interviews can be very valuable as you adjust your recruiting, retention, and recognition programs to reduce turnover.

WHAT KIND OF ENVIRONMENT DO YOU HAVE?

To obtain a measurement of your company environment, answer the following questions:

1. What is the feeling within your organization?
2. Are people highly motivated and charged up about doing a great job?
3. Do people come to work eager to attack a new problem?
4. Do people help each other solving problems even if they are not directly involved?
5. Do people look forward to working with other members of the organization?
6. Do people feel comfortable asking questions?
7. Are people willing to take chances and possibly make mistakes?
8. Are people able to have a well-balanced home life and still give 110 percent to the company?
9. How would you describe the morale of the employees in your company?

As you think about these questions, you will begin to understand the environment you have created for your employees. It is this environment that will have the greatest impact on the retention of the employees you worked so hard to recruit and hire.

A strong supportive environment that promotes respect and recognition for all people will help to create a positive working

A positive work environment helps to retain employees.

RETENTION & RECOGNITION

environment. An organization that offers support and assistance when people and departments are in need also helps to foster an environment that encourages other people to share and work together. A company that encourages employees to balance home life and work life creates an environment in which everyone understands the need to pitch in when necessary because the company is willing to do the same for the individual when necessary.

THE COST OF EMPLOYEE TURNOVER

The cost of employee turnover has a direct impact on your ability to recruit and retain the best candidates for all your available jobs. Every time you are faced with replacing an existing employee due to turnover, you are wasting money you could be spending more productively. When you are looking to turn the red bottom line into a black bottom line, you may find some black ink with better retention of your employees.

To reduce your employee hiring costs, you must first begin to think in a strategic manner. Consider the long-term goal of your company and how you want to get there. What are the incremental steps along the way? What can you do independently? What will need the assistance of other people to be accomplished? How much of your operating budget can you dedicate to this effort? What do you expect this investment to achieve? Will you be able to measure your success?

When you have gone through the strategic thinking process you can then begin analyzing specific situations. The details of specific situations will change, but your strategy will remain the same.

For example:

Have you priced classified advertising in your local newspapers recently? If you have, you know how expensive it can be to advertise in the help wanted section of a newspaper. The greater the distribution, the more expensive the rate.

Print advertising is the most prevalent form of first-line recruiting for companies. Scan any help wanted section of a newspaper and you have an immediate snapshot of which companies are growing rapidly and which companies are managing poorly.

> Employee turnover is a waste of company funds used in hiring another employee.

RETENTION & RECOGNITION

Companies place adds for two basic reasons:
- To staff vacated/empty positions.
- To staff a newly formed position.

The up-front cost is the same for both scenarios but the return on investment is dramatically different. Let's explore the difference.

SCENARIO 1

A growing company has forecast future sales and recognizes the need to support these sales with additional staff. The company identifies the staffing need; develops a job profile, job description, and job specifications; and then moves into a recruiting mode.

Generally, a classified ad is placed with the local urban and suburban newspapers. Sometimes a headhunter/recruiting firm is engaged to assist with acquiring new talent. The cost of a service such as this can range from 10 percent to 40 percent of the first-year salary of the individual hired.

This company is planning ahead to ensure the increased sales forecast will be appropriately supported by additional staff. The new employee salary and benefits, as well as the cost of recruiting for this position, have all been included in the business forecast. A talented person has an exciting position and a well-run company has a quality new employee. Everyone wins!

SCENARIO 2

A company needs to replace an existing position.

A company has maintained steady sales with minor fluctuation. An employee resigns or is fired from this position. The existing job profile, job description, and job specifications may be reviewed to determine if any adjustments are necessary.

Almost invariably, the company will place a classified ad in an urban and suburban newspaper. If the position has turned over or changed frequently, the company may choose to go directly to a headhunter or recruiting/search firm for assistance. The company believes that the recruiting/search firm will help solve the problem for them.

It becomes obvious very quickly that the problem is not just finding qualified candidates.

> Money is spent more wisely in hunting for new positions than hiring for existing positions.

RETENTION & RECOGNITION

In both scenarios the initial expenses are very similar. Until we dig a little deeper.

When we look at the return on investment in Scenario 1, we recognize increased revenues and a growing organization. The cost of hiring a new staff member is a small portion of the value of increased sales and has been considered in calculating the compensation for the new position.

In Scenario 2 the organization is not experiencing any dramatic increase or decrease in growth. The cost of recruiting the new employee increases the basic overhead because it is not linked to added growth.

Although the actual dollars expended are the same, the financial impact is dramatic.

COST OF TURNOVER EXAMPLE

Let's imagine a situation where an employee has given two weeks' notice.

The administrative office employee earns $800 per week, not including any benefits and incentives they may be eligible for. The employee has given two weeks' notice so we can be fairly sure that this employee has been thinking about leaving for at least four weeks prior. In most cases it is fair to say that during these six weeks the employee's productivity will not be at 100 percent. In fact he or she may be functioning at only 50 percent productivity. Even the very best employee will be preoccupied with a variety of tasks that must be completed prior to starting the new job. Many of these tasks will not be related to your company or the job you are paying this person to complete while in your employ. There is a definite decline in the productivity and the value you will receive from this employee during these six weeks. Needless to say, in many cases the six weeks may be months. Frequently an employee will make a decision to leave an organization many months prior to the date he or she finally leaves. You must be prepared to calculate the cost of this reduced productivity during this time.

While we are examining this issue, consider the impact an employee might have on an organization if that person is thinking about leaving. As you know, employees talk among themselves and share information, even when it may be somewhat sensitive. It is fair to expect that other people, not including you, will know that a co-worker is planning to leave well before the two weeks' notice date. During these weeks and sometimes months, the departing employee can do serious damage to the organization. Well-placed comments and criticism can begin to create a negative climate that makes it easier for the person to leave and may oftentimes lead to other people resigning.

As this employee prepares to leave the company you will need to recruit, hire, and train a new employee. Depending on your recruiting strategy, you may have a new employee ready to fill the position, and you can arrange for the resigning employee to train the new employee. If that is not possible, you must then have another employee train the new employee while still doing his or her own work. Clearly, the productivity in both cases will be greatly reduced. The exiting or transfererred employee will be pressed to maintain the level of productivity and quality, and the new employee will not be getting focused, dedicated training for the job he or she was hired to fill.

Meanwhile, the employees doing the training may begin to resent the fact that they have to do double work and not get double the pay. Morale is affected, and frequently a company will begin to see an "attitude" problem.

There is a direct cost here, and it is yours! All this reduced productivity will cost your company plenty.

The cost of the example we just described would be as follows:

Four weeks of reduced productivity @ 50% productivity	**$1,600**
Two weeks' notice period @ 50% productivity	**$800**
Recruiting and advertising expenses	**$1,000**
Interviewing costs	**$2,000**
Training for new employee, 4 weeks @ $800/wk	**$3,200**
Trainer salary @ 25% for 4 weeks ($1,000 salary)	**$1,000**
Total Cost	**$9,600**

RETENTION & RECOGNITION

Try to keep as many of your employees as possible. Try to make each employee a highly productive member of the organization. Try to keep all your employees working with you. By retaining your employees you will ensure the retention of the knowledge, skill, and abilities that are your best method of keeping and increasing your client and customer base.

THE ROLE OF EMPLOYEE RECOGNITION

Studies on studies have shown that employees have very specific needs, as do all people. Most of the time managers and business owners think that the only thing an employee wants is more money. In reality that is very far from the truth.

In studies of thousands of employees in a variety of business environments a consistent theme emerges. People are more concerned with being recognized for the work they do than for any other issue. The next most important concern for employees is knowing that they are part of "the big picture," that they are "in on things," and that they are included in the overall process of the business.

The bottom line is that people want to be valued, respected, and recognized for what they contribute to the organization. People are proud and want to experience recognition for whatever they do. At first glance this seems easy enough to accomplish. But as a manager and/or owner of a company you must seriously consider the strategy you will employ to achieve this sensibility of recognition.

In reality, employees are not as concerned with money as people think. In the list of the ten most important concerns for employees, money was rated right in the middle.

First and foremost, employees want recognition, involvement, and honest concern about their welfare from their employer.

Interestingly, in the past, most managers and owners have thought employees were not at all concerned about being in on things or knowing what was going on. It is obvious that we have a lot to learn about each other.

> Many employees leave a company because they do not feel involved or valuable.

RETENTION & RECOGNITION

Look at this list of the top three issues that motivate employees:

- Full appreciation for work done
- Feeling of being "in on things"
- Assistance with personal problems

When examined, you will recognize that you, alone and with no budget, can give employees just what they want. It doesn't cost anything to say "thank you for doing such a fine job." It doesn't cost a cent to inform your employees that a new product or service or system will be rolled out on a particular date. It doesn't cost you any hard dollars to ask employees about the health of their family or if they have resolved a personal problem of which you are aware.

In reality, the issues most important to employees are the issues most easy for an organization to supply. But they must be supplied in a fashion that is sincere and consistently applied. You cannot make employee recognition a program that happens at a certain time each year with bells and whistles and fancy awards. The creation of a positive employee recognition strategy demands an ongoing commitment to employees as people and as partners within the company. It must be real and it must be a part of the day-to-day culture of the organization. The annual awards ceremony will be meaningful and have impact if it is really the highlight of an organization that demonstrates recognition and respect for all employees all the time.

Employees will respond with enthusiasm and energy when they know they are valued. They will contribute at higher levels of productivity and creativity when they know they are recognized and valued. They will accept new challenges and will transform problems into opportunities when they know, when they feel, when they experience, recognition, and respect from their manager.

Many organizations try to create employee recognition programs without first establishing the foundation of valuing and respecting employees. When an employee recognition program is just a program and not part of the fabric of the company, it fails to

> By investing time in the emotional well-being of employees, managers can avoid turnover later on.

RETENTION & RECOGNITION

achieve its objectives. When the program is an extension of the company culture and sensibility, the program has great impact.

Employee recognition programs can be whatever you want them to be. They should reflect your personal style. If you feel that athletic, outdoor activities are important and valuable, build your employee recognition program around that theme.

For example:

The owner of ABC Company is a woman who is extremely health-conscious. She is dedicated to healthy eating, exercise, and an active lifestyle. She has established a business that supplies cleaning services to a wide range of clients and has more than a hundred employees.

Her employee base is split equally between male and female. The population is 70 percent nonexempt and 30 percent exempt. Most of the nonexempt employees have direct contact with the clients.

As an incentive when employees are hired, they are offered the opportunity to join one of a number of health clubs that have preferred rates with ABC Company. At the time of hire the company offers the new employee the opportunity to join a club with a preferred rate negotiated by the owner. After three months with ABC Company, employees who signed up for the health club are given a bonus, which pays for their initiation fee at the health club. After one year with the company the employee will have 25 percent of the health club membership fee paid for by the company. After two years the company will pay 50 percent of the health club fee. After three years the company will pay 75 percent of the health club fee. Once the employee has been with the company for five years the company pays 100 percent of the health club fee.

The owner is very interested in keeping her employees healthy and motivated to continue working for ABC Company. To achieve this objective she also utilizes other strategies.

She sponsors monthly workshops on nutrition and invites specialists into the company to present information and demonstrate

> Being concerned about the health of employees gains their trust and encourages them to perform well.

RETENTION & RECOGNITION

products. Employees are given time to attend these workshops and are encouraged to participate.

ABC Company has an annual outing at a major park that allows for a wide variety of family activities. A cross section of employees are selected to plan and execute this annual event within a defined budget. All employees are invited with their families. At this outing, employees are given T-shirts or hats that designate the number of years they have worked with the company. Everyone gets something, even the family members. The owner recognizes how important the family members are for the productivity of each employee.

WOW! You may be thinking that this is a very large price to pay for recognition. But the alternative will likely be even more expensive if you consider the high cost of turnover and the routine replacement of the people, knowledge, and skills within your organization.

Not all employee recognition needs to cost money. You can take some very simple actions and achieve great results. When you combine all the actions together in a comprehensive strategy you are setting a course for success.

Here are some additional suggestions for recognizing employees:

- Create a vehicle for employee to recognize other employees who help them in ways that are frequently overlooked—personal recognition for the person who always is there to help out in a crunch.
- Develop a program to recognize teams that work especially well together to achieve a defined objective. Make the guidelines measurable and linked to the business objectives.
- Reinvent and consistently follow the employee-of-the-month program that most companies have had in the past. The key is to keep it going and to make the award meaningful. How are they recognized? How does everyone learn about this? Do all the employees of the month get together at certain times of the year?

> Even small gestures of gratitude can greatly improve employee morale.

RETENTION & RECOGNITION

- Create employee-of-the-month focus groups where those employees are asked to assist with business problem solving and creative strategic development.
- Periodically surprise everyone with a special award: the Just Because You Did a Great Job Award. Pretty soon people will begin doing the kinds of things you appreciate in the hope they'll receive one of the coveted Just Because You Did a Great Job Award. It's a great way to develop your company culture quickly.
- Rather than having a discipline procedure that only tracks problems and performance issues, have a performance development policy. Let this performance development policy offer managers the opportunity to praise employees when they reach a new milestone in   personal professional development. No longer will people fear the personnel file, they will want to get statements of positive development put into their file.
- Don't forget the tried but true 5-10-15 year seniority awards, plaques, and events. Again the key is consistent application of these procedures, especially when times are not so good and cash flow is low. This is not the time to skimp on these awards. People need to have some sense of security during the really slow business times.
- It may simple, but a friendly note to say "thank you" goes a long way. Consider writing notes to people you catch doing something the way you want it done. Again the key is to make it personal and to consistently follow through.

> Reward employees for outstanding service and longevity.

QUESTIONS AND ANSWERS

1. **What if I don't have a budget to implement a recognition program for my department?**
   Even with limited or no budgets, supervisors and managers can make a difference. Consider walking up to employees when you see them doing a task correctly and letting them

RETENTION & RECOGNITION

know that you appreciate their effort. Write that same employee a note that will get copied to your boss, so that the employee knows other people have been informed. At staff meetings use the good work of employees as a role model for others in the work group. None of these costs anything except your time and determination.

2. **What happens when exit interviews tell me something about one of my managers and how they have been negatively impacting the organization?**

Start by reflecting on what you have heard and/or read in the exit interview. Consider the source and the circumstances. Then take more than a few minutes to reconstruct your history of supervision of the manager in question. Do you really know what has been going on his or her department? You may be shocked to realize how little you know about your own operation. Once you have done all your research and reflection, have an open conversation with the manager in question regarding the issues presented in the exit interview. Use the exit interview information as a steppingstone to an honest, direct, and valuable conversation about the manager's job duties, the value of the employee in question, and how you can work better together to retain more productive employees.

3. **I don't have time to organize employee recognition events and I don't have a large enough staff to do all the work to bring a program together. What do I do?**

First you'll need to decide what you think you want. Then you'll need to communicate that need to your staff, including all employees, and ask for their help. Create a volunteer task force to develop a plan of action for you to review. Based on the plan of action, create a work team or committee to make the idea come alive. Allow your own employees to create a program that will respond to their needs while staying within your original expectation and any budget you determine to be appropriate.

> Take information gained in an exit interview and use it as a base for research into potential problem in the company.

RETENTION & RECOGNITION

4. What does it mean if I cannot hold on to my employees?

At first blush it sounds like you should reread this chapter. More than likely you have a number of issues that are challenging your organization. It could be your management style, or your compensation program, or your work environment, or your policies and procedures. You should begin by asking some of the people who once worked for you. Call them and ask them to be honest with you. Let them know you are sincerely concerned. They will be happy to hear from you.

5. What can I do if I don't get any recognition as an employee?

It may be time for you to start blowing your own horn. You should take every opportunity to promote the good work you do for your company. Without going overboard, let management know of your successes by sending a note to your supervisor thanking that person for his or her help making a particular project so very successful. Send a copy to that person's boss. Everyone will be happy to hear good news and you will have name recognition with the next level of management.

6. Is there anything I can do when I realize I missed an opportunity to recognize someone's contribution?

Yes, there is. Go directly to the person and say, "I'm sorry, but I forget to let you know how much I appreciated the work you did on . . ." Then take a few minutes to explain why you thought the issue warranted your attention and comment. Again apologize for missing the opportunity the first time and ask the person to let you know when he or she plans take on a similar project. Let the person know that maybe you might like the opportunity to work with him or her on a future project.

7. Should I ever pay someone not to leave the company?

Before you take out your wallet, find out why the person is leaving. If it is a money issue and you know you haven't been paying the person fairly, you might want to rectify the

> It is never too late to recognize the contribution of an employee.

RETENTION & RECOGNITION

situation. The damage may already be done and you may be throwing money at a lost cause, or maybe this information will help benefit a larger group of people and turn the situation into a very positive improvement for the company. The best thing to do is to learn as much as possible about why the person is leaving and then make an informed decision from that point.

8. **Is there ever any case where it is acceptable to have turnover?**

   You will always experience turnover. Turnover is not just a sign of poor management practices. Sometimes turnover is a sign of developmental learning, with people moving on to other job opportunities in other companies. Sometimes employees are looking for more growth and your company cannot offer the growth. In many cases these same employees will return to your company with greater skills and abilities and will help you move to the next level of company-building.

9. **I have an annual recognition program but only half of my employees show up. Why?**

   Maybe the program is considered a joke by the employees. If the recognition program is not supported and promoted by you and the entire company, then the employees realize that it and they are not very important. Why would anyone want to go to an event for unimportant people?

10. **How do I incorporate bonuses into my recognition program?**

    You can do it in any way you might like. One simple way is to link bonuses to the seniority of the person in the company. You could also link the bonus to the person who achieved the greatest success with whatever you are recognizing with the program. You may want to physically tie your bonus program to your recognition program, allowing for every employee to receive something. It doesn't hurt to make people feel special and to let others share the success of specific individuals.

STREETWISE advice

- **Good employee retention is more than cost savings. It is the value of keeping the knowledge base within your company.**

- **Your turnover percentage is your best thermometer of the health of your business. Monitor this rate religiously.**

- **Have your payroll department maintain accurate and easy-to-access information regarding turnover.**

- **Keep track of your recruiting and advertising expenses.**
  The costs for recruiting and advertising, job fairs, flyers, and any incentive programs should be tracked very carefully. You will need this information to determine the success of your programs and to establish future budgets for recruiting and retention and recognition.

- **Get your policies and procedures in order. You will keep more of your good employees with clear policies and procedures.**

- **Set up a process for conducting exit interviews regularly and consistently.**
  The data collected will be invaluable to your business efforts.

- **Periodically, you may wish to conduct an employee attitude survey.**
  This tool will give you a good window into the way in which your rank-and-file employees are thinking. An ounce of prevention is worth a pound of cure.

> Be aware of the employees' attitude, to fix problems of morale before they become too negative.

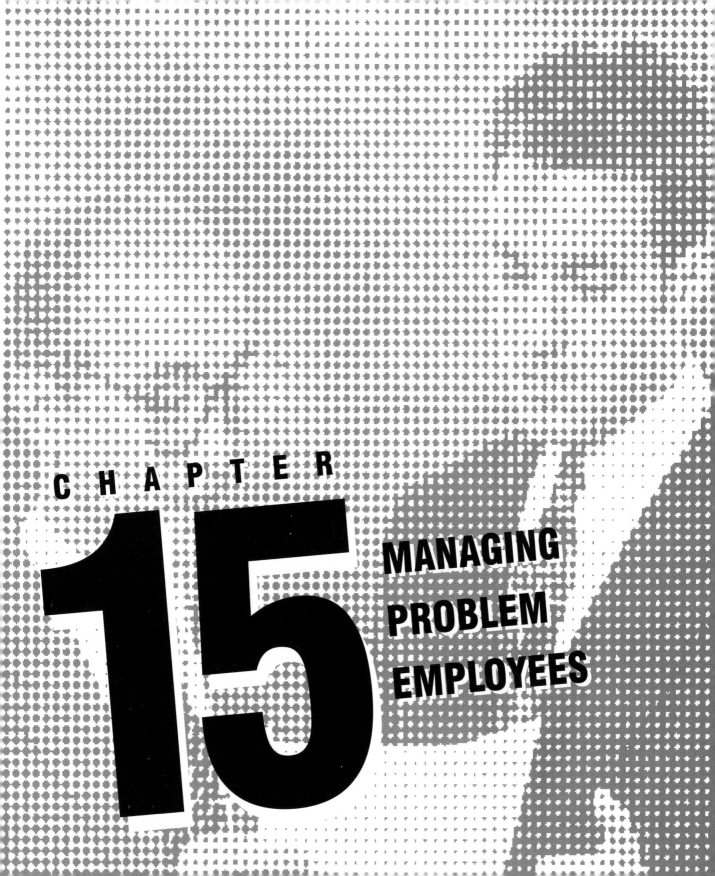

CHAPTER

15

MANAGING
PROBLEM
EMPLOYEES

Y ou can turn around the performance of *almost* any problem employee. Virtually everyone wants to succeed at work, give it their best effort, and get along with people too. When shortcomings or problems arise, they can almost always be overcome with some additional coaching or with a positive, but frank discussion of the issues at hand. As much as possible, you want to leave people with the feeling that you are helping and supporting them, not reprimanding them.

MANAGING PROBLEM EMPLOYEES

MAKING VALUE JUDGMENTS

In any situation, as part of a manager-employee relationship, the potential for a clash of motivations, fears, competencies, and communication styles is always present. For instance, you might be a direct communicator who takes action quickly. But an employee who reports to you may need time to methodically weigh alternatives before responding to your question or inquiry. As a result, you may mislabel this employee as slow, incompetent, rigid, or that all-encompassing word *difficult*.

IMPACT ON THE COMPANY

When you have a disagreement with a difficult employee, the impact can be felt throughout the company even more so by employees who are not vocal about their unhappiness over any particular issue. Your difficult employee will ignore your message and obviously make it tough for you to lead and ensure continued productivity if the disagreement spreads and affects other employees. This is especially true if other employees, whether or not they are vocal, view you, the manager, as the source of the difficult employee's problems.

TAKING CONTROL

You need to take control—that is, *take control of the situation, not the person*. You can be proactive by learning techniques to head off difficult situations before they become disasters. By learning to "read" others, you can objectively describe behaviors, then create and implement solutions. Think of resolving these one-on-one situations as a dance; until now you and your difficult employee have been tripping each other up. Now you must take it upon yourself to lead and hope that the employee decides to follow.

You take control of a difficult situation when you commit to learning results-oriented communication skills such as listening proactively, asking open-ended questions, and matching your words with your body language. These skills will enable you to persuade your difficult employee to buy into your goals and objectives.

> By taking control of a bad situation, you can work to find the best solution with minimal damage to the rest of the company.

MANAGING PROBLEM EMPLOYEES

MANAGEMENT QUESTIONNAIRE

Before looking at the answers and commentary, go through the following questionnaire to see if your perception of how individuals respond to particular questions and statements matches with the their true response. Choose the answer that matches your gut reaction to each statement.

1. What generally happens when you ask a question that starts with "why"?
   - The person gets defensive. _____
   - You get a direct answer quickly. _____
   - You begin to open a dialogue. _____

2. Asking people to get involved with providing a solution to a difficult situation . . .
   - takes too much time. _____
   - gives away authority. _____
   - motivates them to achieve. _____

3. Comparing someone's actions to those of a controversial, well-known figure . . .
   - provides a point of reference. _____
   - belittles the person. _____
   - puts the person in his or her place. _____

4. Asking an employee a question such as "What's the real issue?". . .
   - gives too much credence to his or her bad behavior. _____
   - can reveal more problems than you want to deal with. _____
   - opens dialogue and holds him or her accountable for his or her behavior. _____

5. Describing someone's performance as "weak and unacceptable" . . .
   - provides valuable information. _____
   - focuses his or her attention on performance issues. _____
   - is considered, in part, a value judgment. _____

MANAGING PROBLEM EMPLOYEES

6. Providing step-by-step instructions . . .
   - is sometimes appropriate and necessary. _____
   - is too time-consuming. _____
   - provides measurable results. _____

7. People who let their personal problems affect their professional work are . . .
   - undisciplined. _____
   - unprofessional. _____
   - human. _____

8. Accommodating and changing the rules for one person . . .
   - causes everyone to feel entitled to special privileges. _____
   - paints the organization as compassionate. _____
   - hinders organizational progress and productivity. _____

9. You supervise a former peer and suspect his or her behavior to be motivated by jealousy. You should . . .
   - say to yourself, "It's the employee's problem, not mine." _____
   - ask him or her if your assumptions are correct. _____
   - give a little leeway while he or she adjusts to the new situation. _____

10. Communicating assertively . . .
    - means being aggressive. _____
    - means that you are being straightforward with the person. _____
    - puts your needs before that of the employee. _____

MANAGING PROBLEM EMPLOYEES

SCORING AND INTERPRETING YOUR RESPONSES

Now review the questions again, this time scoring your answers as indicated for each question. Compare your answers with the scoring and review the commentary on the best response to each statement.

1. What generally happens when you ask a question that starts with "why?"
   - The person gets defensive.   3 points
   - You get a direct answer quickly.   1 point
   - You begin to open a dialogue.   0 points

Commentary *When you start a question with "why," employees feel threatened or at the very least defensive about their actions and look to confront you rather than explore the issue with you. You may get, from time to time, a direct answer such as "I don't know" or "I'll have to look into that," but from a purely emotional standpoint, employees will feel like you are backing them into a corner. Thus the first response is most appropriate.*

2. Asking people to get involved with providing a solution to a difficult situation . . .
   - takes too much time.   0
   - gives away authority.   1
   - motivates them to achieve.   3

Commentary *One of the most rewarding aspects of managing a difficult situation successfully is cooperatively working toward a solution with a difficult employee. He or she will feel like a part of the solution rather than the source of a problem and will be more motivated to work out solutions to future problems with you without resorting to difficult behavior.*

3. Comparing someone's actions to those of a controversial, well-known figure . . .
   - provides a point of reference.   1
   - belittles the person.   3
   - puts the person in his or her place. 0

> When an employee feels threatened, they become defensive and confrontational.

MANAGING PROBLEM EMPLOYEES

Commentary *When you make light of a well-known or controversial individual in the context of a conversation with your difficult employee and his or her actions, it only serves to make a difficult situation even worse. Thus the second response is most appropriate.*

4. Asking an employee a question such as "What's the real issue?"...
   - gives too much credence to his or her bad behavior.   0
   - can reveal more problems than you want to deal with.   1
   - opens dialogue and holds him or her accountable for his or her behavior.   3

> Open dialogue between manager and employee can help avoid hostile confrontations.

Commentary *The third response is best because by using the word "what" you immediately open a dialogue with your difficult employee and avoid a hostile confrontation. It is also possible that your difficult employee may reveal problems that you do not want to hear or deal with immediately, so the second response is possible but not as likely.*

5. Describing someone's performance as "weak and unacceptable"...
   - provides valuable information.   0
   - focuses his or her attention on performance issues.   1
   - is considered, in part, a value judgment.   3

Commentary *If you simply labeled someone's performance as "unacceptable," then the second response would be appropriate. By adding the word "weak," however, you enter the realm of making value judgments with respect to an individual's performance without any clear reasons behind the comment. Thus, the third response becomes a valid response.*

MANAGING PROBLEM EMPLOYEES

> Realizing the human limits to our work performance helps avoid confrontations.

6. Providing step-by-step instructions . . .
   - is sometimes appropriate and necessary.   1
   - is too time-consuming.   0
   - provides measurable results.   3

Commentary. Because our professional lives are becoming more hectic with each passing day, as managers, the second response might seem to be most appropriate. However, when working with a difficult employee, you sometimes need to provide additional guidance to help that individual succeed in his or her position. For that reason, the third response is best.

7. People who let their personal problems affect their professional work are . . .
   - undisciplined.   1
   - unprofessional.   1
   - human.   3

Commentary. While you may feel that anyone who brings his or her personal life to work is unprofessional or undisciplined, the third response is the most appropriate choice because there will always be times when even the most disciplined employee will carry some personal baggage to work. It is unavoidable.

> Flexible and reasonable managers breed flexible and reasonable workers.

8. Accommodating and changing the rules for one person . . .
   - causes everyone to feel entitled to special privileges.   0
   - paints the organization as compassionate.   3
   - hinders organizational progress and productivity.   1

Commentary. The normal tendency here is to go with the first response because one's natural reaction is, Why should the company bend the rules for any one individual? The fact is that by

MANAGING PROBLEM EMPLOYEES

demonstrating the ability to be flexible and recognizing an individual employee's special needs, a manager will go a long way toward turning a difficult employee into a more cooperative and productive employee and help everyone feel the company is a compassionate, caring organization.

9. You supervise a former peer and suspect his or her behavior to be motivated by jealousy. You should . . .
    - say to yourself, "It's the employee's problem—not mine."   0
    - ask him or her if your assumptions are correct.   3
    - give a little leeway while he or she adjusts to the new situation.   1

__Commentary.__ The second response underscores the importance of keeping an open dialogue between you and the difficult employee to make sure your insights into the employee's behavior are correct. It is tempting to give the employee some room to maneuver while he or she gets used to having you as a boss. But it is more effective to keep open lines of communication and try to find the underlying reasons for the difficult employee's behavior and attitude toward you.

10. Communicating assertively...
    - means being aggressive.   0
    - means that you are being straightforward with the person.   3
    - puts your needs before that of the employee.   2

__Commentary.__ Some people equate being assertive with being aggressive. Rather, communicating assertively suggests that you are being open and honest in a direct manner with your difficult employee. Thus, the second response is the best response to this statement.

MANAGING PROBLEM EMPLOYEES

HOW TO SCORE YOURSELF.

If you scored 25–30
Consider yourself an excellent communicator. You "read" people well, are perceptive, and deal with difficult situations appropriately.

20–25:
You have a good foundation. You're well on your way to successfully working with difficult situations. Begin to observe yourself while you're communicating, and actively ask yourself if your responses are constructive and productive. Think before speaking.

Under 20:
Challenge yourself to learn all you can about listening empathetically, making nonjudgmental statements, and taking time to resolve conflicts in a win-win approach. Remember, there are more viewpoints and approaches than just your own.

DEALING WITH PROBLEM EMPLOYEES

LACK OF SKILLS

First try to ascertain if the employee really lacks the skills necessary for the satisfactory performance of his or her duties, or if another issue is negatively affecting his or her ability to perform. Often, when a manager assumes that someone cannot do a job for lack of skill, the real problem is centered on sloppiness. And sloppiness is almost always correctable.

If the problem is skill-oriented, decide whether there is something you or the company can do to improve the employee's skills. Can a coworker help bring the employee up to speed? Would a professional seminar be worthwhile? Would studying a book or instructional software help?

You also need to evaluate how important the deficient skill actually is within the performance scope of the particular job. Consider how strong the employee might be in other aspects of job

> A skill-oriented problem can sometimes be corrected through education and training.

MANAGING PROBLEM EMPLOYEES

performance. A shop floor manager, for instance, may be not be great at giving performance reviews but absolutely terrific at scheduling and maintaining production runs and inventory management. Obviously his or her strengths far outweigh the weaknesses in effectively carrying out the primary responsibilities of the job. It is often okay to have an employee with a serious weakness, as long as you are aware of the problem area and the employee compensates for one skill deficiency with a super skill strength.

If, despite all considerations, you feel that an employee should not remain in the current position, think about moving him or her to another area or level of responsibility within the company. There are two advantages to this strategy. First, since you already know where the employee's strengths and weaknesses lie, you have a good idea of what capacity he or she might satisfactorily perform in—much more so than you would for a new employee, for instance. Second, it is demoralizing for other employees to see a coworker fired, especially if that employee was trying hard at the job.

SLOW PACE

A slow work pace can be among the most difficult problems to resolve unless you have standards or goals against which to compare actual performance.

For most nonprofessional positions, you can create standards, or minimum quantitative measures of output. For example, warehouse workers may be expected to pack so many orders every day. Data entry people may be expected to process so many entries each day. Salespeople may be expected to make so many calls to new accounts, make so many face-to-face contacts, or close so many dollars in revenue each day.

The work of professional employees, on the other hand, generally does not lend itself to quantitative performance standards. However, you can usually set specific time goals for when you expect projects to be completed. For example, you may expect an accountant to accomplish month-end book closings within a three-day period at the end each month. You may expect a software engineer to write a particular program within two weeks. You may expect a

> Specific time goals can help motivate workers with slow paces.

MANAGING PROBLEM EMPLOYEES

graphic designer to design and lay out a specific small catalog within a three-week time frame.

If an employee doesn't measure up to a preset or measurable goal, the next step is a closed-door meeting with the employee. During this meeting, present, in an encouraging manner, the facts in as simple a fashion as possible. For example you may say, "You are packing ninety-three orders per average day, whereas our standard is one hundred thirty-five. How do you think you can increase your output?" Or, "Together we set a time frame of three days at month's end in which to close our monthly accounting books. It is typically taking four. Is there some way in which we can work toward the original goal?"

If you are pleasant and encouraging, the employee will probably say something like "Gee, I thought I was working at a pretty good pace, but I am confident that I can work at a little faster clip." In this case, say, "This sounds great. I'm glad to hear it!" Then follow up and be sure the employee knows exactly where he or she stands at the end of each day. Chances are such employees will reach a higher performance level. If not, have them monitor themselves and record their progress every hour or day, as may seem applicable to the task. Consider having peers work with them and help them along. Or consider having the employee make progress reports to you at various intervals.

Sometimes an employee will tell you during your first meeting or during subsequent meetings that the standards or goals that have been set are not realistic, fair, or possible. In this case (assuming you don't agree with the assertion), promptly issue the employee a written warning and plan on terminating his or her employment unless the attitude and performance improve quickly.

SLOPPINESS

Sloppiness is one of the most common workplace problems. Examples include missing errors when proofreading company literature, mispacking orders, entering shipping addresses incorrectly, and performing inaccurate accounting work. Sloppiness most quickly

> A one-on-one meeting with an employee to help set positive goals is valuable in correcting bad performance.

MANAGING PROBLEM EMPLOYEES

surfaces in clerical work, but it is also prevalent in the work of many professionals–although it is much more difficult to detect!

For the first incidence or two of minor sloppiness, you should kindly point out the error to the employee. Don't comment, but watch the person's work more carefully.

If the problem proves to be recurrent or is more serious in nature, you need to sit down with the employee outside of earshot of his or her coworkers. Be positive. Remember that the employee probably has no idea that his or her work is sloppy. Most people take pride in their work. But be candid. Tell the employee that you are concerned about the work and cite specific examples of sloppiness. Relate the clearest or most serious infractions that you have evidence of. Don't discuss marginal problems or ones that you have little evidence of. This can lead to arguments and a feeling of unfair treatment. The point is to assist an employee in performing up to snuff, not to demoralize him or her.

Encourage feedback, but expect to hear something like, "These are isolated examples. Everyone makes errors and basically my work is fine." At this point, don't get into a long discussion about how serious or representative the cited problems are. Instead, shift to telling the employee how important his or her work is to the company. Let the person know how important it is to eliminate all errors and sloppy work, no matter how infrequently it may occur or how insignificant it may seem to be. Try to end the meeting on as positive a note as possible.

Keep observing the employee's work. If, after a few days, the work patterns are improving, be sure to compliment him or her. If the sloppiness continues, conduct another closed-door meeting. There is good chance that the employee is capable of better work and is simply refusing to recognize the existence of an ongoing problem. In this second meeting make a judgmental statement such as, "I am concerned about the overall errors or sloppiness in your work." Again, bring up the most clear or flagrant examples.

For a nonprofessional or entry-level employee, assign someone with good or exemplary work habits, especially in the problem

Even while criticizing an employee, try to remain positive.

MANAGING PROBLEM EMPLOYEES

> Sometimes a manager has to go out of his or her way to establish communication with a difficult employee.

employee's area of weakness, to work side by side with the problem employee for a small portion of each day. Have the "monitoring" employee suggest specific steps for achieving performance improvement. Have the monitor provide continuing feedback. Personally monitor the work of a professional employee. Discuss any progress, or lack of it, every few days.

As long as an employee has the basic skills necessary to effectively perform in the job, sloppiness can be overcome in almost every case. It only takes the efforts of a manager who is willing to invest time and who tries, no matter how frustrating it may be, to adopt a coaching rather than a reprimanding approach.

DIFFICULT TO MANAGE

An employee who is difficult to manage can make your life absolutely miserable. Such a person can be every bit as disruptive to the forward progress of your company as an employee who lacks the skills or initiative to do the job well.

The first thing you should do with a difficult employee is bite your tongue and try to woo him or her. Go out to lunch and try to develop a positive rapport with the person. Often there is some issue that is causing the negative behavior he or she is exhibiting. Many times employees will be very reluctant to discuss these issues, whether they are professional or personal in nature. A casual, relaxed setting may put them at ease. They may open up and tell you what's really bugging them.

Often the underlying causes of employees' negative behavior patterns are quite simple. They may have the perception that they are not appreciated. They may feel that they have not been complimented adequately for work well done. They may feel that they deserve more attention. Remember, you should always be liberal with compliments. Key employees especially need attention from you. But this is advice that is easier to give than heed.

On the other hand, sometimes a difficult-to-manage employee's behavior is the result of personal problems—an ailing parent, a runaway child, a divorce, or financial difficulties. In this case you want to show that you understand the predicament. If at all possible, offer

MANAGING PROBLEM EMPLOYEES

the employee time off or an adjustment in work hours so he or she can focus on resolving the personal dilemma.

However, if the problem is ongoing and is having a serious negative impact on your workplace, you need to let the person know that some sort of resolution is imperative.

If the problem persists, have a formal, closed-door meeting with the employee and address in a forthright manner the most obvious examples of his or her inappropriate behavior.

If an employee remains difficult despite all attempts at building rapport or providing help, you need to make a careful assessment. Be honest with yourself. Do you simply dislike the employee in question? Are the difficulties you are experiencing perhaps minor in character? If this is the case, drop the matter. But if the employee is truly exhibiting behavior problems that seriously disrupt the workplace, you need to take further action. Consider issuing a written warning that details the specific problems as clearly as possible.

If, after issuing such a warning, the employee's bad behavior persists, you may feel that the only solution is termination. Consult with an attorney before dismissing the employee. You need to know whether you have a strong enough case to withstand a potential lawsuit for wrongful firing. An employee who has been fired for issues relating to difficult behavior is much more likely to sue you than an employee fired due to poor work performance.

> Before considering the termination of an employee, utilize meetings and warnings to correct the problem.

TARDINESS

Many good, hardworking people have a tendency to be habitually late.

Unless being precisely on time is crucially important, don't bring up the tardiness issue with an employee who is occasionally late. Such employees will appreciate your tacit understanding and they will take it as a sign of your trust in them. Of course, if the employee is a security guard and you are operating a nuclear power plant, any display of tardiness could be serious. Use your judgment!

On the other hand, an employee who is habitually late can have a demoralizing effect on other employees who arrive for work on time. Furthermore, habitual lateness is a infectious disease. Soon

MANAGING PROBLEM EMPLOYEES

many employees may exhibit tardy behavior. Why do some otherwise great, hardworking employees have a problem being on time? Who knows?

The key question is, Where do you draw the line on tardiness? If a person is ten or more minutes late more than five times within a given month, it's time for a brief chat.

Assuming that the employee's job performance is satisfactory in all other respects, say something like, "Linda, overall I really enjoy having you on our team. I would really appreciate it, however, if you could cut back on your tardiness. I can understand being late on occasion for whatever or even no apparent reason. But enough is enough. Can I count on you for a little improvement in this area?"

Virtually all tardiness problems disappear after a gentle talk. Unless the problem is extremely severe, stick to a very light approach. But sooner or later you will encounter an employee who feels he or she shouldn't have to work on a schedule. One employee actually told me that she felt "professionals" should be able to come and go within the workplace whenever they pleased. She saw absolutely nothing wrong with arriving two hours late. Well, now she can still come and go whenever she pleases—she just can't do it at *our* workplace!

> Tardiness is a problem that can usually be solved with open communication.

MANAGING SCENARIOS

SCENARIO 1: SLOW PERFORMER

Setup

In this scenario, a new city editor chastises a beat reporter for not delivering stories in a particular format. The new format is supposed to help the reporters get their stories done faster with less hassle. The implication in this case is that the reporter is slow and not smart enough to adapt or understand the new format, causing him to consistently miss his deadline.

MANAGING PROBLEM EMPLOYEES

Weak Method:

City Editor: Jim, I've told you on several occasions that we're using a new format to enter and create copy. By not using this format, you've once again missed deadline.

Jim: It's impossible to use your format. It's too confusing and more complicated than the old format. As for missing the deadline, I was working until 1:00 A.M. when the mainframe went down.

City Editor: It's always an excuse with you. Last time it was traffic. Today, the computer. Jim, you're too focused on minute, insignificant details. Your stories also lack punch. The new format is easy to use; a child of six could understand it.

Jim: Are you saying I'm not smart enough to follow this format?

Strong Method

City Editor: Jim, you've missed deadline again for the fourth time in eight weeks, and you've again failed to use the new format I implemented for reporters.

Jim: I want to go the extra mile and do the best job I can on each story. That means checking every fact and covering all the details. I admit I've had some trouble making decisions on what should be in each story.

City Editor: It seems like you're too caught up in the details. Your need to strive for perfection causes you to sacrifice quality. That's why the new format is so useful. The reader will always be able to get the most from your stories if you use the new format.

Jim: I guess it's obvious that I've struggled with the new format. You're a new editor, and I'm just not used to your methods. As for missing deadline, didn't you get my note about the computer crashing?

City Editor: Yes, I did. That explains this deadline. But what about future deadlines? We need to determine how to

> Refrain from insulting or instigating a troublesome employee.

MANAGING PROBLEM EMPLOYEES

alleviate your need for perfection so you can adopt my new format.

Commentary

In the second example, the manager stated the situation in measurable and observable terms so there was no denying the facts. He also involved the employee in the solution by asking for feedback. He took time to hear out the employee's explanation, then asked for input on how to solve the problem. Jim will now feel motivated to change because there's a level of understanding instead of an accusation or a demanding "why" question.

SCENARIO 2: OFFICE GOSSIP/TROUBLEMAKER

Setup

In this illustration, a manager deals with an employee who is an office gossip and a troublemaker, someone who doesn't mind "stirring the pot" and who takes shots at management for what he perceives to be a lack of attention to issues that are important to him.

Weak Method

Manager: Once again, I have to hear it from third parties that you're questioning authority. It's always something with you. Now it's our bathrooms. Last week, you got people shook up about the possibility of our canceling the Christmas party. Even if it were true, you had no business speaking on behalf of upper management when you didn't have the facts.

Warren: You know, it's always the same old song with you guys. You're so busy covering for one another, you forget about everyone else. Morale stinks around here—WE NEED THAT PARTY! As for the bathrooms, have you taken a look at the mess that's been building up in there? They are deplorable!

> Always try to remain open-minded and neutral when confronting an employee.

MANAGING PROBLEM EMPLOYEES

Manager: Look, I'm just trying to get the job done. I'm not managing a federal agency here. And all you're doing is making my life difficult.

Strong Method:

Manager: Warren, it's come to my attention that you're unhappy with the condition of the bathrooms and have made your feelings known to other employees. This has been upsetting to them.

Warren: They should be upset. The bathrooms are a disaster. Who told you, anyway?

Manager: Who told me is not the issue. Perhaps the bathrooms do need work. The point is, you should have come to management. Instead, you went to the employees, accusing management of not caring about their welfare. You know, you seem to be upset about a number of issues lately. What's up?

Warren: Like you care?

Manager: I wouldn't be asking if I didn't care. What I am saying is that I am willing to open a dialogue here as long as we can discuss the issues and stay away from rumors and innuendo. okay?

> Management should try to establish a feeling of trust in order to work with the employee to generate a solution.

Commentary

The manager sees that Warren's behavior is not caused by one isolated incident. This "troublemaker" may have a big chip on his shoulder because he feels underpaid or underappreciated. Or he may be a social crusader who belongs in another field. The manager is willing to establish an environment of trust to gain some insight into Warren's true motivations. He didn't belittle him or the issue by calling him names, and he asked Warren to address "the issues."

The challenge will be for the manager to be consistent. This employee apparently has felt unsafe for whatever reason to go directly to management to work with them to fix the problem . . .

MANAGING PROBLEM EMPLOYEES

and it will be a while before this crusader feels comfortable telling management his real concerns. The manager is at least opening the door at this point. This scenario may conclude with the employee leaving because he is unhappy at the job, and that could be best for all concerned. Managers should not feel the need to save the world.

SCENARIO 3: LACKS SKILLS

Setup

In this scenario, an accounting clerk who lacks verbal communication skills is asked to take on the responsibility of calling on delinquent accounts to collect funds. The manager is unaware of the employee's fear of rejection and lack of verbal skills and berates him for not succeeding at the task.

Weak Method

Manager: Ray, I've been looking at some of the numbers from our call collections, and frankly, these numbers look atrocious! Can't you pick up the phone and get these guys to ante up?

Ray: Hey, I'm no call wizard. Besides, I was hired for my numbers ability, not to harass customers into paying bills.

Manager: That's a weak and unacceptable excuse. Everyone here has the ability to get on the phone and get what they need when they need it. We're a for-profit company, not a charity. Delinquent accounts add up to less money for the bottom line. Do I have to translate?

Ray: Are you saying my job's on the line? That's ridiculous. You ought to try dealing with some of these jokers. Trying to get money out of them is like trying to squeeze blood from rocks!

Manager: Squeeze harder. We need to get our accounts squared away.

> Berating and negatively criticizing an employee does not encourage an improvement in performance.

MANAGING PROBLEM EMPLOYEES

Strong Method

Manager: Ray, I've been reviewing the collection accounts and have noticed that several accounts are still delinquent. Collecting these funds is key for the overall profitability of the company. We need to make sure our customers know how important it is to keep their accounts current. Can you help me understand what's causing this problem?

Ray: Well, calling on these accounts has been difficult because it's time-consuming and often frustrating when the customer doesn't comply. I'm also concerned that my productivity in other areas will diminish as a result.

Manager: As I mentioned, it's vital that we stay on top of these accounts. Would it be helpful if I outlined or developed a script for you to use when you make the calls? We could work on it together so you feel comfortable with the language.

Ray: That would be great.

> Patience and a willingness to teach skills can help turn a problem employee into a productive one.

Commentary

Managers often assume that other employees have the same skill set they themselves possess, so it is not unusual for these managers to falsely assume that an employee's performance problems are due to a lack of effort and initiative rather than a lack of skills. Sometimes managers have to deal with employees who lack even the basic skills and confidence to do seemingly routine tasks because of mental, emotional, or social conditions. While it can be trying, patience is in order. The manager should walk the employee through specific steps that will increase the employee's confidence to accomplish the task at hand. Focusing on the problem rather than the person will help Ray change his behavior and respect his manager as a teacher, not as a disciplinarian.

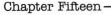

MANAGING PROBLEM EMPLOYEES

SCENARIO 4: TARDINESS

Setup

In this example, a manager confronts an employee who is habitually late for no apparent reason. The manager does not have complete information on why the employee is late and finds out only after he confronts the employee.

Weak Method

Manager: John, it's eight forty-five. Everyone here arrives at 8:00 A.M. You know the policy, yet you continue to come in forty-five minutes late.

John: We have too many rules around here.

Manager: Look, John, I don't want to spend a lot of time on this. The fact is that others manage to arrive at 8:00 A.M., and I want you here at that time as well.

The unhappy employee leaves the office and later that afternoon the manager's phone rings.

Manager *(answering the phone):* Hi, this is Sam.

Other manager *(on phone):* Hey, Sam, this is Jim. Listen I heard that John McMartin has his house up for sale. Seems he bought a place in Oakville, about an hour and a half from here. I'm curious—is he leaving the company?

Strong Method

Manager: John, it's come to my attention that you recently moved into a new house in Oakville. With the traffic and distance, I now understand why you've been late recently. I wish you had come to me.

John: I've been so busy with the move and trying to stay on top of my work that I couldn't find the time. My wife found a job in Crydertown, about three hours from here, so we decided to relocate to Oakville to split the difference in commuting distance.

> By researching the facts of a situation, a manager can avoid a needless confrontation.

MANAGING PROBLEM EMPLOYEES

Manager: Dealing with a move is always a challenge, especially when distance is involved. I know you can handle your workload. Is there anything I can do to help?

John: Well, if I could work from 9:30 A.M. to 6:30 P.M. and skip lunch, I know I could make it here even with the traffic and distance. Knowing I wouldn't technically be late would reduce my stress once I got here.

Manager: Now that I know the situation, I understand what you have had to deal with regarding your new house. Adjusting your schedule is the least we can do to support you. Please keep me updated, okay?

Commentary

Unfortunately, since the employee chose not to share his personal troubles, the manager had nothing to go on and reacted negatively to the tardy behavior. Once he got the information, he was sincerely supportive. He asked the employee how he could help. Mr. McMartin's request to come in an hour and a half late is reasonable. His peers undoubtedly will understand, and stress for all will be reduced. The manager concluded by asking that he be kept posted, which underlined the sincerity of the offer of support.

SCENARIO 5: JEALOUSY OVER A PROMOTION

Setup

In this scenario, we see a manager dealing with an employee who was formerly a peer but who now reports to him. The manager is upset because the employee doesn't seem to take direction and consistently demonstrates an indifferent attitude toward the manager's requests for action.

> Open communication between employees and managers can help avoid confrontation.

Weak Method

Manager: Craig, I noticed you're still using the old invoicing forms. I thought we agreed that we would use the new

MANAGING PROBLEM EMPLOYEES

> When communicating, a
> manager should be honest
> and open, yet refrain from
> making judgments or
> placing blame.

forms. Now all of our new billing information is going
to reflect our old policy.

Craig: I decided that until we properly notify customers of the
changes, it would be rude to send out the new invoices.

Manager: Craig, it's not your decision to make. I told you that
management created the policy at last month's meeting.
I'm responsible for implementing their wishes.

Craig: Since they made you supervisor, you've been spouting
the party line. I can't believe it. I don't even want to
have coffee with you. What's with you?

Manager: I might ask the same question of you.

Strong Method

Manager: Craig, you're still using the old invoicing forms. We
agreed that the new forms would be in place by now.
The billing is still going to reflect our old policy. I need
to know the reasons so I can explain the delay to upper
management this afternoon.

Craig: I decided that until we properly notify customers of the
changes, it would be rude to send out the new invoices.

Manager: Craig, it's not your decision to make. I told you management created the policy at last month's meeting. But
you know what? I don't think this is the real issue.
We've been friends a long time, and I admit this is a difficult conversation to have, but it seems to me that
since I was promoted you've been distant. I'm concerned that you're sabotaging yourself with some of the
actions you're taking against me. You've always been a
valuable team player. If you're having a problem with
me, let's get it out on the table.

Craig: Okay. Okay. I admit I have hard feelings. We started at
the same time, and we have the same expertise. I resent
the fact that I wasn't given a shot at the promotion.
They didn't even consider me. One day you're my peer;
the next you're my boss. It's a lot to handle.

MANAGING PROBLEM EMPLOYEES

Manager: I understand how you feel. If I were in your position, I might feel the same way. But if you want to succeed at this company, you need to be a team player and learn to adjust. In the long run, it will only help your professional development if you work with me in resolving these issues before they become major problems.

Commentary

With this kind of open dialogue, undoubtedly the employee will learn a lot from his friend, and the friendship on and off the job will flourish. Change is hard, but both the manager and the employee have a lot to gain by keeping communication lines open. The manager correctly pointed out to the employee that by openly sabotaging the manager's efforts, he would only end up hurting himself in the long run.

> Try and be award of the employee's situation in order to come to an equitable solution.

COMMUNICATION SKILLS

- **Observe.**
  Communication is a two-way operation that involves sending and receiving signals. Empowered communicators learn to receive signals so they can be proactive rather than reactive to what they send. When communicating, step into the shoes of the other person. Read body language, tone of voice, statements, and silences. Investigate the employee's motivation and fear.
- **Ask open-ended questions.**
  Remember, your goal is to get enough information so you can work with the person to resolve problems and increase productivity. A yes/no (or closed) question will only give you a yes or a no answer. A question that begins with "why" puts people on the defensive. Think about how you react when asked questions such as, "Why were you late? Why do you act like that?"

MANAGING PROBLEM EMPLOYEES

Who, what, where, and how questions involve the other person. "What leads you to make that decision? How can we work together on solving this problem? Who else is affected when you're late? When do you think you can start working toward this new goal?" It takes practice to self-edit and reframe your questioning techniques because we're conditioned to accuse and assume, not to accumulate information.

- **Listen intensely and avoid solving others' problems.**
So often our good intentions prompt us to provide solutions to people's problems when they don't actually want advice, but instead simply want to be heard. Comments such as, "That must be painful for you. You sound angry. It seems like you're feeling frustrated" might seem weak and even ineffectual if you're used to communicating directly and giving orders. But the up-front investment is worth the results generated by this kind of listening. Once people feel genuinely heard, they'll entrust you with more information, which is what you want because it gives you control.

- **Frame your responses using the I-language technique.**
Essentially you are taking responsibility for your feelings. You are not, I repeat NOT, blaming the employee for his or her actions, but you are pointing out how his or her behavior affects your feelings. To begin, comment on observable factual behaviors and state the consequences. Finish with involving the employee in a collaborative resolution.

  Here's an example: "When you give me your reports at the last minute *[fact]*, I feel frustrated because I must rush and wonder if I'm not catching errors and I end up barking at you *[give consequences that matter to him or her]*. I wish you would give me more lead time *[ask for behavior change in terms of 'start doing a' versus 'stop doing b']* so that we'll both be less stressed *[state the benefits]*. What do you think?"

- **Match your words to your body language.**
If you're honest, your body language will confirm it. If you're feeling angry and denying it, your tone of voice might give

Being honest about the ramifications of the employee's actions upon both the manager and the company, can avoid placing blame and judgment on the employee.

MANAGING PROBLEM EMPLOYEES

you away. Be honest, then do a body check to make sure your words match your nonverbal gestures. Otherwise you won't be taken seriously.

QUESTIONS AND ANSWERS

1. **What happens when no matter what I say or do, an employee will not budge from his or her position?**
   This situation can be extremely frustrating, especially when you feel you're right! When someone won't accept your expertise, opinion, or advice, simply take a breath, and say the following in the tone of voice you'd use to ask someone to pass the salt, "That's interesting, but I don't see it that way." Or, "You may feel that way, but I don't, and we're all entitled to our feelings." This is called "fogging," and it deflates the power of the argument. The discussion has nowhere to go. You aren't agreeing nor disagreeing. It's very disarming.

2. **What can I do when a whole department is "difficult"?**
   Call a staff meeting. Set an agenda, but make it your goal to have the group develop creative solutions. Make sure the meeting is not a gripe session but a constructive, problem-solving session. Be a facilitator. Try not to defend yourself when accusations fly. If you can't stay dispassionate, consider bringing in a neutral third party to facilitate.

3. **How do I handle someone who constantly undermines me in public?**
   Remember, "silence implies consent," so don't ignore the problem. It will take great restraint to speak up in a neutral voice when internally you're feeling angry, violated, or challenged. But acting professionally, it's appropriate to say, "Let's meet at my desk in ten minutes to discuss this in private." That gives you time to calm down and collect your thoughts. Make sure to use the I-language technique when you meet.

> To avoid an escalation of tempers, address problems as soon as they arise.

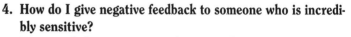
MANAGING PROBLEM EMPLOYEES

4. How do I give negative feedback to someone who is incredibly sensitive?

No one relishes criticism. Be honest with yourself, and be objective. Are you passing a value judgment and disapproving of someone's performance or behaviors based on your set of values? Or is the person not living up to previously established, measurable, obtainable goals and objectives? If the performance can be measured and observed, discuss it from that vantage point. Always ask the employee how he or she thinks he or she is performing, and include him or her in the plan to correct or better the performance. Never label the person lazy or incompetent. Point to a specific incident, and approach the subject from a point of wanting to coach the person, not reprimand him or her.

5. How can I learn to say "no"?

First, realize that what you really want is to say "yes" to yourself. Sometimes managers are so busy being caretakers and martyrs that they let their own needs get shelved. This is draining and ineffective. Learn to be emotionally honest. In other words, don't lie to yourself. Don't say or do something you don't mean. This is a particular challenge for new supervisors who are managing former peers and don't want to appear authoritative.

6. Can humor alleviate a difficult situation with a problem employee?

The secret to humor is to use a universal example that teaches a lesson with laughter. But be tasteful. Remember, ethnic, racial, violent, age, and gender jokes are inappropriate in today's workplace. As far as self-deprecating humor goes, be careful; too much will lower your credibility.

7. How do I show workaholics and perfectionists that they don't add much more to the company's success by working so hard but, instead, damage themselves?

The self-esteem of these employees is tied up with what they do rather than who they are, and they can never do enough

MANAGING PROBLEM EMPLOYEES

to satisfy their inner critics. They define achievement by endurance and set few boundaries. They may even hold a grudge against others who don't burn the midnight oil like they do—and you might be one of them!

You can help these employees by working with them to set achievable goals so they know when it's okay to stop. Remind them that working harder is not necessarily working smarter. Point out times when, in an effort to be perfectionists, they actually held up production. Coach them into participating in social group activities. Encourage them to take their jobs seriously but themselves a bit more lightly.

> Work with employees to achieve reasonable goals.

8. **How do I get buy-in from someone who resists change?**
Some of us are risktakers who embrace change. Others loathe it and cling to the status quo as if it's a lifeboat during a violent storm at sea. And let's face it: Unwanted change is turbulent. At the core of the resistance is fear. It's your job to listen empathetically and ask questions that allow the person to name those fears. Perhaps the employee does not want to learn how to use a new software program. Maybe he or she has a fear of failure, looking dumb, or messing up the system. Maybe he or she never learned to type and fears losing valuable information, working longer hours, showing his or her age, or being replaced by a machine? Until you find out the employee's fears, you'll continue to meet with resistance.

> Rather than lecture, use listening as a two-way dialogue to get employees to see alternatives.

9. **What do I do with someone who is constantly negative?**
Negativity in the workplace has reached such proportions it's practically considered an epidemic. The term "negaholic" has been coined to point to its addictive aspect. It's dysfunctional, counterproductive, and contagious, yet to the negaholic it's strangely familiar. It's more comfortable for that individual to stay that way than to consider the temporary pain of change. And yet as a manager, you want them to change for the good of the entire organization. Don't lecture or patronize these people. They don't want advice. Instead, consistently help them see the alternatives, and more importantly, help

MANAGING PROBLEM EMPLOYEES

them see the benefits of considering those alternatives. To open a dialogue, say something like the following: "I have noticed you've been talking to a lot of people about your perceptions that things are bad around here. My feeling is that we are either part of the problem or part of the solution. What can we do together to get you involved with generating solutions?" When people can answer the question "What's in it for me?" they begin to consider changing their behavior—slowly.

10. **How do I handle the know-it-all expert?**
When "know-it-alls" challenge you, it takes a toll on your credibility. When they challenge their peers, it diminishes and demoralizes the team spirit. Unfortunately, they are sometimes right. But often they are spouting out erroneous statements with such authority that listeners take them as fact. Again, depending on the subject matter, this could undermine your personal credibility and the intentions of the organization. Be consistent. When you feel their information is correct, simply acknowledge their expertise. When you need to point out the erroneous information, question firmly but don't confront.

STREETWISE advice

◆ **Learn as much about yourself as possible.**
Know your own hot button: What is your threshold for tolerating different behavior patterns? Establish what motivates you and notice how it differs from your employees. For example, you may be motivated to get recognition for doing excellent work; an employee who works for you may be motivated to come to work for the socializing rewards. Remember, it takes all types. What type are you? A driver? An influencer? A people pleaser? A perfectionist? Be aware of the differences, and try to use them to create a more flexible working relationship between you and your employees.

◆ **Be assertive.**
Assertive is not passive and not aggressive. It's simply communicating directly and appropriately. It's about knowing what you want and thinking enough of yourself to assert your needs. When you are honest and up-front with your words and actions, you're neither lying in an attempt to be overly nice and protective (i.e., passive!), nor are you denying your anger to the point of one day blowing up—in other words, being aggressive. Asserting yourself allows you to hold your ground without putting the other person down, creating a win/win situation for both parties.

◆ **Do not try to solve a problem that is too tough to handle.**
Ask for help from resources with more expertise than you have. Don't feel you have to solve your employees' problems. You might be a terrific line manager but an inadequate therapist—and that's because you're a manager, not a human service provider. Don't bite off more than you can chew. Once you've listened, asked caring questions, involved the person in a possible solution, but still failed to reach a resolution, call in the troops: the human resources department, your company's employee assistance program, or your own manager.

◆ **Learn that you cannot change others.**
You can change your own behavior and hope that by serving as a model, employees will follow your lead. Do yourself a favor and understand that ultimately people do what they want to do despite your best wishes and intentions. Protect yourself by learning to deflect their negative behaviors, and don't take them personally. So often, out of self-defense and perhaps low self-esteem, we make false assumptions. It takes a self-assured person to dig in and ask information-gathering and constructive questions that lead to mutually satisfying results.

◆ **Be flexible.**
When you think about all the ways we are different as human beings, it's easy to see how we view the world through different glasses. We are different in age and gender and sexual preference; our upbringing, environment, education, values, and culture all define us in one way or another. Learn to accept the differences even if you don't agree or condone others' choices. Your life will be a lot less stressful!

> Addressing a problem in an assertive manner establishes an open line of communication.

16

FIRING
PROBLEM
EMPLOYEES

No one enjoys firing people. But getting someone out of the organization who just can't do their job or who is a de-motivator can give a huge boost to the performance of the business. The general tendency is to put off the decision to make a firing, because it's not an easy issue. But procrastination just makes it worse for you, for the organization, and perhaps even for the employee, who may get a fresh start someplace else.

FIRING PROBLEM EMPLOYEES

O f all confrontations with an employee, the response you get from firing someone is the most difficult to predict. One employee may thank you for giving him or her the opportunity to work with you, while another may attempt to engage an immediate supervisor in a fist fight.

You need to prepare carefully before firing someone. You need to be ready to become fully engaged in what may become a very demanding encounter.

How you handle a firing will have a tremendous impact on how the employee feels about himself, you, and your company. This will, in turn, effect your chance of being sued. In addition, a poorly handled firing will have a negative impact on morale throughout your entire organization.

THE DECISION TO WAIT ON A FIRING

How much time should you give an employee to improve his or her performance? There really aren't any specific guidelines. One thing to take into consideration, however, is the employee's length of service with your company. Loyalty does count. Give an employee who has served you for several years a few months to work out his or her performance deficits.

Remember too, that when you fire a long-term employee the negative effect on the morale of other employees will be far greater than, say, if you were to fire a recent hire. And when you work together with long-term employees in an effort to help them improve their job output, and ideally keep them gainfully employed, you create goodwill throughout the company.

On the other hand, if an employee shows poor work habits, has unsatisfactory skill levels, or displays attitude problems during the provisional ninety-day employment period, don't hesitate to fire him

> Consider the loyalty of an employee before firing them for poor performance.

FIRING PROBLEM EMPLOYEES

or her. (But beware of the legal risks—the courts do not recognize "provisional" employment periods.)

THE DECISION TO FIRE

While firing should definitely be a last-resort measure, many managers, especially newly minted ones, hesitate to terminate an employee until it is long overdue.

As demonstrated throughout the section on problem employees, by carefully working with an employee many performance shortcomings can be resolved. An employee's job achievement can be improved through care.

If these "gentle" tactics don't work, however, you must move on to a firm verbal warning that makes mandatory a work quality or attitude improvement and cites specific suggestions for effecting such an improvement. If that fails, issue a written warning. Some people just require the jolt of a firm warning to shift their work performance into high gear.

Of course, during the period when you are working with an employee in an attempt to improve their performance, you run the risk of having them decide to seek employment elsewhere. This risk increases if a written warning is handed down. If the employee quits or submits his or her resignation, that's okay. It is a lot easier to lose weak performers through their own proactive decisions.

HOW TO FIRE AN EMPLOYEE

After you have taken all of the preliminary steps, considered all of the potential ramifications, legal and otherwise, and have made the difficult decision to let someone go, stick to it. Don't torture yourself. Don't prolong the firing. It is, after all, inevitable.

Only the worker's direct supervisors, and any witnesses that will be present at the termination meeting, should be told about the termination decision in advance. An advance leak of a firing can only worsen the situation.

In the past, late Friday afternoon was considered the optimum time to let someone go. Today, earlier in the day or even the week is deemed appropriate. Some companies that take this approach offer

> Stick to your decision to fire an employee, and do it as soon as is feasible.

FIRING PROBLEM EMPLOYEES

the employee the option of either remaining for the rest of the day or week, or leaving immediately with pay for the workday.

When you are ready to proceed with the termination, call the employee into the office. Approach him or her with "I have something to discuss with you."

After the employee and any other managerial personnel or witnesses have gathered in your office, get to the point quickly. Briefly explain to the employee that he or she is being fired. Summarize the main reasons for the firing, recap the warnings that have been issued, and the opportunities extended to improve his or her performance record. Give the person a check for monies due. If you are offering severance pay, detail the severance offer and present the employee with the forfeiture document to be signed if the severance is to be paid. Explain any continued work options. Offer to let the employee clean out his or her office or desk now, or have you mail any personal belongings to him or her later. If the employee elects to have you mail his or her belongings, have two people oversee the cleaning process to be sure that all of the employee's personal possessions are mailed.

Show appropriate sympathy for the employee, but not empathy. Do not waiver and change your mind. Do not overstate any aspect of the employee's performance.

Answer any question the terminated employee may have, even if he or she interrupts you. A termination is extremely emotional. Don't be surprised if the employee doesn't hear the basic message or doesn't understand the details of his or her firing. You may have to restate all or part of the termination.

As long as the employee doesn't lose control, extend him or her every reasonable courtesy. Certainly give the person an opportunity to say good bye to coworkers. He or she will only call these people up on the phone later anyway.

If the employee does lose control and becomes verbally abusive, ask him or her to vacate the building. Don't get upset. Remember, no matter what you think of the employee, that person is being terminated. He or she is leaving, not you.

> Be open in communicating with the employee, but do not compromise your position.

FIRING PROBLEM EMPLOYEES

Even if you or someone else in the office can overpower a suddenly violent discharged employee, the risk of a lawsuit is huge. The one time I did call the police, the employee fled the building before they arrived. But the (Boston) police told me its policy was not to refuse cancellations on this type of call because all too often the discharged employee returned with a weapon. In this case, the employee did return with his dog—but the dog was about the size of a miniature poodle, with about the same level of ferociousness.

The odds of you or another employee being endangered during a firing is slim, but you do need to be prepared for the unexpected.

SEVERANCE

First, by law, you need to immediately remunerate a terminated employee for any unused vacation or personal time, all regular and overtime hours worked, and previously unpaid, earned bonuses and any other earned pay.

When you fire an employee, even if he or she has only been with you for ninety days or less, for any just cause short of confiscating the queen's jewels, you should pay severance. It is decent, remaining employees expect you to have done it, and it makes you look better in the worst of situations. It also decreases your risk of a lawsuit.

Many firms that pay severance offer two weeks pay. Others pay two weeks plus one week for each year of service the employee has given to the company. Still others are considerably more generous, particularly to employees who held senior positions. In this case, six months' to a year's pay is not atypical and is predicated on the assumption that a senior-level employee will have a more difficult time obtaining a new and equal job than will an entry-level employee.

While it is nice to pay out a lot of money to departing employees, if you own a small business, you need to be concerned about staying in business and paying your remaining staff members. But whatever you decide to do regarding severance pay, in all termination situations, severance for similar positions with similar service time should be consistent. If you continually change your severance policies, you are only adding to your legal risks.

> Paying the employee severance is not only proper but may circumvent lawsuits later on.

FIRING PROBLEM EMPLOYEES

You should only pay severance, however, if the employee agrees to sign a document that forfeits their right to sue you for wrongful termination. Don't be cheap in this lion's pit of potential danger. Have a lawyer draw up the release document so that it is, as much as possible, bullet proof. You should give the employee twenty-four hours to review, sign, and return the document to you, otherwise it may not hold up in court should the employee decide to sue you anyway. If the employee is age forty or over you must, by law, grant the person twenty-one days to review such a document.

LEGAL RISKS

Thanks to your friends in the federal government, you need to carefully consider any potential termination from a legal perspective. If you aren't sure where you would stand legally should a terminated employee bring suit, consult an attorney before you take any action against that employee. To do otherwise would be "penny wise and pound foolish."

While there aren't any laws in the United States that take away the right of employers to fire employees for cause, including unsatisfactory quantity or quality of work, you still face a significant legal risk every time you fire someone.

Why? Once you fire an employee you have typically engaged the person's fury. This person seldom believes that his or her performance was as poor as you have claimed. Someone who decides to pursue "justice" through the courts will generally claim discrimination. Women, anyone over the age of forty, physically challenged persons, minorities, gays, and many other groups are protected by law from discrimination. Some form of legal discrimination protection blankets just about 80 percent of our national work force.

Courts, especially juries, tend to be highly sympathetic to fired employees. This sympathy is magnified if the fired employees remain unemployed or if they are older workers.

AVOIDING A LAWSUIT

The first way to avoid getting sued is to be sure that you and all other supervisors understand discrimination law. Go one step further

> The threat of a lawsuit is a very real factor a manager must consider when firing an employee.

FIRING PROBLEM EMPLOYEES

and be sure that all supervisors really believe in the importance of fighting discrimination—both on a practical and a subconscious level.

You need to remember that abiding by the law and being able to prove to a hostile jury that you have done so are two very different things. If you end up in court, you need to have a rock-solid case against any employee you fire. You should take whatever preventive steps you can to avoid the possibility of a suit altogether.

Create a paper trail long before termination is seriously considered. Write summaries regarding specific performance problems that were cited via direct verbal warnings to the employee and file a copy in his or her employment records. Be sure that you have issued the employee at least two written warnings.

If the employee knows and appreciates that you have tried to work with him or her towards improving such job performance, this can decrease the chance of a lawsuit.

How you handle a problem employee's performance reviews are critical. The recent reviews should not be positive. This is often a problem because employers, supervisors, and managers hesitate to write and present to an employee a negative review, even if such a review is warranted. If, during the review process, you give into the human temptation to say something like "your work really isn't all that bad" or "I know your work is improving," you are planting the seeds of a discrimination suit.

Another potential problem you should be aware of is how you handle reference calls for a former, and fired, employee. If you give out any information on such an employee, other than dates of employment and a salary confirmation, you risk a lawsuit. There was even an instance where a company lost a suit brought by a terminated employee because a good reference was supplied but the employee felt, and the jury agreed, that the reference wasn't good enough!

> Be sure to document employee performance and keep track of written warnings.

FIRING PROBLEM EMPLOYEES

SCENARIO: TERMINATING AN EMPLOYEE

The following dialogue provides an excerpt from a firing that involves an employee who had sincerely tried to do his job but just hadn't been able to perform at a satisfactory level. Note how the manager shows patience and expresses sympathy but does not offer false praise or waiver in his decision.

In this excerpt one manager is handling the termination procedure. It is good practice, however, to have another manager present. Ideally, the second manager should not be someone the employee reported to either directly or indirectly. If the firing does not go smoothly, the second manager can be called upon as a witness should any legal action ensue at some later point.

Manager:	Tom, please have a seat.
Tom:	Thank you.
Manager:	Tom, I know that you have tried hard to succeed at your job. Nonetheless, for some months now, your overall performance has not been satisfactory. There are too many instances of errors in the accounts payable reports and your attempts to carefully check over each report have slowed down the pace of your work considerably. We cannot retain you in this position and we must let you go.
Tom:	You mean, I'm fired?
Manager:	Yes, that is correct. I am very sorry that this did not work out.
Tom:	I know I can do the job. Give me another chance. I really like working here.
Manager:	Tom, we have given you at least two written warnings and several verbal warnings.
Tom:	But my supervisor says the quality of my work is improving.
Manager:	While the number of errors has decreased, the quality is still not satisfactory. And in working to decrease the

> When terminating an employee, having another manager present reduces the risk of hostile confrontation.

Streetwise

FIRING PROBLEM EMPLOYEES

amount of errors your work pace has become unsatisfactory. I know you have tried . . . but it's still not working out.

Tom: What about another position? I've never really liked payables. How about the entry-level position in accounts receivable? I'll really give it my all.

Manager: Tom, it's time to move on. We all like you here. This is a difficult decision for all of us. But the decision has been made. We truly wish you the best.

QUESTIONS & ANSWERS

1. **Should I consider rehiring a fired employee?**
Probably not. An employee who has been fired for cause is much more likely to have a poor attitude toward your firm than a fresh hire. Even if the problems that led to the firing have disappeared, don't rehire.

2. **Any there any specific steps suggested to avoid an age discrimination suit?**
In addition to the steps suggested throughout this section that should be observed prior to and during a firing, consider hiring an older individual to replace the fired employee. This isn't an ironclad guarantee of winning an age discrimination suit, but it sure won't help the plaintiff's case!

3. **Is it better to fire several people at the same time?**
If you have decided to fire more than one individual, it is best to fire them simultaneously. If you effect the firings piecemeal, remaining staff members will wonder, "Who's going to get the ax this week?"

4. **Should I announce the reasons for a firing to others?**
No. There's already enough risk involved in a firing. When customers or vendors call, instruct the receptionist or other personnel to simply say "John Doe is no longer with us.

FIRING PROBLEM EMPLOYEES

Sally Smith has taken over his duties. May I connect you with her?"

If the firee was a key manager, you may feel compelled to detail the reasons to other managers. This is OK, but don't reveal anything that you can't substantiate. Avoid negativity and insist that the topic remain confidential.

5. Should I fire someone who is leaving soon anyway?
Often, but not always, employees who have given notice slow down their work pace in the period before their actual departure. If you aren't happy with this, ask them, sincerely, if they would prefer to leave earlier.

If the employee would like to continue in your employ until the announced departure date, encourage him or her to keep up their work pace, but don't push the employee to leave earlier. The legal risk for the company and the trauma that may be caused to other members of your work force are good enough reasons to avoid a firing in this instance. Besides, the employee has done you the courtesy of giving you advance notice of departure.

6. What can I do to avoid a lawsuit after firing someone?
If you are seriously concerned about this possibility, contact an attorney that specializes in employment law. Depending on the situation, the steps the attorney recommends may include paying your standard severance pay package, offering extra severance pay in exchange for signing a legal release, carefully documenting the reasons for the termination, promptly processing unemployment claims, promptly sending the employee any personal belongings left behind, and paying the employee any past due wages at the same time as the separation as mandated by law.

> Keeping the reasons for termination confidential can avoid further risk of lawsuit.

STREETWISE
advice

- **Don't take firing lightly.**

  Usually, even a very weak job performance can be brought up to a satisfactory level. Firing, on the other hand, involves a significant legal risk. It also has a traumatic impact on other members of your staff, even if they understand and appreciate the reasons for the termination.

- **Don't hesitate to consult with counsel.**

  If you have any questions regarding a firing, consult with an expert employment attorney prior to the termination. You may save yourself the legal fees of a post-firing lawsuit.

- **Plan what you are going to say.**

  If you don't carefully plan out what you are going to say during a firing, and stick to it, chances are you will offer kind words regarding their work performance. This can lead to legal action. During a firing, you don't want to even hint at anything positive in the person's job performance.

- **Be calm.**

  Even if the employee you are firing irritates you, don't let on. If he or she lashes out verbally, don't get excited. Soon this person will be gone and will no longer be your problem.

- **Be humane.**

  Treat the employee you are firing as kindly as possible during the termination process. This is a very traumatic experience for them. Being kind, without conveying anything positive about their job performance, can assuage this trauma. And, of course, it can decrease the odds that someone will bring a wrongful firing suit against your company or place negative phone calls to your remaining staff.

- **Avoid surprises.**

  Give weak employees every opportunity to improve their work performance or attitude before opting to let them go. If you can prove that you have given them every possible chance, there will be less grounds for a lawsuit. Plus, other employees will feel less threatened by the implications of the firing.

  Additionally, employees who have been aware for some time that their continued employment is on the line will find the actual firing less traumatic. It may well be that they will feel "clued," and will seek and find employment elsewhere before you can fire them.

  At all costs, you want to avoid firing someone who has no idea that his or her job is in jeopardy.

- **Have a strong paper trail.**

  Good documentation of poor work performance or attitude is essential in defending against a wrongful firing suit. Make a record of any verbal warnings you have given to the employee and, if possible, issue written warnings to him or her well before the firing. Negative performance reviews are a must.

> Be humane and kind without unduly complimenting work performance.

INDEX

INDEX

INDEX

INDEX

INDEX

INDEX

Streetwise Managing People is also available as a software product!

Designed for Windows®3.1, Windows®95, and Macintosh®

Master the Art of Managing People

Perhaps the most important skill in determining your success in business is your ability to manage people. Through a powerful set of interactive tools—questionnaires, self-assessments, and video scenarios—**Managing People** will help you increase employee morale, job satisfaction, and productivity. You will learn to:

- ▶ Resolve Conflicts Smoothly;
- ▶ Build Your Leadership Skills;
- ▶ Successfully Manage Difficult People;
- ▶ Coach Your Staff to Success;
- ▶ Effectively Manage Change;
- ▶ Motivate Your Staff to Go the Extra Mile.

SPECIFICATIONS

CD-ROM (Win/Mac Multimedia) Version: CD-ROM drive
3.5" Disk (Win Lite) Version: 3.5" disk drive

Windows: Windows 3.1 or higher, Windows NT, or Windows 95 • 386 PC (486 or Pentium recommended) • Sound Blaster or compatible audio • 4 MB RAM (8 recommended) • 5 MB free hard disk space

Macintosh: System 7.0 or higher • Performa, Quadra, Centris or Power Macintosh • 4 MB RAM (8 recommended) • 5 MB free hard disk space

Also available at software retailers nationwide:

How to order: If you cannot find this software at your favorite retail outlet, you may order it directly from the publisher. Call for price information. BY PHONE: Call 1-800-872-5627 (in Massachusetts 781-767-8100). We accept Visa, Mastercard, and American Express. $5.95 will be added to your total order for shipping and handling. BY MAIL: Write out the full title of the software you'd like to order and send payment, including $5.95 for shipping and handling to: Adams Media Corporation, 260 Center Street, Holbrook, MA 02343. 30-day money-back guarantee.

Visit our exciting job and career site at http://www.careercity.com